The Scottish Children's
System in Action

*For Rebecca, Rachel, Paul, Niamh,
Joseph, Luke and Xosia*

The Scottish Children's Hearings System in Action

by

Brian Kearney MA, LLB
Sheriff of Glasgow and Strathkelvin

Tottel publishing

Published by
Tottel Publishing Ltd
Maxwelton House
41–43 Boltro Road
Haywards Heath
West Sussex
RH16 1BJ

Tottel Publishing Ltd
9–10 St Andrew Square
Edinburgh
EH2 2AF

ISBN 978-1-84592-056-2
© Sheriff Brian Kearney 2007
First published 2007

British Library Cataloguing-in-Publication Data
A catalogue record for this book is available from the British Library

Typeset, printed and bound in Great Britain by
M & A Thomson Litho Ltd, East Kilbride, Scotland

Preface

Sometimes people working in one discipline are unaware, or only partially aware, of the principles and procedures which apply in other disciplines, even where they are engaged in a common purpose. I think this may be true of our Children's Hearings system. Some lawyers have a limited knowledge of what happens at hearings and some of those working in the hearings system have a limited knowledge of what happens when a case originating in a hearing has to be dealt with in court. The general public has only a very general idea of what goes on in either forum.

It is the purpose of this book to remedy this by tracing the history of two imaginary cases on their journeys through the hearings and court proceedings in order not only to show how the rules and procedures work in action but also to give some impression of how the various participants think, act and interact. It is not the aim to provide a comprehensive textbook, dealing with the provisions affecting every contingency – to have attempted this would have been a practical impossibility – but it is hoped that most of the more commonly encountered situations are covered.

For obvious reasons I have tried to ensure that the various rules are obeyed and that best practice is observed and this sometimes leads to a degree of unreality. Many children's hearings are not as tidy as those depicted here. The over-all purpose is to explain what is being done and why. Sometimes this is achieved in the Notes which form the running commentary, sometimes by footnotes and occasionally by judicial pronouncements. Not many sheriffs feel it necessary to explain their decisions in such detail as is sometimes done in this text. In some instances the procedures are explained by conversations between the professionals. It is of course not to be assumed that every such conversation would cover all the matters represented here but I believe that they are typical of the discussions which take place in practice.

It would not have been possible for me to have come near to achieving my objective without massive help from others. Pre-eminent among these are Mr Brian Lister and Miss Pauline Proudfoot of SCRA. Mr Lister has been a constant adviser from the beginning and a meticulous proof reader at the end. Miss Proudfoot provided many crucially helpful suggestions and also read the proofs. Sheriff Carole Cunninghame also read the proofs and made a number of very useful suggestions. Sheriff Margaret Liddell read the text at an earlier stage and gave helpful advice, particularly about the rules now governing the solicitor-client relationship. In the early stages I had useful discussions with Miss Anne Marie McGinlay, solicitor, now with SCRA, and Mrs Moira Mackinnon, Principal Officer (Child Protection), Glasgow City Council. I must also thank the Scottish Safeguarders Association and, not least, members of the Sheriff Clerk's staff in Glasgow for much helpful advice on matters of practice. I am also most appreciative of the skill of the staff of Tottel Publishing Ltd in setting up the text and for their patience in waiting for it. I am most grateful to Sheriff Principal James A Taylor for having permitted the taking of photographs of the Children's Hearings suite here and to Mr Kevin Meechan, of the Sheriff Clerk's staff, for his expertise in taking them. I acknowledge an immense debt of gratitude to all who have helped me and saved me from many errors, but of course the responsibility for the book and any errors which remain is mine.

I must conclude by thanking my wife Elizabeth for her patient forbearance during the lengthy period when this book was being written and for her support throughout.

Brian Kearney
Glasgow
October, 2007

Children's Hearings Suite at Glasgow Sheriff Court

Children's Crèche at Glasgow Sheriff Court

Contents

Table of Cases

Table of Statutes

Table of Statutory Instruments etc

[References are to page number]

Table of European Materials

Introduction – A bird's eye view of hearings system

Historical perspective

Until the introduction of the Children's Hearings system in 1971 juveniles – persons under 16 – who were accused of all but the most serious crimes were tried in the 'Juvenile Court' which was simply a modified version of the sheriff sitting alone in summary procedure. Charges of the most serious nature, such a murder, were tried under 'solemn procedure' before a jury. There was growing dissatisfaction with this arrangement and in 1961 a committee was set up 'to consider the provisions of the law of Scotland relating to the treatment of juvenile delinquents and juveniles in need of care or protection or beyond parental control and, in particular, the constitution, powers and procedure of the courts dealing with such offenders, and to report.' The committee was presided over by Lord Kilbrandon, a Scottish Law Lord, and reported in 1964[1].

The Kilbrandon committee, having been charged with the task of considering the powers and procedures of the courts advanced recommendations which, surprisingly to some, involved the virtual removal from the courts of jurisdiction in cases wherein children were said to have offended. The Report stated at paragraph 71: 'The shortcomings which cause dissatisfaction with the present juvenile court system (and this is no reflection on those who serve in such courts) seem to us to arise essentially from the fact that they seek to combine the characteristics of a court of criminal law with those of a specialised agency for the treatment of young offenders, proceeding on a preventive and educational principle.' The Committee proposed the setting up of what it called 'juvenile panels' of lay persons which would decide on the measures to be taken where appropriate grounds had been admitted or proved. Where there was no agreement as to the existence of such grounds the matter would be remitted to the sheriff for decision. If that decision were that the grounds existed then the sheriff would return the matter to the panel who would decide on the measures required for the child. As to the principles to be applied by panels in making their decisions the Committee stated: 'in our view, referral should be made for one reason only, namely, that *prima facie* the child is in need of special measures of education and training ... panels should be empowered to assume jurisdiction to order such measures for any child under 16 in respect of whom, on a referral, one or more of the following circumstances is shown to apply, namely, his falling into bad associations or moral danger; his being the subject of criminal neglect or an unnatural offence...; his having violated the law as to crimes and offences; his

---

1. Children and Young Persons, Scotland (1964), Cmnd. 2306 HMSO ('The Kilbrandon Report').

failure to attend school; his parent or guardian having abandoned him ... or who is of such habits and mode of life as to be unfit to have control of the child.' In short, Kilbrandon made two revolutionary proposals; separation of 'trial' from disposal and declaring the needs of the child to be the central principle for disposal.

The Social Work (Scotland) Act 1968 substantially followed the Kilbrandon proposals and by 1971 the relevant rules and structures were in place and the system got under way. The Children (Scotland) Act 1995 and relative Rules, which now govern the system, made important procedural changes, but the system set out in the 1968 Act remained substantially the same.

Proposals are afoot to effect further changes by way of the Children's Services (Scotland) Bill but the basic system will remain. The document 'Draft Children's Services (Scotland) Bill Consultation[2]' recalls that in May 2003 the Scottish Ministers 'set out a Partnership Agreement commitment to: "Review the Children's Hearing's system and improve the current service. Scotland has led the world in developing a system which puts the child at its centre, involves local people in deciding what is the right thing to do and focuses on the care and welfare of young people. We will hold on to those fundamental principles. It is now, however, time to review the system to ensure that it has the right set up and adequate resources to ensure that it does the best possible job to protect children."'

The Children's Panel

The 'Children's Panel', as enacted[3], comprises not, as in the Kilbrandon terminology, the tribunal dealing with children, but the pool of persons recruited by the local authority from whom that tribunal, called the 'hearing', is drawn. The panel members are appointed by the Scottish Ministers, who act with the assistance of the Children's Panel Advisory Committee ('CPAC') which has the task of advising Scottish Ministers on such appointments and on the administration of the Panels. The various CPACs play an active rôle, in association with Universities, in the pre-appointment and continuing in-service training of Panel Members. Panel Members may be removed by the Scottish Ministers, but their independence is protected by the provision that their removal must have the consent of the Lord President of the Court of Session[4]. Panel members are now appointed for three-year periods, with the possibility of renewal. They are unpaid volunteers, but are entitled to expenses. Each panel has a chairperson who is responsible for convening panel members to hearings.

---

2. Scottish Executive, December 2006 ISBN 0-7559-5237-5, paragraph 3.5
3. Children (Scotland) Act 1995, s 39(1) and Sch 1.
4. Tribunals and Inquiries Act 1992, s 7(1)(e) and Sch 1, para 61(a).

Children and Relevant Persons

A 'child' for the purposes of the system is a person under the age of sixteen years, a person under 18 who is subject to a supervision requirement[5], and a child who has been subject to an order corresponding to a Scottish supervision requirement granted in England, Wales or Northern Ireland[6].

The persons having parental rights and responsibilities for the child – generally but not always the biological parents of the child – are dubbed by the Act 'relevant persons[7]'.

The Children's Reporter

The person responsible for considering whether a child should be referred to a hearing, and, if the decision is made so to refer, to effect the referral, is commonly referred to as The Children's Reporter, although that term has no statutory foundation. The statutory officer is the Principal Reporter who is appointed by, and answerable to, the Scottish Children's Reporter Administration ('SCRA')[8]. The Principal Reporter may delegate to officers appointed by SCRA any of his functions except that of reporting annually to the Administration[9]. The independence of the Principal Reporter and the officers appointed by him is secured by provisions for appeal to Scottish Ministers in the event of dismissal by SCRA and the provision that SCRA may not give directions to reporters in any matter affecting the exercise of their professional functions[10]. There are no prescribed qualifications for reporters. In practice most have legal or social work qualifications or both.

For administrative purposes SCRA has divided Scotland into four regions, with each sub-divided into smaller areas. Each region is led by a 'Reporter Manager', and the smaller areas are led by 'Authority Reporters'. The Principal Reporter works from SCRA headquarters in Stirling where also work senior administrative, policy making and training staff.

Social Work Departments – Social Services Departments

The Kilbrandon Report has envisaged that the decisions of children's hearings would be implemented by a 'matching field organisation' and proposed the creation of a new 'social education department'[11]. This was not enacted as such and the main 'field work' is carried out by social workers employed by local authorities in Social Work Departments, now often called Social Services Departments. The key rôle of the local

---

5. Children (Scotland) Act 1995, s 93(2).
6. Children (Scotland) Act 1995, s 33.
7. Children (Scotland) Act 1995, s 93(2)(b), definition of 'relevant person'.
8. Local Government etc (Scotland) Act 1994, s 128(4).
9. Local Government etc (Scotland) Act 1994, ss 128(5) and 131(2).
10. Local Government etc (Scotland) Act 1994, ss 129(1) and 128(8).
11. The Kilbrandon Report, paragraph 241.

authority is reflected in the provision that the reporter may request the local authority to investigate and report on any child who may appear to require to be referred to a children's hearing[12].

The criteria for entering the system – The Grounds for Referral – The Welfare Principle

Before a child can become subject to the jurisdiction of a children's hearing there must be evidence that one or more of the 'Grounds for Referral' set out in section 52(2) of the Children (Scotland) Act 1995 exists in relation to that child. These include the classic 'care or protection' categories which have been with us since early in the twentieth century, such as the child 'falling into bad associations' or being 'exposed to moral danger,' being likely to suffer unnecessarily or being neglected or abused by those who should be caring for him or her, and the child failing to attend school regularly without reasonable excuse. Another ground is the commission of an offence by the child, but this is listed in the midst of the 'care or protection' grounds, thus reflecting the welfare-oriented philosophy which underlay the approach of the Kilbrandon Committee which is now echoed by section 16(1) of the Children (Scotland) Act 1995 which requires courts and hearings, when making decisions about a child, to regard the child welfare throughout his or her childhood as their paramount consideration. The right of the Crown to prosecute children accused is preserved[13] but this is only exercised in relation to very serious crimes and the Lord Advocate has issued directions as to the type of crimes for which children may be prosecuted[14].

The procedures for entering the system

The Children's Reporter is the sole channel into the system. Any person who has information giving him or her 'reasonable cause to believe' that a child should be dealt with by a hearing may pass the relevant information to the reporter[15]. A local authority which has information which 'suggests' that a child should be dealt with by a hearing, and is, after such investigation as may be appropriate, 'satisfied' that a child should be dealt with by a hearing, must pass the relevant information to the reporter[16]. In practice most notifications originate from the police. Notifications are also made by social work, schools, doctors and other health professionals, and parents. Notifications from members of the public, such as concerned neighbours, are rare but not unknown. In certain circumstances criminal[17] and civil[18] courts may refer children to the reporter. On receiving any such

---

12. Children (Scotland) Act 1995, s 56(2).
13. Criminal Procedure (Scotland) Act 1995 s 42(1).
14. See Kearney B, *Children's Hearings and the Sheriff Court*, second edition (Edinburgh 2000), at paragraph 1.26.
15. Children (Scotland) Act 1995, s 53(2).
16. Children (Scotland) Act 1995, s 53(1).
17. Criminal Procedure (Scotland) Act 1995 s 48.
18. Children (Scotland) Act 1995, s 54.

notification the reporter must investigate and decide on whether or not a hearing should be arranged[19]. Where a child has been made the subject to one of the emergency protection procedures, the most common of which is the Child Protection Order ('CPO'), the reporter must be notified and may arrange a hearing[20].

The procedures of the hearing

A hearing can never 'try' a case in the sense of examining the evidence and deciding if grounds are established or not. At the appropriate stage[21] a hearing must find out if the child and the relevant person(s) understand and accept the grounds for referral. Where the grounds are understood and accepted[22] (or later held as established by the sheriff) the hearing, after considering all the information, in the form of reports and the like, and discussing the matter with the child and the relevant person(s), being careful to take appropriate account of any views of the child[23], may dispose of the case by imposing (or not) a supervision requirement[24]. A supervision requirement may name a place other than the child's home as a place where the child is to reside, and may in certain circumstances specify that the child shall be liable to be kept in secure accommodation[25]. Hearings have powers, in certain circumstances, to order the detention of children while a case is pending[26].

Where the grounds are understood but not accepted[27] or where the grounds are not understood by the child[28] the hearing, unless it decides to discharge the referral, directs the reporter to make an application to the sheriff to hear the evidence and make a finding as to whether or not the ground which has not been accepted or has not been understood is established by that evidence – thus the other key Kilbrandon principle – separation of 'trial' from disposal, is secured.

The procedures before sheriff

In Scotland the judge presiding in the local court is known as the sheriff. Sheriffs are qualified lawyers of standing, either solicitors or advocates, holding the Queen's commission. They have extensive criminal jurisdiction and almost unlimited civil jurisdiction. When appearing before the sheriff in relation to a case after a direction by a children's hearing the reporter

---

19. Children (Scotland) Act 1995, s 56.
20. Under, where a CPO is involved, s 57(5) and 59(1) and (2) of the Children (Scotland) Act 1995.
21. Special preliminary procedural steps must be taken in relation to children entering the system by way of the emergency protection procedures such as CPOs.
22. Children (Scotland) Act 1995, s 65(5).
23. Children (Scotland) Act 1995, s 16(2).
24. Children (Scotland) Act 1995, s 70.
25. Children (Scotland) Act 1995, s 70.
26. Children (Scotland) Act 1995, ss 66 and 67.
27. Children (Scotland) Act 1995, s 65(7).
28. Children (Scotland) Act 1995, s 65(9).

will bring forward witnesses who are able to speak to evidence justifying the relevant grounds of referral which have not been accepted or have not been understood[29]. The child and the relevant persons have the right to be, and very frequently are, represented by lawyers, generally paid for by free Legal Aid. The procedure in which the sheriff hears the evidence is known as a 'proof' which is the legal term used for a 'trial' in civil matters – and this reflects the legal position that the proceedings before the sheriff are civil and not criminal in nature. The sheriff may appoint a safeguarder[30] for the child or, by virtue of common law powers, a curator *ad litem*, where he or she thinks this is necessary to secure the interests of the child.

The proof takes place in the sheriff's private room. Witnesses give their evidence on oath or affirmation. The witnesses for the reporter may be cross-examined by or on behalf of the other parties. The others may bring forward witnesses who may be cross-examined. The parties or their representatives then address the court and the sheriff considers and decides the case. In all cases except where the child is accused of an offence the standard of proof is the civil standard of the balance of probability. Where the ground for referral is that the child has committed an offence the criminal standard applies[31] and the sheriff must be satisfied 'beyond reasonable doubt' by corroborated evidence before the sheriff can uphold the ground. Where the sheriff upholds at least one ground for referral he or she directs the reporter to arrange a hearing to decide what is to be done. Where the sheriff does not uphold any ground of referral he or she discharges the referral thus bringing the referral proceedings to an end.

The sheriff also has a rôle in relation to decisions by hearings. A child or relevant person can appeal to the sheriff on the ground that a substantial decision of a hearing is not justified in all the circumstances of the case[32].

All substantial decisions by the sheriff (except in relation to CPOs) may be appealed by any party on a point of law to the Sheriff Principal or the Court of Session[33]. There are now important provisions enabling the sheriff court to review the decision of a sheriff at a proof where new evidence has come to light[34]. These provisions are only rarely invoked, but when they are a long and complex hearing of evidence can result.

---

29. Act of Sederunt (Child Care and Maintenance Rules) 1997, SI 1997/291, r 3.47.
30. Children (Scotland) Act 1995, s 41.
31. Children (Scotland) Act 1995, s 68(3)(b).
32. Children (Scotland) Act 1995, s 51(1)-(10).
33. Children (Scotland) Act 1995, s 51(11)-(15).
34. Children (Scotland) Act 1995, s 85.

Part I
The McPerlin Children

The McPerlin Children

Dramatis Personae – as at mid-January 2006

Samantha Transom (later known as Samantha McPerlin).
Aged 12 years, 5 months; born 15 August 1993. Attending Kirklenton Academy, in First Year.

Jacqueline (Jackie) Transom (later known as Jackie McPerlin).
Aged 10 years, 6 months; born 10 July 1995. Attending Kirklenton Primary School, in Primary 6.

Graeme McPerlin.
Aged 1 year, 8 months; born 2 June 2004.

Sharon Transom, known as McPerlin.
Aged 28; born 25 August 1977. Married to Donald McPerlin about 5½ years on 10 July 2000. Sharon works at the check-out at the Caremore Supermarket in Kirklenton. Mother of Samantha, Jackie, and Graeme.

Donald McPerlin.
Aged 44; born 3 January 1962. The father of Graeme.

Rorie McLansing.
Aged 29; born 23 March 1976. Boyfriend and, later, partner of Sharon from late 1992 till 1999. The father of Samantha and Jacqueline.

Susan Ralbie or Transom.
Aged 45; born 30 June 1960. The mother of Sharon.

Hugh Transom.
Aged 46; born 1 February 1959. Husband of Susan Ralbie or Transom and father of Sharon.

Chronological Table

Late Summer, 1993 to late Summer, 1995

Samantha Transom was born on 15 August 1993 to Sharon Transom, the father being Rorie McLansing, six months older than Sharon. They were initially boy-friend and girl-friend for some two years, and then Samantha and Jacqueline were the product of their relationship. Sharon and Rorie separated in 1999. Rorie McLansing leaves the district and emigrates, leaving his partner and children unsupported.

10 July 2000

Sharon Transom and Donald McPerlin marry.

Spring to early Summer, 2004

Sharon has several months in hospital awaiting birth. Samantha accumulates a substantial number of absences from Kirklenton Primary School.

2 June 2004

Graeme McPerlin is born to Sharon and Donald McPerlin

Late Summer, 2004

17 August 2004. School session commences, with Samantha due to go into Primary 7, but no Samantha. The school makes inquiries with no clear result. The Reporter for Kirklenton is notified. He commissions an Initial Assessment Report and a School Report.

6 September 2004. Samantha returns to school and continues to attend normally.

LENTONSHIRE COUNCIL

Social Work Services Department
Kirklenton Office
8 Laverock Road
Kirklenton LE6 4DV

Tel: 012104 545 554; Fax: 012104 545 555

INITIAL ASSESSMENT REPORT

Subject: Samantha McPerlin, date of birth 15th August 1993, at present in Primary 7, Kirklenton Primary School.

Address: 19, Glenview Cottages, Bruaich, Kirklenton, LE29 4QW.

Household

Mother: Sharon Transom or McPerlin. Aged 28; born 25th August 1977, employed as a check-out assistant at the Caremore Supermarket in Kirklenton.

Stepfather: Donald McPerlin. Aged 42; born 3rd January 1962. Not in employment.

Samantha McPerlin. Aged 11 years 1 month; born 15th August 1993, when the mother was in a stable relationship with Rorie McLansing who is Samantha's father. Subject attends Kirklenton Primary School, in Primary 7.

Sister: Jacqueline (Jackie). Aged 9 years 2 months; born 10th July 1995, when mother was in said relationship with Rorie McLansing, who is her father. Attends Kirklenton Primary School, in Primary 5.

Half-brother: Graeme. Aged 3 months; born 2nd June 2004; child of Mr and Mrs McPerlin.

Basis of Report

This report was compiled by the writer on the basis of:

- A preliminary meeting at Kirklenton Primary School on 31st August 2004 with Miss MacKay, guidance teacher.

- Two visits to the family home, on Friday 10th and Monday 13th September 2004.

On the first visit the writer interviewed the child Samantha and Donald McPerlin. The child's mother was at work in Caremore in Kirklenton, where she is employed at the check-out. I asked if an interview could be arranged at a time when the mother was free and was told that she had the afternoon off on the following Monday. I called at about 2 p.m. on Monday 13th September 2004 when I interviewed both Mr and Mrs McPerlin. On this occasion I did not see the child Samantha because she was at school.

Analysis of Family Background

Bruaich is a village of some three thousand inhabitants situated three miles to the north of Kirklenton. It was a coal mining village until the pit closures in the mid 1980s when most of the employment was related to that industry. Mrs McPerlin's father, Hugh Transom, was a miner as was Angus McLansing, the father of Rorie McLansing, who is Samantha's biological father. Both Hugh Transom and Angus McLansing were made redundant in 1984. Neither has worked since. Donald McPerlin was a 'checker' in the pit, which the writer understands to have been a reasonably well-paid post, and he was made redundant at about the same time. He set up a business as a car repairer with his redundancy money and had some success, and married Sharon, who is some sixteen years his junior, in the summer of 2000. However the business failed in the following year. Sharon is now the wage-earner and is hopeful of getting promotion to supervisor in the supermarket where she works. The writer has the impression that 'playing second fiddle', economically, to a woman considerably younger than himself has had a slightly depressing effect on Donald McPerlin, who was brought up in an ethos of male superiority, not to say dominance.

The Child Samantha McPerlin

Samantha was born on 15th August 1993, after a difficult birth, with the mother suffering considerable loss of blood. She has attended mainstream schooling in Kirklenton Primary School and is at present in Primary 7. Her performance is academically high. She is a reserved child with only limited interest in games and, while in no sense a sulky child, has few friends and no close friend or friends among her school contemporaries.

Ground for Referral

Up to the summer term of 2004 Samantha's attendance at school, while scattered with one or two unacceptable periods of absence, was considered to be reasonably satisfactory. Her quick mind easily caught up with lost time and therefore the absences did not cause serious concern. In the summer term of 2004, however, she incurred absences amounting to 93 out of a possible 110 half-days and, after the appropriate procedures, the reporter was informed and the writer was requested to investigate and this report is the result. Samantha did not return to school for the first week of the new term but she has now returned and has attended regularly since 6th September 2004 and has made good progress academically.

The class teacher agreed that Samantha had been more than usually reserved during those classes which she attended at this time. At first she had been unwilling to communicate about her absences, but, in one of her attendances towards the end of the summer term, when Samantha had (unusually for truanting children) come in for an exam, she had explained that she had been off because her mother was in the maternity hospital awaiting the birth of a baby (Graeme, born 2nd June, 2004) having been admitted about three months before the expected birth because of the complications attending the birth of Samantha and Jackie. With the consent of the child's mother the writer checked with the Blackmore Memorial Infirmary and they confirmed that Mrs McPerlin, the child's mother, had indeed been admitted for observation on 13th April 2004 and had remained in the Infirmary until a week after the birth of Graeme.

Samantha's mother and her husband are most supportive of Samantha and speak highly of her behaviour at home and her performance at school. Mr McPerlin is vocal in his praise for Samantha at the time when his wife was in hospital expecting Graeme. He states that she 'virtually ran the house', making sure, for example, that Jackie was ready to be collected by the school bus every day. The writer checked with the school which confirmed that Jackie had had no material absences during this period. The school is apologetic that it did not pick up on the oddity that Samantha was persistently absent from school while Jackie was attending normally. Mr and Mrs McPerlin now seem to realise that allowing Samantha to take over so much of the running of the house while the mother was in hospital was inappropriate, although they still tend to justify this, or at least mitigate it, by reference to Samantha's ability to 'catch up' quickly owing to her obvious maturity and intelligence. On being pressed by the writer, however, they now seem to accept that this was wrong and should not ever happen again.

Assessment and recommendation

The explanation given to the writer that the absences were caused by the child helping out during a family crisis seemed to the writer to be an accurate one. It is corroborated by the fact that in the new term, after an initial absence, she has had perfect attendance. The writer was a little concerned that the 'father' of the household had apparently been unable or unwilling to perform this rôle and when questioned about this Mr McPerlin was reticent, as he was about most matters. The writer's impression was that being a 'house-husband' is not something which comes naturally to the males in a community such as this. Sometimes Mr McPerlin seemed unduly reticent but Mrs McPerlin confirmed the writer's initial impression that the losing of his job as a miner and the subsequent failure of his car-repair business has had a marked de-skilling effect upon Mr McPerlin, with consequent reluctance on his part to participate in any inquiries which bear upon this situation, for which he blames himself.

Fortunately the maturity and natural intelligence of Samantha has enabled her to catch up completely with her school work. The school reports that she is if anything more reserved than before and even more of a 'loner' but this is readily attributable to her having been away from school for nearly a whole term. The rest of the family are fully supportive and would not welcome social work intervention.

Weighing all these matters the writer can see no rôle for social work intervention at this stage. The school is aware of the position and will monitor Samantha's emotional as well as academic development. For all these reasons the writer would suggest, with respect, that neither formal intervention in the form of a referral to a hearing under section 52(2)(h) of the Children (Scotland) Act 1995, nor informal voluntary work by the Department, is indicated in the present case.

Marcia Drummond
Social Worker

29th September 2004

---

12 October 2004 – in the Reporter's office

The reporter has now considered the Initial Assessment Report and has come to the conclusion that formal intervention is not required. He writes to Samantha, Mr and Mrs McPerlin (as 'relevant persons') and the school (as the person who brought the matter to his notice) that he has decided that a children's hearing does not require to be arranged and that he does not consider it appropriate to refer the child to the local authority for advice, guidance, or assistance of the child and her family under Chapter 1 of Part II of the Children (Scotland) Act 1995[1].

---

1.   Children (Scotland) Act 1995 section 56(4).

*Note [1]   **Relevant persons.** Until the Children (Scotland) Act 1995 the biological mother and father of a child were referred to as 'parents' and, in order to allow for persons in loco parentis, section 30(2) of the Social Work (Scotland) Act, 1968 provided that for certain purposes 'parent' should include guardian and section 94(1) of the 1968 Act (the interpretation section) gave 'guardian' an extended meaning, including any person recognised by a court or a hearing as having for the time being the custody, charge, or control of the child. This was perhaps somewhat artificial, involving as it did the possibility of referring to someone as 'parent' when s/he manifestly was not the parent. It had however the advantage of allowing one, in the (fairly normal) situation where the parents were the parents of referring to them as such. It is not known if the somewhat illogical provisions of the earlier Act caused any real problems but the drafters of the Children (Scotland) Act 1995, as is the way with revisers[2], were impelled to try to improve by changing, and hit upon the idea of trying to bring all the kinds of person having relevant rights and responsibilities for a child under the same umbrella and called this umbrella 'relevant person'. Section 93(2)(b) of the 1995 Act provides that 'relevant person' means:*

'(a)   any parent enjoying parental responsibilities or parental rights under Part I of this Act;

(b)   any person in whom parental responsibilities or rights are vested by, under or by virtue of this Act; and

(c)   any person who appears to be a person who ordinarily (and other than by reason only of his employment) has charge of, or control over, the child'.

By virtue of section 3 of the Children (Scotland) Act 1995, as amended by section 23 of the Family Law (Scotland) Act 2006, which came onto force on 8 May 2006 the principal shelterers under the umbrella of 'relevant person' are:

- *a child's mother, whether or not she is or has been married to the father;*

- *a child's father if married to the child's mother at the time of conception or subsequently (the father being regarded as married even if the purported marriage was (a) voidable or (b) void but wrongly believed (whether by error of law or of fact) in good faith to be valid by the mother and father);*

- *any person, including an unmarried father, in whom is vested parental rights or responsibilities under the Children (Scotland) Act 1995, s 11(2)(b) or s 11(2)(h) or of the Law Reform (Parent and Child) (Scotland) Act 1986 ('the 1986 Act'),*

---

2.   The late, learned, and much loved Professor W A Watson was wont to remark, 'There is no passion which beats stronger in one man's breast than the desire to change another man's draft'.

s 3(1) (which is a provision analogous to s 11 of the 1995 Act but repealed by that Act) or any other order, disposal or resolution affecting parental responsibilities or rights;

- *a child's (unmarried, presumably) father who has entered a formal agreement in appropriate form and registered in the Books of Council and Session with the mother whereby he becomes vested in parental responsibilities as at the date of such registration; and*

- *an unmarried father, who has been validly appointed as guardian of a child under a testamentary disposition in terms of s 7 of the Children (Scotland) Act 1995;*

- *the biological father of a child married to the mother at the time of the child's conception or subsequently;*

- *the biological father of the child who, though not married to the mother at the time of the child's conception or sub-sequently is registered under an appropriate Registration of Births etc statute[3]. (This provision does not have retro-spective effect, so it only applies to births registered after 8 May 2006.)*

It should be noted that an unmarried father is not ipso facto a relevant person – hence the elaborate provisions as to how an unmarried father may acquire the status of relevant person. A long-term foster carer may arguably be regarded as ordinarily, and other than by virtue of his employment, having charge of, or control over, a child, and by virtue of this to be a relevant person. It has now been decided that a foster carer by virtue of a supervision require-ment is to be regarded as 'ordinarily' having the care and control of the child in terms of section 93(2)(b) of the Children (Scotland) Act 1995 and is consequently a relevant person[4].

*Note [2] **The reporter's decision.** The considerations to which the reporter must have regard in deciding whether or not to take this type of case to a hearing or to refer for advice, guidance and assistance under s 56(4)(b) of the Act include[5]:–*

- *the seriousness or otherwise of the alleged offence(s) against the child;*

- *the presence or absence of risk to the child;*

- *the attitude of the family – e.g. how seriously those in the family not accused of offending are concerned by the allegations of the offence;*

---

3.   Listed in section 3(1A) of the Children (Scotland) Act 1995, as amended.
4.   *S v N* 2002 SLT 589, 2002 FamLR 40; Extra Div; sub nom *JS and TK v MN* 2002 GWD 9-275.
5.   The Scottish Children's Reporter Administration ('SCRA') has issued a 'Framework for Decision Making for Reporters', available on SCRA's website (at www.scra.gov.uk). What appears here, while broadly consistent with the SCRA 'Framework', represents the writer's interpretation of the rôle of the reporter at this stage.

- *the attitude of the child;*

- *the presence or otherwise of addiction and/or aggression;*

- *the age of the child;*

- *the state of relationships within the family; and*

- *how the child is regarded in school and how she or he is getting on in school.*

- *the reporter's assessment of the value of the advice of the social worker*

- *the principle, enacted in s 16(3) of the Children (Scotland) Act 1995 that a requirement or order should be made in relation to a child only where making the requirement or order concerned would be better for the child than not making any order or requirement[6].*

Reporters and hearings, as public authorities under section 6 of the Human Rights Act 1998, require to comply with those provisions of the European Convention on Human Rights which that Act incorporates into our law such as Article 6 ('Right to a fair trial') and Article 7 (No punishment without law') and Article 8 ('Right to respect for private and family life)[7]. Reporters must accordingly have regard to these provisions of the Convention.

Early September 2005

Mrs McPerlin realises she is pregnant again.

Late December 2005

Mrs McPerlin tells the family, including Samantha, that she is pregnant, that the new baby is due at the beginning of June 2006, and that, because of the difficulties surrounding Graeme's birth, she will probably have to go into hospital for the last few weeks of her pregnancy.

Social Work Notes of Marcia Drummond

13.01.06 at 4.15 pm. Phone call from Samantha McPerlin, d.o.b. 15.08.93. Reminded me that I had prepared report re alleged truancy in late summer 2004. She wants to talk to me about a confidential matter. Emphatic that I not to come to home or school. Can come to office any Tuesday or Thursday afternoon when usually goes with friends to

---

6.   This principle is frequently referred to as the 'minimum intervention' principle. The writer prefers to refer to it as the 'no non-beneficial order' principle – see Kearney, *Children's Hearings and the Sheriff Court*, second edn (2000) paragraphs 2.20 and 25.12. Professor Kenneth McK Norrie, however, defends the 'minimum intervention' usage in his *Children's Hearings in Scotland*, second edn (2005) page 123.

7.   For the texts of these Articles see Appendix 2.

Swimming Pool in Kirklenton. Says very important but not immediately urgent. I have panel hearing on Thursday coming so suggest Tuesday 17th Jan and this is arranged.

Going to disclose physical or sexual abuse?? Re-open file. See my IAR 29.09.04. Check Child Protection Register – no entry for any of family. Notify Candice[8], who confirms arrangement OK and asks to be kept informed.

17.01.06 at 4.30 pm. Samantha interviewed. I explain that I may not be able to keep what she says secret if steps have to be taken to protect her or others. She accepts this. I mention that it may be necessary to have a joint police/social worker interview, possibly recorded on closed circuit TV, which I cannot arrange today. Samantha v mature and sensible and understands. She cannot stay long. I tell her I will note her statement in long-hand and she, without prompting, stated as follows, which I have typed up from my hand-written notes which I have preserved in the file.

> *Note [3]   What follows, as Marcia Drummond has made clear in her notes, is a 'Statement' by the child, that is it represents the words of the child unfiltered by the mind of the statement taker. It is not what Scottish lawyers call a 'precognition' and English lawyers a 'proof of evidence'. A precognition, unlike a statement, is usually a paraphrase by the interviewer of what the witness has said. This distinction is an important one and Marcia Drummond is right to make clear that what she is recording is a statement, because it has potentially a high evidential value. The reason for this is that section 2(1)(b) of the Civil Evidence (Scotland) Act 1988 allows for the admissibility, for the purpose of proving any matter contained within it, of 'a statement' by any person whose oral evidence would have been admissible, and section 9 of the same Act defines 'statement' as including 'any representation (however made or expressed) of fact or opinion but does not include a statement made in precognition'. Why this 'protection' is afforded to precognitions is explained by Lord Justice-Clerk Thomson, with characteristically sardonic wit, in Kerr v HM Advocate 1958 JC 14 at 19: ' ...one reason why reference to precognition is frowned on, is that in a precognition you cannot be sure that you are getting what the potential witness has to say in a pure and undefiled form. It is filtered through the mind of another, whose job it is to put what he thinks the witness means into a form suitable for use in judicial proceedings. The process tends to colour the result. Precognoscers as a rule appear to be gifted with a measure of optimism which no amount of disillusionment can damp'. The importance of having a 'statement' (as opposed to a precognition) which can be set up under the 1988 Act was illustrated in F v Kennedy (No. 2) 1993 SLT 1284, 1992 SCLR 750. In this case it was held to be acceptable to use a child's*

---

8.   Candice Roberts is Marcia Drummond's Senior in the Department.

statement to supplement the evidence which the child had given in the proof before the sheriff even although the child had <u>not</u> been asked about the subject matter of the statement while giving evidence. Marcia emphasises that she has preserved her original hand-written notes. It is no longer obligatory, again thanks to the 1988 Act, to produce the 'best evidence' in the form of the actual notes taken at the time, but it is good practice to preserve such notes and to bring them to court in order to be able to produce them to rebut any suggestion in cross-examination that the typed version has been subjected to the optimistic filtration to which Lord Justice-Clerk Thomson refers.

STATEMENT (17th January 2006)

by Samantha McPerlin, d.o.b. 15.08.1993,
19, Glenview Cottages,
Bruaich, Kirklenton.

I want to tell the full story about what happened when I was off school in the summer term of 2004. Everything I told you about looking after the house while mummy was in hospital was true but it was not the whole truth. What I didn't tell you was that on most Saturday nights my stepfather, whom I call Donald, would come up to my bedroom after a night's drinking in the pub and come into my bed and fondle me under my nightie. He would pull up my nightie to round my neck and touch and rub the tops of my legs at what I now know to call my vagina. He would also fondle my chest. He sometimes tried to get me to fondle his private parts but I always resisted this because I found that to be particularly unpleasant. He never forced me further, partly, I think, because he was too drunk. He would sometimes fall asleep in my bed and waken up hours later and then creep away to his own bedroom. It was only when drunk that he would come to me in this way. I think he missed physical contact with my mother. He did not threaten me in any way but I didn't tell anyone about it because I didn't want anything to happen which would upset mummy and perhaps cause her to lose the baby. After mummy came back he never came back to me and I thought it best to keep quiet. I would have kept on keeping quiet except that when I heard that mummy was pregnant again and might have to go into hospital for four to six weeks before the birth which is expected to be at the beginning of June. I realised that Jackie was about the same age now as I was then and I was afraid that Donald would try this again. I think he did something to Jackie at New Year when he was very drunk, because on the morning after Hogmanay Jackie was very upset about something and burst into tears and said something about 'Daddy' (as she calls Donald) which I didn't properly hear and she then clammed up about it. I think I would be able to look after myself if Mummy was away and that I could protect Jackie if I was there, but I would be afraid he would try it on with Jackie at some time when I could not protect her and I know this would damage Jackie far more than it damaged me, for she is young for her age while I have always been old for my age. Even when I was 10 I think I was able to cope with all this much better than I think many other girls of my present age could. You have asked me if there were any witnesses to what he did to me but of course there could be no witnesses. Jackie was in the house but in another bedroom and was always asleep when this happened. I am really worried for Jackie and hope you will be able to do something. I do not want to discuss this with my mother since I do not think she would believe me. She always sticks up for Donald. I do not think she would co-operate with any of your enquiries. I do not know what will be for the best in the long run but at present, and with the prospect of mummy being away from home for a long time both Jackie and I would like to avoid being in the house with Donald alone, even if this meant us having to live somewhere else.

18.01.06. Report meeting with Samantha to Candice who says she will fix meeting with Tony[9] the next Monday.

19.01.06. Case discussion about Samantha. Just Candice and I with Tony in the chair. All agree that situation extremely serious. Probably not urgent since mother unlikely to go to hospital before beginning of April, but always risk of earlier admission to hospital and of repetition of the actions disclosed. Decided to ask police to consider investigation. Candice to contact Sgt. Doreen Kilpatrick of the Family and Child Unit.

Minute of Case Discussion held on Monday 23.01.06.

Children

Samantha Transom/McPerlin 15.08.93.
Jacqueline (Jackie) Transom/McPerlin 10.07.95.
Graeme McPerlin 2.06.04.
Address: 19, Glenview Cottages, Bruaich, Kirklenton, LE29 4QW

Present:

Tony Maclagan	Area Manager, Kirklenton
Marietta Nimmo	Health Visitor, Bruaich
Isabella Mackay	Class Teacher, Kirklenton Primary School
Doreen Kilpatrick	Sergeant, Family and Child Unit, Lentonshire and Muirbrachlan Police Service
Miriam Stevenson	Constable, Family and Child Unit, Lentonshire and Muirbrachlan Police Service
Marcia Drummond	Social Worker, Lentonshire Council
Candice Roberts	Senior Social Worker, Lentonshire Council

---

9.   Anthony Maclagan is the Area Manager of the Kirklenton Office of the Lentonshire Social Services Department.

Apology:

Kenneth Warrender, Head Teacher, Kirklenton Academy

Summary of discussion

Marcia Drummond advised that Samantha's mother, Sharon McPerlin, had been referred to the department in 1993 because Sharon had been under age when Samantha was born and that no action had been taken beyond some voluntary work with the family. Sharon had just left school and initially had brought up Samantha at her parents' home but in 1994 had set up house with Rorie McLansing, then aged 18, and the couple had remained together till 1999 with another child, Jacqueline (Jackie) being born on 10th July 1995. Sharon and Rorie had split up, amicably enough, in 1999 and Sharon had started going about with Donald McPerlin, a man sixteen years older than herself, and they got married on 10th July 2000. There was one child of this marriage, namely Graeme, born 2nd June 2004. Samantha had come to the attention of the department in the summer of 2004 because of absence from school but no action had been taken. Marcia laid before the meeting her report dated 29th September 2004 and its contents were noted by all present.

Marcia went on to advise that Samantha had on 17th January 2006 disclosed incidents of sexual abuse of herself by Donald McPerlin during the summer of 2004 at the time when Sharon was in hospital before the birth of Graeme and possible sexual abuse of Jacqueline at New Year time 2005/2006. Marcia read out the statement she had taken from Samantha.

Marietta Nimmo advised that she had known the family since the birth of Sharon in 1977. She knew Sharon well, not only as Health Visitor but as someone to pass the time of day with – Bruaich being a small and fairly tightly knit community where almost everybody knows everybody else. Sharon is a responsible woman. Although she had left school without any special qualifications she is well-informed and articulate. She is ambitious to 'get on' and has well-founded hopes of promotion to a managerial post in the Caremore supermarket chain. There is one respect in which Sharon is less than balanced, and that is Donald. His car repair business collapsed in about 2001 when Donald was convicted after trial of drunk driving and heavily fined and disqualified for four years. Although it was a serious case with a very high reading – hence the heavy fine and the long disqualifica-tion – Sharon defends Donald and accuses the police of having 'framed' him, even although she was in the car with the children at the time. She is very bitter against the police and the authorities in general. Apart from this Marietta has had no serious concerns about the family. She confirmed that Sharon would require to go into hospital for a period before the birth of her fourth child. Asked by Tony if there was any likelihood of Sharon having to go to hospital before May of this year Marietta stated that while she had no definite infor-mation this possibility could not be ruled out.

Isabella Mackay advised that when at Primary School Samantha was intelligent and very hardworking, with high marks in all subjects. She was however very reserved and, with hindsight, Isabella regrets that she did not look more closely into the reasons for Samantha's absence in the summer term of 2004. Jacqueline was less academically accomplished than Samantha, but still above average. She was more out-going than her older sister but Isabella had noticed that she had become markedly quieter during the first two weeks of the present term and this was alarming in view of what Samantha had disclosed.

Sergeant Doreen Kilpatrick advised that this case had many of the typical features of potentially very serious child sexual abuse. The abuse was associated with the absence of the abuser's partner and, as this absence was likely to be repeated, she thought that action must be taken. In view of Marietta's suggestion that Sharon might be admitted to hospital at any time Sgt Kilpatrick opined that action should be taken urgently. In any event it was necessary to interview and possibly medically examine Samantha and Jacqueline as soon as possible and there was evidence to suggest that the parents would not make them available. Sgt. Kilpatrick suggested getting a CPO. She pointed out that s 57(2)(c) of the Children (Scotland) Act 1995 allowed for the granting of a CPO where there were reasonable grounds for suspecting significant harm and that enquiries were being frustrated by access to the children being denied. She concluded by saying that she will be conferring with her superiors with a view to making a report to the procurator fiscal.

On being asked about the possibility of Mr and Mrs McPerlin allowing access to the children for the purpose of investigations Marietta stated her view that neither parent would allow this. Marcia confirmed that this was her view also. Marietta justified her view by her experience of the mother's anti-authority stance in relation to the conviction of Donald. All the children had been in the car at the time and her defence of her husband indicated that she would take his part even where the children were at risk. Marcia based her view on the statement by Samantha that her mother 'always sticks up for Donald' and the elaborate measures taken by Samantha to avoid letting her parents know that she was in touch with the department.

Tony stated that the sense of the meeting so far was that compulsory measures under the Act would have to be taken. He commented that the evidence of probable significant harm was quite strong but expressed the opinion that the evidence that access to the children was required 'as a matter of urgency' was less compelling and asked Candice if she thought there was enough to persuade the sheriff at Kirklenton that a CPO was necessary – might this not be a case where the less invasive Child Assessment Order (CAO) might be appropriate?

Candice advised that there had been very few CAOs taken out throughout Scotland. She stated that the evidence of serious sexual abuse of Samantha was strong – the evidence here was stronger than the highly inferential evidence which had led to the Place of Safety Order being granted by the sheriff in the famous 'Orkney' case. Accordingly the department owed it to the children to take action which would avoid repetition of abuse of which there was unequivocal evidence from one source (Samantha) and possible evidence from another source (Jackie). The strength of this evidence more than made up for the less strong (but real enough) evidence of 'urgency'. Candice added that in the circumstances there could be no case made out for applying for an Exclusion Order under section 76 of the Children (Scotland) Act 1995 since it was fairly clear, in view of the mother's defensive stance in relation to her husband, that there would be no person in the home willing and able to 'police' such an order as required under section 76(2)(c) of the Act.

Commenting that the sense of the meeting seemed clearly to be in favour of applying for a CPO in respect of Samantha and Jackie, Tony asked for views as to whether Graeme (d.o.b. 02.06.04) should be included in any order. Of course the working principle, based inter alia on the work of Finkelhor (e.g. Finkelhor D, (1984), *Child Sexual Abuse*, New York: Free Press) was that a child sex abuser was a danger to all children, but Graeme was a male toddler and the father's own child and the information from Samantha was that it was females at or about the age of puberty whom Donald abused. If an order were applied for in respect of Graeme, would an 'at birth' order have to be applied for when Sharon's new baby arrived? If all three, and then all four, were looked after by the local authority, could they be kept together?

Candice advised that a foster placement was available for the two girls, but unfortunately it could not take Graeme or any future arrival. A placement was available for Graeme but it could not take any future child. Both placements were in Kirklenton and fairly near each other. Both could offer long-term fostering if required. Candice stated her view that the principle that a child abuser was a danger to all children should be adhered to and that therefore Graeme should be included. The ground of so doing could be explained to the sheriff and it would be for her or him to make the decision. The question of any future arrival could be addressed nearer the time, by which time court action would probably have been taken by the parents to try to displace any orders which had been granted.

Marcia indicated her agreement with Candice's summation, as did Sgt. Kilpatrick and Constable Stevenson.

Tony said that the sense of the meeting was that a CPO should be applied for in relation to Samantha, Jacqueline, and Graeme as soon as possible and this was **agreed**. Tony asked Candice and Marcia to prepare the necessary papers and proceed with the applications.

(Signed) *Anthony E Maclagan*
Area Manager, Kirklenton

Note [4]   A Child Protection Case Discussion such as this is of crucial importance. Clear decisions should be reached, with the next steps clearly defined, including specification of the actions to be considered by identified professionals. The role of the Chair has been described as 'pivotal' and the keeping of accurate minutes with appropriate phrasing and emphasis is essential[10]. The minutes should be circulated amongst participants for approval and, if need be, correction, and the final version sent to participants and any person who was invited but could not come. The perceived inadequacy of the management of Child Protection Case Conferences in the Caleb Ness case led to the authors of the report on that case to make important recommendations as to good practice[11].

Wednesday, 25 January 2006, morning

The foregoing minute is typed in the Social Work Office and e-mailed and posted to the offices of the other participants with the request that they, as a matter of urgency, confirm that the contents correctly narrate what took place or, alternatively, suggest any proposed changes. A copy is also sent to Mr Warrender, who presented his apologies. In the event no suggestions for changes are received. In the meantime, having regard to the relative urgency of the situation, the social workers, reasonably confident of the accuracy of the minute in all material particulars, go ahead with the preparations for a CPO, without waiting for replies from the other participants.

OBTAINING THE CHILD PROTECTION ORDER

Wednesday, 25 January 2006 – later in the morning

Marcia Drummond, in accordance with good practice, phones the Authority Reporter, Hector Somerville, advising him briefly of the situation, including the decision of the Case Discussion, and tells him of the Council's intention to apply for CPOs for the three children before the end of the week. The Authority Reporter (who is of course independent of the local authority) offers no concluded view on the proposed course of action. Marcia confirms that she will, immediately on any CPO being granted, give notice to Mr Somerville's office[12], and Mr Somerville mentions that not only should a copy of any CPO be sent[13], but also <u>a copy or note of any supporting evidence, written or oral, which has been presented to the sheriff under section 57(3)(c) of the Children (Scotland) Act 1995</u>. Mr Somerville tells Marcia that the case reporter will be Laura

---

10.   Cf Stevenson, Olive, *Case Conferences in Child Protection*, in Wilson, K and James, A, *The Child Protection Handbook* (1995) Ballière Tiindall, London, at page 234 and *passim*.
11.   Susan O'Brien QC, Dr Helen Hammond, Moira McKinnon, *Report of the Caleb Ness Inquiry*, October 2003, Edinburgh, paras 9.2.1 to 9.36.
12.   Children (Scotland) Act 1995 s 57(5)
13.   Act of Sederunt (Child Care and Maintenance Rules) 1997, SI 1997/291 r 3.32(b)

Cameron and asks her to remember that any CPO requires to be implemented (or at least attempted to be implemented) within twenty four hours of its being granted[14] and, therefore, that it is important that Laura Cameron be told of the precise time of the granting of any CPO and also the precise time of implementation or attempt at implementation. Marcia confirms that she is aware of these provisions and will comply with them. Mr Somerville confirms that the case reporter, Laura Cameron, will be informed immediately his office hears of any CPO being granted and thanks Marcia Drummond for giving him advance notice.

> *Note [5]   Once a CPO has been granted the reporter must keep the case under review and ensure that a child shall not be kept subject to the CPO, or conditions or directions made thereunder, where, having regard to the welfare of the child, he considers that, in the light of a change of circumstances or further information, the conditions for the making of a CPO, or of conditions or directions therein, are no longer satisfied and, in this event, must notify the person who implemented the order and the sheriff who granted it[15]. This is why the reporter requires to be put in the same position as the sheriff was when granting the CPO in the first place – hence the need, noted in the underlined passage in the foregoing, for the reporter to be aware of the basis of information which is to be laid before the sheriff who is to be asked to grant the order. (Otherwise the reporter could not know if there had been any change of circumstances.)*
>
> *The provisions about CPOs in the Children (Scotland) Act 1995 and the associated Rules are complex and the provisions in relation to timescales are particularly demanding, yet there have been comparatively few examples of things going wrong owing to rules having been disregarded, by time limits having been missed, or otherwise. It is thought that this is, at least in part, thanks to the professionals' enjoying with each other relationships of mutual respect which enable conversations such as this to take place. The reporter, as the 'expert' dealing with the details of the Act on a daily basis should not be shy of sharing his or her expertise with other workers in the field. The social worker, while also expert in the field, should, where there is, as here, a good working relationship, welcome and not resent having his or her understanding of these provisions confirmed.*

Thursday, 26 January 2006, morning

Marcia Drummond prepares, and Candice Roberts revises, the Application for a Child Protection Order, using Form 47, contained in Schedule 1 of the Act of Sederunt (Child Care and Maintenance Rules) 1997.

---

14. Children (Scotland) Act 1995 s 60(1).
15. Children (Scotland) Act 1995 s 60(3) and (5).

Note [6]   This application, although to a degree urgent, is not being treated as having the high degree of urgency which would attach if a child were in imminent danger of significant harm or of becoming imminently liable to being removed from a place of safety, such as a hospital for example, where an application is made to remove a baby immediately after birth. In applications having that high degree of urgency the application would be prepared as soon as practicable, often enough by the 'Out of Hours' team of social workers.

Rule 3.30

FORM 47

APPLICATION FOR A CHILD PROTECTION ORDER BY LOCAL AUTHORITY

Section 57 of the Children (Scotland) Act 1995

Case No: 8B 2/06
Date Lodged: 26.01.06

Application to the Sheriff at Kirklenton

For a Child Protection Order under Section 57 of the Children (Scotland) Act 1995

Part 1   DETAILS OF APPLICANT AND OTHER PERSONS WHOM THE APPLICANT BELIEVES SHOULD RECEIVE NOTICE OF THE APPLICATION

APPLICANT

Lentonshire Council, per Marcia Drummond, Social Worker, Social Work Department, 8 Laverock Road, Kirklenton, LE6 4DV. Tel: 012104 545 554. Fax: 012104 545 555.

CHILDREN

*Samantha McPerlin,
d.o.b 15.08.1993, girl*

*Jacqueline McPerlin,
d.o.b. 10.07.1995, girl*

*Graeme McPerlin,
d.o.b 02.06.2004, boy*

All children reside at 19 Glenview Cottages, Bruaich, Kirklenton, LE29 4QW

RELEVANT PERSON(S)	*Sharon McPerlin, (Mother)* *19 Glenview Cottages, Bruaich,* *Kirklenton, LE29 4QW* *Donald McPerlin, (married to mother* *of Graeme – person ordinarily having* *charge of all 3 children)* *19 Glenview Cottages, Bruaich,* *Kirklenton, LE29 4QW*
SAFEGUARDER	*(Not applicable – no safeguarder* *known to have been appointed)*
THE PRINCIPAL REPORTER	*The Principal Reporter, per Hector* *Somerville, Authority Reporter,* *Scottish Children's Reporter* *Administration, 17 Laverock Road,* *Kirklenton LE6 7EK.* *Tel: 012104 545 700.* *Fax: 012104 545 710*
ANY OTHER PERSONS WHO SHOULD RECEIVE NOTICE OF THE APPLICATION:	*None*

Note: Information to be provided in Part 3 where applicant does not wish to disclose the address or whereabouts of the child or any other person to persons receiving notice of the application.

Part 2   INFORMATION ABOUT THE APPLICATION AND ORDERS SOUGHT

GROUNDS FOR MAKING APPLICATION

Previous referral to department (in September 2004) of child Samantha in respect of absence from school April to June 2004 when the mother was in hospital for an extended period expecting baby (Graeme).

Subsequent information (17th January 2006) from Samantha that she was sexually abused by Donald McPerlin when absent from school April – June 2004).

The mother is again expecting a baby and is again going to be in hospital for an extended period.

Samantha's younger sister, Jacqueline (d.o.b. 10.07.1995) is now about age Samantha was two years ago. Samantha has reported circumstances suggesting that Jacqueline may have been abused by Donald over New Year period (ie around 1st January 2006) and is apprehensive that she may be targeted when Mum has to go to hospital later this year.

Health visitor has reported that Sharon is very anti-authority, and tends to take Donald's part even where children's interests are involved, citing her failure to accept Donald's conviction for drunk driving on an occasion when she and children were in the car.

Samantha has confirmed that her mum always supports Donald.

OTHER APPLICATIONS AND ORDERS WHICH AFFECT THE CHILD

None

SUPPORTING EVIDENCE

The following evidence is produced –

1.   *Initial Assessment Report dated 29th September 2004.*

2.   *Statement by Samantha dated 17th January 2006.*

3.   *Minute of Case Discussion held 23.01.2006.*

Part 3   DETAILS OF ORDER SOUGHT AND ANY TERMS, CONDITIONS OR DIRECTIONS

ORDER SOUGHT: *The applicant requests the sheriff to make a Child Protection Order in respect of the children:*

Samantha Transom aka McPerlin, d.o.b. 15.08.1993
Jacqueline Transom aka McPerlin, d.o.b. 10.07.1995
Graeme McPerlin d.o.b. 02.06.2004

TERMS AND CONDITIONS TO BE ATTACHED TO ORDER

In terms of section 57(4) the applicant seeks an order to

(a) Require Mrs Sharon Transom or McPerlin, 19 Glenview Cottages, Bruaich, Kirklenton LE29 4QW, Mr Donald McPerlin, 19 Glenview Cottages, Bruaich, Kirklenton LE29 4QW, and any other person in a position to do so to produce said children or any of them to the applicant;

(b) Authorise the removal of the said children by the applicant to a place or places of safety and the keeping of the said children at that place or places;

DIRECTIONS IN RELATION TO THE EXERCISE OR FULFILMENT OF PARENTAL RESPONSBILITIES OR PARENTAL RIGHTS

In terms of section 58(4) and (5) the applicant seeks the following direction(s) –

That the applicant be granted the parental responsibility of having the child Jacqueline examined by a suitably qualified paediatrician within the Blackmore Memorial Infirmary, Kirklenton.

That the applicant be granted the parental responsibility of securing all normal medical and dental treatment of the said children, Samantha, Jacqueline, and Graeme.

That the relevant persons be allowed supervised contact with the said children, Samantha, Jacqueline and Graeme at such places and for such periods as the local authority shall in its discretion determine

ANY OTHER ORDERS SOUGHT

Non-disclosure of the whereabouts of the children, Samantha, Jacqueline, and Graeme to the relevant persons, Sharon McPerlin and Donald McPerlin

Service of restricted documents on the child Jacqueline, because of the sensitive nature of the subject matter of the application

Dispense with service of all documents on the child Graeme because of his age (one year and six months)

Authorisation for Anthony Edwin Maclagan, Candice Roberts and Marcia Smith Drummond, or any one of them, being officers of the local authority, Lentonshire Council, authorised by said Authority to represent it throughout the proceedings and in all respects suitable so to do, to serve the Order by way of personal service and/or oral service, all in terms of Rules 3.15(3), 3.16(1)(c) and 3.16(2) of the Act of Sederunt (Child Care and Maintenance Rules) 1997, owing to the consideration that service requires to be made and that there is not sufficient time to use other methods.

Part 4   DETAILS OF FIRST ORDER SOUGHT FROM THE SHERIFF

The applicant requests the sheriff to:

a Make a Child Protection Order in respect of the said children

Samantha McPerlin, d.o.b 15.08.1993, girl
Jacqueline McPerlin, d.o.b. 10.07.1995, girl
Graeme McPerlin, d.o.b 02.06.2004, boy

on the terms and conditions set out in Part 3 of the application, and subject to the directions sought in Part 3 of the application.

b Order the applicant forthwith to serve a copy of the Child Protection Order, and a copy of the application, on

i.   *The child Samantha, together with a notice in Form 50*

ii.   *The persons listed in Part 1 of this application , together with a* notice in form 51;

<u>and</u> order the applicant forthwith to serve on the child Jacqueline the following document only, namely, notice in Form 50.

c *Order that the addresses of the said children, Samantha, Jacqueline, and Graeme should not be disclosed in the application*

d *Dispense with service on the child Graeme for the following reason: his young age (1 year and 6 months).*

Signed *Marcia S Drummond*   Date: 26th January 2006.

Marcia Smith Drummond, Social Worker, Social Work Services Department, 8 Laverock Road, Kirklenton, LE6 4DV. Tel: 012104 545 554. Fax: 012104 545 555.

Note [7]   Note that this application is made under section 57(1) of the Children (Scotland) Act 1995 – application by 'any person' who can satisfy the sheriff that there are 'reasonable grounds to believe' that the child is at risk – as opposed to s 57(2), which empowers a local authority to ask for a Child Protection Order where it has 'reasonable grounds to suspect' such risk. A local authority is of course included in the category 'any person' and therefore where, as here, there is substantial information, notably the statement of Samantha, as to the risk, the local authority has decided to use s 57(1) the conditions of which are somewhat less demanding in that s 57(2) requires the local authority to satisfy the sheriff that its enquiries are being frustrated by access to the child being unreasonably denied, whereas the parallel provision in s 57(1) is simply that the sheriff must be satisfied 'that an order under this section is necessary to protect the child from such [i.e. significant] harm (or such further harm)'.

Thursday, 26 January 2006

2 pm

Marcia Drummond phones the Sheriff Clerk's office at Kirklenton Sheriff Court and advises that an application for a Child Protection Order will be made in the afternoon. It is arranged that the application will be heard at 2.30 pm.

2.10 pm

Miss Drummond then phones the Reporter's office and tells Laura Cameron that the CPO application is to be heard that afternoon and that if any CPO is granted she will ensure that the paperwork is with Miss Cameron no later than first thing on the following morning.

2.30 pm – In the Sheriff Clerk's office

Candice Roberts and Marcia Drummond arrive at the Sheriff Clerk's office and hand in the Application Form and accompanying papers. (They also have with them the whole Social Work file on the McPerlin family). The sheriff clerk depute 'books' the application, i.e. records it in the Books of Court, takes a copy of all the documents for record purposes and takes the principal documents to Sheriff Grey's chambers. The sheriff reads the papers in preparation for the meeting with the social workers.

2.45 pm

Sheriff Grey phones the sheriff clerk depute and says she is ready to see the social workers. The sheriff clerk depute brings them into Sheriff Grey's chambers. The social workers introduce themselves and confirm that they are authorised by the local authority to make the application.

> *Note [8]   Generally in court proceedings[16] only an advocate, or a solicitor advocate or solicitor holding a current valid practising certificate, is entitled to represent a party, sign court papers and appear on a party's behalf in court. However rule 3.21 of the Act of Sederunt (Child Care and Maintenance Rules) 1997 empowers a person who is not thus qualified to represent any party in these proceedings provided s/he can satisfy the sheriff that s/he is a 'suitable person' and is authorised by the local authority to act as its representative. Some local authorities use solicitors from their legal department to present applications. Where social workers are used they are usually issued with an 'identification card', which certifies that the bearer is authorised by the local authority under rule 3.21.*

Sheriff Grey, who, since this is a hearing in chambers, is not robed, invites the social workers and the sheriff clerk to sit round the table. She indicates that she has read the papers but would like the social worker closest to the case to explain briefly the background to the application. (Sheriffs do not generally administer the oath at this stage, and it is thought that this is correct, since the sheriff is receiving 'information' and not 'evidence'. The sheriff will note the substance of what is said in her notebook.)

Marcia Drummond summarises the history, referring mainly to the contents of the statement by Samantha. The sheriff asks whether there is any real need for a Child Protection Order, having regard (a) to the consideration that it will be some time before the mother will be admitted to hospital and (b) the issue of whether it might be possible for an attempt to be made to have the children seen and interviewed by consent of Mr and Mrs McPerlin.

---

16. Special rules apply in Summary Causes and Small Claims – also in relation to certain public officials.

Note [9]   Although, as noted in paragraph [6] supra, this is an application under s 57(1) of the Act, and therefore the sheriff does not need to be satisfied that access to the child is being unreasonably denied, this does not prevent the sheriff, in the exercise of her wide discretion, from inquiring about this point. If need be the sheriff could justify her question by reference to the provision in s 57(1)(b), which requires the applicant to satisfy the sheriff that the Child Protection Order is necessary for the protection of the child from significant harm.

Candice Roberts takes up the discussion and submits, in relation to (a), that, although it is likely that the mother will not go into hospital for some time, there is a real possibility that she could be admitted earlier and also submits, saying this is perhaps more important, that the information that Donald seems to have molested Jacqueline over the New Year period, gives cause for immediate concern. In relation to (b) she argues that the application is justified by referring to the health visitor's impression that the family will not co-operate, coupled with Samantha's opinion that Sharon will always 'stick up for' Donald.

The sheriff acknowledges these points and goes on to ask if, in the event of the Child Protection Order being granted, the local authority will be able to keep the children together.

Note [10]   In considering whether or not to grant a Child Protection Order the sheriff is explicitly required to have regard to the first of the 'Section 16 principles', namely the 'paramountcy' principle – that the welfare of the child throughout his/her childhood shall be the court's paramount consideration[17]. It is well-known to sheriffs that it is generally in the interests of children for the family to be kept together and social workers should be ready to deal with such a question.

Candice Roberts states that extensive inquiries have been made and that, while it will be possible for the girls to be placed with the same foster-carers, the baby Graeme will require to be placed separately. The sheriff expresses great concern at this. Miss Roberts emphasises that every attempt has been made to find a placement which could accommodate all three children but without success. Sheriff Grey thinks about the possibility of asking the sheriff clerk to phone the Lentonshire's Director of Social Work on this point, but, impressed by the detailed information which the senior social worker has been able to give regarding the efforts which have been made, decides not to do so.

Note [11]   How far does it do for a social worker to argue with such an august person as a sheriff? The answer is the same for social workers as for other professionals appearing before sheriffs – if you have prepared the matter properly (as Miss Roberts has

---

17. Children (Scotland) Act 1995 s 16(1).

evidently done in this case) then do not be afraid to 'fight your corner' firmly but, of course, courteously!

Sheriff Grey then asks about the views of the children. Marcia Drummond states that Samantha is clear that there is a considerable threat to Jacqueline and that she, Samantha, is generally uneasy about the situation at home. She is very mature for her years and has come to the conclusion that things can only get worse. She is resigned to leaving home, perhaps for a substantial period of time. Marcia Drummond has not spoken directly to Jacqueline but Jacqueline has told Samantha that she, Jacqueline, is much more ambivalent. She is young for her age and hopes that everything will work out all right without the necessity of having to leave the family home. Samantha has also said that Graeme, now eighteen months and very conscious of what is going on around him, is very attached to his mother and would be totally 'destroyed' if he were separated from her. If he were <u>also</u> to be separated from his half sisters he would 'never get over it', in Samantha's phrase.

Note [12]   The making of a CPO is <u>not</u> one of the procedures in relation to which the sheriff requires to observe the 'consulting the child' principle[18] (although in considering the granting of a Child Assessment Order the sheriff would require to observe this principle[19]). Presumably this is because where a sheriff is satisfied that there are reasonable grounds to believe, or even suspect, that a child is or is likely to be at risk of significant harm if not removed, it is difficult to figure a situation wherein any wish of the child to stay at risk could prevail. However, there is no rule of law or practice preventing the sheriff from taking the child's views into account, and Sheriff Grey takes the view that it is generally necessary to ascertain any views of children in order to get as comprehensive a picture as possible. The sheriff is also aware that if a Motion to Set Aside or Vary the order is lodged under section 60(7) of the Children (Scotland) Act 1995, then the consulting the child principle will come into play[20]. The sheriff consequently wishes attention to be focused on the children's views at as early a stage as possible. The news about the likely effect on Graeme vindicates the sheriff's broad approach.

The sheriff asks whether it would not be preferable to grant the more limited Child Assessment Order under section 55 of the Children (Scotland) Act 1995. Candice Roberts replies that this has been considered but that the extremely definite information from Samantha indicates that there is real danger to the girls and that a Child Protection Order is necessary and should be obtained right away rather than at a later stage. The sheriff asks if the possibility of an Exclusion Order has been considered. Candice Roberts and Marcia Drummond explain between

---

18.   Children (Scotland) Act 1995 s 16(4)(b)(i)
19.   Ibid.
20.   Children (Scotland) Act 1995 s 16(4))(b)(ii)

them that this has been considered but rejected because the information about Sharon being inclined to stick up for Donald has led the department to the conclusion that there is no 'appropriate person' in the household able to take responsibility for the order[21] (to 'police' the order in the commonly used phrase). The sheriff presses the social workers on whether they individually (as opposed to echoing the views of the department) take this view and they confirm that they do.

> *Note [13]   The last question is not necessarily typical of questions which every sheriff might ask but Sheriff Grey has a particular interest in social work practice and has read and agrees with the conclusions in The Report of the Inquiry into Child Care Policies in Fife (HMSO Edinburgh 27th October 1992) emphasising (e.g. at paragraph 26 on page 627) the importance of the critical ability and professional expertise of the individual social worker. The other questions, however, are matters which all sheriffs are likely to ask about, and the social workers here would have supplied the information even unasked.*

The sheriff returns to her concern about the position of baby Graeme. Accepting that it is not practicable to place Graeme along with his half-sisters, is it really necessary to include Graeme in the order at all? The allegations about Donald, if true, do not suggest that his inclination lies towards molesting male toddlers and this seems to be supported by the fears of Samantha that her younger sister's approaching the age of puberty makes her particularly vulnerable. The social workers concede that this sounds plausible but refer in general terms to the research of Finkelhor indicating that it is the relative weakness rather than the gender of the child which tended to motivate the paedophile. Sheriff Grey indicates that, in the absence of very clear information that Graeme is at real risk, her mind is working towards granting CPOs for the girls but not for Graeme. She observes that the logic of granting a CPO for Graeme would lead to the granting of a CPO for the new baby once he or she were born. The social workers do not allow themselves to be drawn into a discussion of this point but confine themselves to maintaining their application for all three of the McPerlin children. They add that they would like the addresses at which the children are to reside to be kept from Mr and Mrs McPerlin and they suggest that contact should be ordered to be under supervision of and at the discretion of the local authority. They also ask for an order dispensing with service on Graeme and Jacqueline. The sheriff indicates her agreement with the proposals about not revealing the new addresses of the children and the proposals for contact. She also agrees that service of any order on Graeme would be inappropriate because of his age, but says she is inclined to think that service on Jacqueline should not be dispensed with since she, though less mature than Samantha at her age seems mature enough to understand and in any event she will hear about it anyway from Samantha and therefore it would be as well that she should receive notification 'in her own right' so that she may feel properly involved in a process which vitally concerns her. The social workers indicate no objection.

---

21.   Children (Scotland) Act 1995 s 76(2)(c).

Note [14]   By indicating in advance the way her mind is working both in relation to the substantive applications and the ancillary motions Sheriff Grey is following good practice in that the applicants are given the opportunity to state their positions. It is also good sense from the sheriff's and the social workers' point of view, since allowing matters to be discussed openly reduces the chance of mistakes or omissions.

The sheriff indicates that she will grant Child Protection Orders in respect of Samantha and Jacqueline but refuse to grant the application for Graeme. She will also grant the motions about residence and contact. The question of serving on Graeme therefore does not arise but she will not dispense with service on Jacqueline.

Note [15]   Has the local authority any recourse against the refusal of a sheriff to grant a CPO? Section 51(15) of the Children (Scotland) Act 1995 expressly excludes a decision of a sheriff on a CPO application from the appeals procedure under the Act. In practice, in a situation such as this one, the department, where a sheriff has refused to grant a CPO, would monitor the situation and, if and when information emerged fortifying the view that Graeme was at risk, it might re-apply to one of the Kirklenton sheriffs, perhaps quoting the words, (which refer to reporters but arguably have relevance to sheriffs) in the Fife Report[22]:

'We believe that in general Reporters, if informed by the Social Worker that he or she cannot protect the child without the assistance of compulsory measures of care, will accept this advice and take the case to a hearing.'

There is no procedure within the Children (Scotland) Act 1995 or other legislation for review of or appeal against the decision of a sheriff not to grant a CPO. In the event of a sheriff continuing to refuse to grant a CPO which an applicant considered essential it may be that application might be made to the nobile officium[23] of the Court of Session. So far as the writer is aware no such Application has ever been attempted.

In the event of a sheriff refusing to grant a CPO it would, it is thought, not be appropriate to re-new the application unless there were a change of circumstances.

3.25 pm – In the Sheriff Clerk's office

The sheriff clerk prepares the necessary documentation. The sheriff signs the Interlocutors and the Orders.

Here is the interlocutor narrating the grant of the order for Jacqueline:

---

22. The Report of the Inquiry into Child Care Policies in Fife, HMSO, Edinburgh 27th October 1992 at page 597.
23. The equitable jurisdiction of the Court of Session to make legal provision for circumstances not provided for in the existing law where the interests of justice so demand.

8B 2/06

Kirklenton 26th January 2006 – at 3.30 pm

In the presence of Fiona Grey, Sheriff

The Sheriff, being satisfied that *Marcia Smith Drummond, Social Worker,* is authorised to act on behalf of the applicant and is a suitable person so to do, and having heard from the applicant on this application, MAKES/ ~~REFUSES TO MAKE~~ a Child Protection Order in terms of Section 57 (1)/~~(2)~~ of the Children (Scotland) Act 1995 in respect of the ~~male~~/female child *Jacqueline McPerlin, born 10th July 1995*; Specifying *c/o Francis and Elizabeth Jamieson, 103 Gresham Road, Kirklenton LE10 7MR* as the place of safety; ~~Dispenses with service on the child~~; all in terms of the copy Child Protection Order attached hereto.

(Signed) Fiona Grey
SHERIFF

The interlocutors granting the application for Samantha and refusing the application for Graeme are, mutatis mutandis, in similar terms.

Here is the Child Protection Order for Jacqueline:

Rule 3.31(2)

FORM 49

CHILD PROTECTION ORDER

Section 57 of the Children (Scotland) Act 1995

IN THE SHERIFF COURT of Lenton *and Muirbrachlan at Kirklenton Case No: 8B 2/06*
At Kirklenton on 26th January 2006.

In the application by *[Insert name and address]*:

Lentonshire Council per Marcia Smith Drummond, Social Worker, Social Work Services Department, 8 Laverock Road, Kirklenton, LE6 4DV

for a Child Protection Order/~~Child Assessment Order~~*, the Sheriff makes a Child Protection Order in respect of the child *[insert name and address (unless order made re non-disclosure), gender and date of birth of child]:*

Jacqueline McPerlin (Female – d.o.b. 10.07.1995) 19 Glenview Cottages, Bruaich, Kirklenton LE29 4QW.

TERMS AND CONDITIONS

*The sheriff orders that *[insert name and address of person(s)]*

Mrs Sharon Transom or McPerlin, 19 Glenview Cottages, Bruaich, Kirklenton LE29 4QW, Mr Donald McPerlin, 19 Glenview Cottages, Bruaich, Kirklenton LE29 4QW, and any other person in a position to do so

is required to produce the said child *Jacqueline McPerlin* to the applicant, *[Insert name and address of the applicant]*

Lentonshire Council, Social Work Services Department, 8 Laverock Road, Kirklenton, LE6 4DV.

*The sheriff authorises the removal of the child by the applicant to **[Insert details of the place]*:

c/o Francis and Elizabeth Jamieson, 103 Gresham Road, Kirklenton LE10 7MR.

a place of safety and for the keeping of the child at that place.

~~The sheriff authorises the prevention of the removal of the child from~~ [Insert details of the place].

*The sheriff orders that the locality of the place of safety should not be disclosed to

Mrs Sharon Transom or McPerlin, 19 Glenview Cottages, Bruaich, Kirklenton LE29 4QW, and Mr Donald McPerlin, 19 Glenview Cottages, Bruaich, Kirklenton LE29 4QW.

DIRECTIONS

*In terms of section 58(1) and (2) the sheriff gives the following direction to the applicant as to contact with the child *[Insert details of any directions]*:

That the relevant persons be allowed supervised contact with the child Jacqueline at such places and for such periods as the local authority shall in its discretion determine.

*In terms of section 58(4), (5) or (6) the sheriff gives the following directions as to the exercise or fulfilment of parental responsibilities or parental rights in respect of the child *[Insert details of any directions]*:

The applicant is granted the parental right and responsibility of having the child Jacqueline examined by a suitably qualified paediatrician within the Blackmore Memorial Infirmary, Kirklenton.

The applicant is granted the parental responsibility of securing all normal medical and dental treatment of the child Jacqueline.

For the purpose of enforcing this order warrant is granted for all lawful execution, including warrant to open shut and lockfast places.

Signed *Fiona Grey*
Sheriff, *at Kirklenton at 3.30 p.m. on 26th January 2006.*

*Delete as appropriate

Thursday, 26 January 2006 at 4 pm

The Social Workers, Candice Roberts and Marcia Drummond, leave the court with the Child Protection Orders and, as pre-arranged, meet with PC Miriam Stevenson and PC Andrew Henderson, both of the Family and Child Unit, and social workers and police drive to the McPerlin household in Bruaich in order to execute the warrants. They arrive about 4.30. Mrs Sharon McPerlin, whose shift work in the supermarket fits in with school hours, is at home with the three children. Donald McPerlin is nowhere to be seen. The social workers are admitted to the house with PC Miriam Stevenson, who is not in uniform. PC Andrew Henderson (who is in uniform) waits in the car. The social workers exhibit the CPOs to Mrs McPerlin and give her a copy of them. Mrs McPerlin becomes very emotional when she realises what is happening and says she will challenge the Child Protection Orders in the courts. Candice Roberts advises that there must be an initial children's hearing on the 'second working day' after the implementation of the orders and that the continuing or otherwise of the orders will be considered by that hearing[24]. She explains that since the orders are being implemented now, i.e. on Thursday 26th January, the 'second working day' hearing[25] will be on Monday 30th January in St Lenton's House, 1 Laverock Place, Kirklenton, LE5 1AA at a time which will be notified to the parents and the girls by the reporter, probably, in the case of the parents, by telephone[26]. Mrs McPerlin asks if she and her husband can be legally represented at the hearing. It is explained by the social workers that she can have someone with her and that that person may be a solicitor, but that as the law stands at present

---

24. Children (Scotland) Act 1995 s 59(2).
25. Children (Scotland) Act 1995 s 59(3), when read with s 93(1) of the Act – 'working day'.
26. Children's Hearings (Scotland) Rules 1996, r 7(5), when read with r 6(2)(a).

there is no provision for free legal aid in cases of this type before hearings since the rules enacted allowing state-assisted legal representation[27] only apply to representation for a <u>child</u> who, in the opinion of the hearing, requires a legal representative in order to participate effectively in the hearing or where a supervision requirement or warrant with authorisation of secure accommodation is in prospect[28]. The social workers also advise that Mr and Mrs McPerlin have the right to apply to the sheriff at Kirklenton to set aside or vary the CPO[29]. They explain that this can be done immediately, provided the application to set aside or vary is lodged in the sheriff court and intimated to the appropriate parties, including the reporter[30] before the 'second working day hearing'[31] and also, in the event of that hearing continuing the CPO, within two working days of the date on which the hearing continues the CPO[32]. They advise Mrs McPerlin to consult a solicitor and offer to give her a list of the solicitors practising in Kirklenton. Mrs McPerlin, who is in course of purchasing her council house from the local authority, and is therefore in touch with a solicitor, says this will not be necessary and the social workers leave with the girls.

Thursday, 26 January 2006 at 4.45 pm

Mrs McPerlin phones her solicitor who says that his firm, which does mainly conveyancing, does not practice in the area of children's law and recommends that she approach Messrs Brodie, Paterson & Co, Solicitors, Kirklenton and ask for Mr Paterson, who is one of the handful of solicitors in Kirklenton who practise in children's law. Mrs McPerlin phones Mr Paterson and they discuss the position. In the course of the conversation Mr Paterson points out that Mr McPerlin, not Mrs McPerlin, is the person actually accused of the offence, and asks if he is to be represented. Mrs McPerlin says she assumed that Mr Paterson could act for both. Mr Paterson indicates that this is a matter which will require to be discussed at the meeting, which they arrange for the following morning.

Thursday, 26 January 2006 at 5.00 pm

In the meantime the social workers take the girls in the first instance to the Social Work office in order to explain what has happened and is likely to happen. They repeat what has already been said in their presence about the right, which they and Mr and Mrs McPerlin possess, to make application to the sheriff to recall or vary the CPOs either right away or if and when the CPOs have been confirmed by the children's hearing. They also arrange for the reporter's office to be telephoned with the news that

---

27. The Children's Hearings (Legal Representation) (Scotland) Rules 2002, SSI 2002/63.
28. The Children's Hearings (Legal Representation) (Scotland) Rules 2002, r 3 (1) and (2). In practice a reporter would try to obtain a legal representative for the child where a secure warrant was anticipated.
29. Children (Scotland) Act 1995 s 60(7).
30. Act of Sederunt (Child Care and Maintenance Rules) 1997, SI 1997/291, Form 52.
31. Children (Scotland) Act 1995 s 60(8)(a).
32. Children (Scotland) Act 1995 s 60(8)(b).

CPOs have been granted for Samantha and Jacqueline but not for Graeme. They explain to the girls that they have arranged for a routine medical examination before taking them to foster-carers and the girls are happy to consent to this and this is carried through.

Thursday, 26 January 2006 at 5.30 pm

The social workers take Samantha and Jacqueline to the foster-carers, who are expecting them, and they settle there.

> Note [16]   *During the period between the granting and implementation of the CPO and the 'initial hearing' under section 59(2) of the Children (Scotland) Act 1995 the reporter will consider if further enquiries should be made into the grounds of referral. For example, in a case involving 'on-going' physical or sexual abuse, the local authority would probably wish to arrange medical examinations(s) of the child by a suitably qualified paediatrician[33] and give any relevant information to the reporter[34]. In the present case it is unlikely that there will be any physical signs of abuse and the reporter, on further reflection, does not pursue such investigations.*

Friday, 27 January 2006 at 9am – In the Reporter's office

Laura Cameron arrives in the office and finds a package marked 'Urgent' which has been hand-delivered. It contains: copies of the CPOs for Samantha and Jackie; notifications in Form 51 to the reporter as a named person; copies of the Applications and the supporting documentary information, viz, the Initial Assessment Report of 29th September 2004, Samantha's statement of 10th January 2006, and the minute of the case discussion of 23rd January 2006; and a hand-written note of the oral information given to the sheriff on the afternoon of 26th January 2006[35]. Laura reads the information and arranges for the CPOs to be registered as formal referrals and has a new file made up for Jacqueline (she already has a file for Samantha). The Department also advises the reporter that they had applied for a CPO in respect of the child Graeme, that this had been refused by the sheriff and that they (the Department) wish to refer Graeme to the reporter. Miss Cameron has a discussion with Hector Somerville and they agree that Grounds for Referral should also be stated in respect of Graeme.

Laura Cameron then phones Marcia Drummond and they have a long conversation going over the following issues:

- Miss Cameron mentions the documents she has received and Miss Drummond confirms that that is what she should have received.

---

33. *Hence the 'Direction' in the CPO: 'The applicant is granted the parental responsibility of having the child Jacqueline examined by a suitably qualified paediatrician within the Blackmore Memorial Infirmary, Kirklenton'.*
34. In practice there is, more often than not, no physical symptom of sexual abuse – cf *W v Kennedy* 1988 SLT 583, sub nom *WW v Kennedy* 1988 SCLR 236.
35. Cf Children (Scotland) Act 1995 s 60(3), the implications of which have been discussed *supra* at [4].

- Miss Cameron asks Miss Drummond to confirm that the CPOs have been implemented by the children having been taken to the place of safety within 24 hours of the granting of the CPOs[36] and Miss Drummond confirms that this was done at 5.30 pm on the same day as the CPOs were granted[37].

- Miss Cameron asks Miss Drummond if there is any new information or change of circumstances since the granting of the CPOs which might affect the continuing competence or necessity of the CPOs or of any of their terms, conditions or directions[38]. Miss Drummond says there is no new information and no material change of circumstances and adds that she will let the reporter's department know immediately should any material new information or change of circumstances transpire during the currency of the CPOs. She confirms, when asked by Laura, that the local authority still thinks that the CPOs are still necessary to promote the welfare of the girls[39].

- Miss Cameron confirms that she will be stating Grounds for Referral for Samantha and Jacqueline and advises that she will also be stating Grounds for Referral in relation to Graeme. For Samantha the Ground will be under s 52(2)(d) [Schedule 1 offence committed against her] and for Jacqueline and Graeme the Ground will be under s 52(2)(e) of the Act [is, or is likely to become, a member of same household as a child against whom a 'Schedule 1 offence' has been committed]. Miss Cameron mentions that the case of Graeme will require to be initiated by serving Grounds for Referral in the normal way of a 'non-emergency case'.

Note [17]   If the social workers had not been able to confirm that the CPO and related conditions and directions were necessary, then the reporter would require to consider whether the CPO was really necessary and consider whether s/he should use the powers vested in him/her effectively to terminate the order[40].

- Miss Cameron confirms that the Initial or Second Working Day hearing[41] (the '2WD hearing', as they abbreviate it in their notes) is to take place in the Hearings suite of the Reporter's office at 2.30 pm on the following Monday (30th January 2006) and asks her to secure that arrangements are made to ensure that the children, both of the relevant persons (Mr and Mrs McPerlin), and any professionals who may be appropriate attend this hearing are notified verbally as soon as possible[42] and if there are any difficulties to let her (Laura) know right away. Miss Cameron suggests that it would be courteous to

---

36. Cf Children (Scotland) Act 1995 s 60(1).
37. It is important the know when the CPOs were implemented as this controls the date of the 2WD hearing – Children (Scotland) Act 1995 s 59(3).
38. Children (Scotland) Act 1995 s 60(3).
39. Children (Scotland) Act 1995 s 57(6).
40. Children (Scotland) Act 1995 s 60(3), (4) and (6)(d).
41. Children (Scotland) Act 1995 s 59, s 59(3).
42. Children's Hearings (Scotland) Rules 1996 r 6(2).

explain that the practicalities of providing another time-slot on the day virtually rule out any latitude in the timing of the hearing but says that since there is the bonus of the intervening week-end she intends to notify separately Mr and Mrs McPerlin and the girls in writing by first class post. Miss Drummond accepts that this approach is sensible.

Note [18]   Once again (cf [5] supra) co-operation between the professionals will tend to avoid mistakes and omissions. It is good practice to have a checklist and use it or some other means to keep a record of such conversations. The reporter and the social worker now go on to discuss more substantive issues specific to this case.

- **Conjoined hearing.** Laura and Marcia agree that there would be no benefit in having separate hearings for the two girls.

Note [19]   The rules[43] imply that a hearing is in respect of 'a child'[44], but it is not mandatory to keep each child's hearing separate and in practice where, as here, there is more than one child and the facts relating to each child are substantially identical, the reporter may convene a single hearing for the children, although at such a hearing the panel members would require to consider each child as an individual.

- **Girls do not want to see Mr and Mrs McPerlin during the 2 WD hearing.** Marcia advises that both girls are adamant that they do not wish to see their parents at the hearing and ask if they can be excused. Laura advises that as this is an 'emergency' type hearing there is no mechanism for having this formally decided in advance since a Business Meeting under section 64 of the Children (Scotland) Act 1995 attracts a requirement of a period of notice of at least 4 clear working days[45]. Accordingly the reporter has no statutory authority to agree to excusing the attendance of the girls in advance of a 2WD hearing. However the protecting of the interests of the children must be addressed. It emerges that the girls are not proposing to refuse to come to the hearing – they just do not wish to be in the same room as Mr and Mrs McPerlin.

- **Managing the hearing – the principles.** Laura confirms that the girls have an absolute right to attend, as well as an obligation[46], but the hearing has the power, in a Schedule 1 offence case[47] or in any case

---

43. Children's Hearings (Scotland) Rules 1996 rr 11 – 21.
44. E.g. Children's Hearings (Scotland) Rules 1996 r 20(2): 'Unless a children's hearing consider the case of a child in the absence of the child, any relevant person and any representative, the chairman shall, before the children's hearing proceeds to consider the case, explain the purpose of the hearing to such persons as are present'.
45. Children's Hearings (Scotland) Rules 1996 r 4(3). For discussion of business meeting, see below at pp 139, 140.
46. Children (Scotland) Act 1995 s 45(1).
47. I.e. a case wherein the ground of referral is that an offence (child abuse and neglect and others) mentioned in Schedule 1 of the Criminal Procedure (Scotland) Act 1995, has been committed against the child, as provided in Children (Scotland) Act 1995 s 52(2)(d).

wherein there would be detriment to the child, to dispense with such attendance[48]. While (oddly enough) there is no statutory obligation on panel members <u>at this stage</u> to ascertain if the girls wish to express their views[49], the hearing will wish to do so having regard (a) to the comparative maturity of the children and (b) to the consideration that the sheriff will require to consider their wishes in any application to set aside or vary[50]. Accordingly it will be advantageous for the girls to be present for at least part of the hearing. As this is a Schedule 1 offence case the hearing has an absolute right to dispense with the attendance of the girls[51] and their attendance could be dispensed with for the parts of the hearing at which the parents were present. Similarly the hearing could exclude the parents from those parts of the proceedings at which the girls were present on the basis that their presence would be likely to cause them significant distress[52]. In effect the hearing could be 'split' to bring it about that the girls could feel 'involved' in the process by their being readily accessible, but without causing them significant distress. Laura reminds Marcia of the necessity of explaining to the girls that the panel members would require to explain to Mr and Mrs McPerlin the substance of what had happened while they were not present[53], and that, as a matter of good practice, the panel members would tell the girls of their obligation to do this. Miss Cameron and Miss Drummond reflect that there is, paradoxically, no provision in the Act or the rules requiring the hearing to advise children of the substance of what has happened when <u>they</u> (the) children were absent, but recall that panel members usually do this as a matter of good practice, at least when such disclosure would not cause significant detriment to the child.

- *Managing the hearing – practical issues.* The two confirm that Marcia will bring Samantha and Jacqueline in by a separate entrance to the building at a different time from when the parents are expected and that they will be kept in a waiting room separate from Mr and Mrs McPerlin.

- *The likely course of the hearing – possibility of legal representation.* Marcia indicates that Mrs McPerlin has mentioned seeking legal advice. Laura responds positively to this, and both note that Mr and Mrs McPerlin and the girls should be reminded of their rights[54] to bring a representative to the hearing. Laura mentions the possibility of the hearing appointing a lawyer to represent either or both of the girls[55] (and thus enable such lawyer to be remunerated

---

48. Children (Scotland) Act 1995 s 45(2).
49. Children (Scotland) Act 1995 s 16(2) and (4)(a).
50. Children (Scotland) Act 1995 s 16(2) and (4)(b).
51. Children (Scotland) Act 1995 s 45(2)(a).
52. Children (Scotland) Act 1995 s 46(1)(b).
53. Children (Scotland) Act 1995 s 46(2).
54. Children's Hearings (Scotland) Rules 1996 r 11.
55. Children's Hearings (Legal Representation) (Scotland) Rules 2002 (SI 2002/63) – conveniently reproduced in Norrie, K McK, *Children's Hearings in Scotland*, second edition 2005, Appendix 8.

by the state[56]) but says she thinks this unlikely because (a) there is no prospect of secure accommodation being recommended by the hearing[57] and (b) there is no obviously complex legal issue at this stage and (c) the girls are relatively mature and not obviously in need of legal representation in order adequately to participate at the hearing[58]. The two agree, however, that Miss Drummond should tell both the parents and the girls about the statutory provisions about representation.

- *The likely course of the hearing – consideration of appointment of safeguarder.* Miss Cameron refers to the obligation of the hearing to consider the appointment of a safeguarder[59] but speculates that the hearing may not wish to do so because of the time constraints. Miss Cameron remarks that the question of appointment of a safeguarder will have to be considered at all subsequent hearings.

- *Papers to be provided to Panel Members, relevant persons and the girls*[60]. Miss Drummond advises that she has already prepared a very brief ('no more than a few pages') report, summarising the case history, recent events, and her recommendations to the hearing in relation to the continuation of the CPOs and their terms, directions and conditions. Laura decides that the only other information she would provide for the hearing under the relevant rule[61] would be: Copies of the CPO Applications (as they contain concise details of the concerns raised in the hearing before the sheriff); and copies of the CPOs themselves <u>with the details identifying the place of safety removed</u>.

Note [20]   Not all the papers in the file need to be submitted – see the terms of rule 5(1) and (2) of the Children's Hearings (Scotland) Rules 1996. Miss Cameron thinks:

1. *The Initial Assessment Report of 2004 is old and not material to the present circumstances.*

2. *The social work notes are not material.*

---

56. *Grant Scheme for Persons Appointed by a Children's Hearing to Act as a Child's Legal Representative* (made under the Panels of Persons to Safeguard the Interests of Children (Scotland) Regulations 2002, SSI 2001/746, reg 10 and The Curators *ad Litem* and Reporting Officers (Panels) (Scotland) Regulations 2001, SSI 2001/477, reg 10).
57. Children's Hearings (Legal Representation) (Scotland) Rules 2002 r 3(1)(b).
58. Children's Hearings (Legal Representation) (Scotland) Rules 2002 r 3(1)(a).
59. Children (Scotland) Act 1995 s 41(1) – the exclusion under s 41(2) of the Act of the possibility of the appointment of a safeguarder 'in relation to proceedings under section 57 of this Act' does not apply to proceedings subsequent to the granting of a CPO.
60. Children's Hearings (Scotland) Rules 1996 r 5.
61. Children's Hearings (Scotland) Rules 1996 r 5(1) and (2) – see particularly the words of r 5(2): 'If the Principal Reporter has obtained any information (including any views of the child given orally to the Principal Reporter by virtue of rule 15) or any document other than a document mentioned in paragraph (1) which is material to the consideration of the case of a child at any children's hearing, he shall make that information or copies of that document available to the chairman and members of the children's hearing before the hearing.'

3.   The statement of Samantha is of the nature of direct evidence and therefore not appropriate for consideration by the hearing.

4.   The contents of the case discussion of 23rd January 2006 could be useful, but it identified the views of individual professionals and was accordingly straying into a field of evidence which had not been fully investigated and which it would not be normal to lay before panel members. Miss Drummond's Report would be the only report lodged for the 2 WD hearing.

5.   The written notes of the submissions to the sheriff were evidential and concerned with legal issues and therefore should not be submitted.

6.   The court interlocutor should not be submitted because it contained information which was excess to requirements at this stage *and also named the place of safety*.

• **Social work presence at hearing.** Miss Drummond confirms that she will attend the initial hearing[62].

They conclude their long discussion by Miss Drummond confirming that her report will not specify the whereabouts of the place of safety and Miss Cameron confirms that her files will be 'flagged' to make it clear that the identity of the place of safety was not to be divulged to the relevant persons.

Same day, Friday, 27 January 2006 at 10.30 am – In the Reporter's office

Laura phones the chairperson[63] of the Lentonshire Children's Panel to advise him that a Second Working Day hearing is to be held in Kirklenton at 2.30 p.m. on Monday 30th January 2006 and he confirms that he will arrange for three panel members, with each gender represented[64], to be in attendance. Laura says she expects to receive the social worker's brief report at the beginning of business on the Monday morning and offers to arrange for copies of this, the CPO applications, and the CPOs themselves to be delivered to the homes of the panel members on the Monday morning. The chairman says he will try to advise Laura of the contact details of the panel members concerned in the course of the day but remarks that if it should prove impracticable to deliver the papers to them during the day it will be enough for the papers to be given to them at least half an hour before the hearing. He says he will ask them to attend at the hearing venue at about 2 p.m.

---

62. Surprisingly, there is no statutory requirement for a social worker to attend at a hearing, but in practice a social worker nearly always attends.
63. Children (Scotland) Act 1995, Schedule 1, paragraph 1.
64. Children (Scotland) Act 1995, s 39(5)

Same day, Friday, 27 January 2006 at 10 am –
In Mr Paterson's office

Mrs McPerlin meets Mr David Paterson, solicitor.

> *Note [21]   Two important 'professional' issues must be addressed by a solicitor on taking on a new client. In the first place, Mr Paterson, like any solicitor, has to pay attention to the recently enacted Solicitors (Scotland) (Client Communication) Practice Rules 2005. These provide that, unless where the client regularly instructs the solicitor in the type of work concerned[65], then the solicitor, when tendering for business, or at the earliest practical opportunity upon receiving instructions, write to the client what may be called a 'Terms of Business' letter explaining: (a) the nature of the work; (b) information about fees where legal aid or legal advice and assistance is not involved; (c) information about legal aid etc where these are involved; (d) a note of who in the firm will be doing the main part of the work; and (e) the identity of the person the client should contact if becoming concerned about how the work is being carried out[66]. Mr Paterson must also, in the situation which presents in the present case, have regard to the Solicitors (Scotland) Practice Rules 1986, rule 3 of which provides: 'A solicitor shall not act for two or more parties whose interests conflict'. This rule merely gives formal recogni-tion of a long-established principle, but since its enactment it is thought that solicitors have become more sensitive to potential conflicts of interest[67].*

Mr Paterson takes the history of the case from Mrs McPerlin. The solicitor confirms the information, previously conveyed to her by the social workers, about bringing the CPO under review. He also advises that Mr and Mrs McPerlin, as 'relevant persons' will be entitled to attend all stages of the proceedings before the hearings and before the sheriff, but that, as the law stands at present, legal representation paid for by the state is only available for hearings before the sheriff because the Children's Hearings (Legal Representation) (Scotland) Rules 2002 do not apply to 'relevant persons'. After ascertaining details about income and the like he explains that Legal Aid may be available in respect of hearings before the sheriff. He also states that in the case of clients who have children's cases involving hearings before the sheriff and hearings before 'the panel', his firm has the practice of representing such clients at the panel hearings without charge, i.e. making do with the legal aid remuneration, including the Legal Aid and Advice provisions which will cover meetings such as the present one. Mr Paterson goes on to explain the likely course of these proceedings, the set-up whereby disputed matters of fact are dealt with by the sheriff, and the structure of the appeals procedure both in relation to

---

65.   Solicitors (Scotland) (Client Communication) Practice Rules 2005, r 4(1).
66.   Solicitors (Scotland) (Client Communication) Practice Rules 2005, r 3.
67.   The interested reader may wish to consult the entire *Solicitors (Scotland) Practice Rules 1986*, reproduced in The Parliament House Book, Part F, pages 271, 272.

substantive decisions of the hearings and of the sheriff. He mentions that
Legal Aid will almost certainly be granted in relation to all the proceedings
in the sheriff court and that no finding for her to pay expenses can be
made against her if she is unsuccessful[68] and that, under the same rule, she
will not be entitled to any award of expenses in her favour if she is
successful.

Mr Paterson advises that if and when, as appears likely, the case goes on,
then the issue will arise as to whether to launch an immediate application
to recall the CPO or to wait for the coming Monday's hearing, Mr
Paterson says that either is possible, but suggests the latter course on the
basis that he would prefer to have the case more fully prepared and
considered than the tight time-scale of an immediate application for recall
would allow. Mrs McPerlin accepts this advice. More generally Mr
Paterson, whose case papers at this time only comprise the Child
Protection Orders, asks Mrs McPerlin in general terms what the reporter's
allegations are and whether she has any information on them. Mrs
McPerlin tells what the allegations are and says that Mr McPerlin strongly
denies all the allegations and that she believes him. She cannot understand
why Samantha should say such things. Mr Paterson says that his first line
of inquiry will be to see how much information the reporter is prepared to
share with him.

Mr Paterson then raises the issue of how, if at all, Mr McPerlin, who
appears to be a relevant person by virtue of being a person ordinarily
having charge of the girls, is to be represented. Mrs McPerlin's first
reaction is that he will probably not wish to be represented, but asks if Mr
Paterson could not act for both. Mr Paterson points out that very serious
allegations are being made against Mr McPerlin and that while it would be
part of his (Mr Paterson's) task to deal with and try to refute these
allegations it would be preferable for Mr McPerlin to be separately
represented, since it is Mr McPerlin who is the person principally blamed
and it will be his solicitor rather that Mrs McPerlin's solicitor who will be
likely to be the main person to 'take on' the reporter in any proof. He also
explains that he could not represent Mr McPerlin since, although there
was no obvious conflict of interest at this stage, a conflict of interest or
other difficulties might arise at some later stage; in any event Mr McPerlin
should be aware that there could be a criminal prosecution and Mr
Paterson's firm does not do much criminal work. Mrs McPerlin, who had
not realised that a criminal prosecution was a possibility, is shocked and
horrified and agrees to advise her husband accordingly. She asks if there is
a solicitor whom Mr Paterson could recommend and he says that Mrs
Mhairi MacDonald has much experience both in children's law and
criminal law and he gives her Mrs MacDonald's contact particulars. Mr
Paterson asks if Mrs McPerlin thinks that Mr McPerlin will instruct Mrs
MacDonald and she replies that she thinks he will. Mr Paterson asks

---

68. Act of Sederunt (Child Care and Maintenance Rules) 1997, SI 1997/291, r 3.19; cf the
    decision of Sheriff Kearney in *The Child BD*, Glasgow Sheriff Court, 16th October
    2006, unrep.

Mrs McPerlin to try to get confirmation of this as soon as possible and also to ask Mr McPerlin to consent to Mr Paterson passing on this information to any person, such as the reporter, having a legitimate interest. Mrs McPerlin agrees to do this.

Mr Paterson says that he will start his inquiries that morning and revert to Mrs McPerlin by phone in the afternoon, by which time the time of the Second Working Day hearing will be known. The hearing will probably be in the afternoon, but Mr Paterson explains that while he himself will be the person in the firm mainly dealing with Mrs McPerlin's case he personally will be unable to attend that hearing since he has at the time of the hearing to be in Edinburgh for a consultation with counsel but his procurator[69], Miss Dorothy Robb, will be able to attend. Mr Paterson introduces Mrs McPerlin to Miss Robb. He asks Mrs McPerlin if she is happy for his firm to act and she confirms that she is.

Mr Paterson concludes the interview by telling Mrs McPerlin that his firm will very soon send out its 'Terms of Business' confirming amongst other matters the issues which have been discussed and asks her to contact him immediately if there should be anything in this document with which she is unhappy or which she does not understand. Mrs McPerlin acknowledges this and the interview ends.

Note [22]   It is not invariably impossible for a solicitor to act for both 'parents' – for example where the grounds for referral do not obviously involve the parents, as where an offence by the child is alleged – but a solicitor must be very careful not to get into the position of having at a later stage to tell the other parent of the need for separate representation. Indeed if that happens the solicitor might have to withdraw from acting for both since she might have received information from one of the parents in the confidential capacity of being that parent's solicitor, thus rendering it improper to continue to act for what would now be 'the other side'. In this case Mr Paterson tactfully does not specify how a conflict of interest or other difficulty might arise, but he knows from experience that mothers sometimes come round to believing the children and that mothers can be accused of colluding with alleged abusers. If Mr Paterson had decided that it was safe to act for both he would come under obligation to explain the potential conflict of interest in the 'Terms of Business' letter, referred to in paragraph [21] above[70].

An immediate application for recall or variation of a CPO would have to be lodged either on the Friday or the following Monday,

---

69. 'Procurator' is a term, employed particularly in the West of Scotland, to refer to a solicitor, including, as here, an assistant solicitor – cognate with, but not to be confused with. the Procurator Fiscal, who is the Procurator of the Fisc, i.e. the state, responsible mainly for prosecution of crime at the local level

70. It is beyond the scope of this work to examine in detail the rules now governing the solicitor/client relationship. Guidance is contained in *Guidance Notes On The Solicitors (Scotland) (Client Communication) Practice Rules 2005* which are reproduced in The Parliament House Book, Part F pages 1336 to 1338.

before the commencement of the children's hearing. On the other hand, an application for recall, if lodged after the hearing has continued the CPO, must be lodged with the court within two working days of such continuation and disposed of by the court within three working days of its being lodged[71].

Same day, Friday, 27 January 2006 at 11.25 am

Mrs McPerlin phones Mr Paterson and tells him that her husband will be instructing Mrs MacDonald and is having a first meeting with her this very afternoon. She says she thinks her husband will probably be in favour of going along with the plan of waiting to see if the 2WD hearing continue the CPOs and then lodge a Motion to Recall or Vary. She confirms that Mr McPerlin has no objection about anyone involved in the case knowing about these matters.

Same day, Friday, 27 January 2006 at 11.30 am

Mr Paterson phones the reporter's office and finds that Laura Cameron is dealing with this case. Miss Cameron says she has a statement from Samantha and is willing to let Mr Paterson have a copy of it[72]. She asks if Mr Paterson intends to apply for the revocation of the CPOs right away or await the result of the Initial Hearing. The solicitor advises that he will await the Initial Hearing and probably lodge Applications to Set Aside or Vary thereafter. He asks about the time of the Initial Hearing on Monday 30th January 2006 and is told that it will be at 2.30 pm. Miss Cameron asks if Mr Paterson can advise as to Mrs McPerlin's position and Mr Paterson passes on the information he has received from his client. The discussion concludes by Mr Paterson confirming that he will accept this conversation as verbal notification of the time and date of the initial hearing and, as such, as sufficient notification to the mother[73]. Miss Cameron says she will notify Mr McPerlin, (or his solicitor if she is in place) and Samantha and Jackie verbally. She says she will also [as discussed with Miss Drummond], since there is time in hand because of the week-end, send written notifications by first class post to the McPerlins and the girls.

> Note [23] Where a CPO has been made and implemented[74] and the reporter has not used his powers under s 60(3) of the Act to discharge the child from the place of safety[75] and, provided no notice has reached the reporter of an application to set aside or vary the CPO[76], the reporter must arrange an 'initial hearing' in order that the hearing may decide whether they should, in the

---

71. Children (Scotland) Act 1995 s 60(8).
72. The reporter has decided that this is a probable production and that it will facilitate the progress of the case to make it available.
73. Children's Hearings (Scotland) Rules 1996 r 6(2).
74. Act s 59(1)(a).
75. Act s 59(1)(b).
76. Act s 59(1)(c).

interests of the child continue the CPO[77]. 'Implemented' means, in the case of an order requiring removal of a child, the day of the removal of the child[78] and, in the case of an order requiring the child to stay put[79], the day of the order itself. In the present case, it means the date on which the children have been removed from home and placed with the foster-parents.

Section 35(2)(a) of the Data Protection Act 1998 excludes from those provisions of the Act prohibiting non-disclosure of personal data any disclosure 'where the disclosure is necessary for the purpose of, or in connection with, any legal proceedings (including prospective legal proceedings) …'. It is thought that this provision, when read along with sections 16(1) and 56 of the Children (Scotland) Act 1995 indicates that there is no objection under the 1998 Act or otherwise to the reporter's 'sharing' with the defence agent (or for that matter the defence agent's sharing with the reporter) information about investigations in relation to the child.

Same day, Friday, 27 January 2006 at 2.30 pm

Miss Drummond e-mails to Miss Cameron:

Report for Second Working Day Hearing

The Children:

> *Samantha McPerlin, d.o.b. 15.08.1993, girl, subject of Report;*
> *Jacqueline McPerlin, d.o.b. 10.07.1995, girl subject of Report;*
> *Graeme McPerlin, d.o.b 02.06.2004, boy (not subject of Report – sibling)*

All children normally reside at 19, Glenview Cottages, Bruaich, Kirklenton, LE29 4QW

Relevant Persons:

> *Sharon McPerlin, aged 28, (Mother)*
> *Sales Assistant in Supermarket*
> *19, Glenview Cottages, Bruaich, Kirklenton, LE29 4QW*

> *Donald McPerlin, aged 44, (father of Graeme, married to mother of the children – person ordinarily having charge of Samantha and Jacqueline)*
> *Unemployed former miner*
> *19, Glenview Cottages, Bruaich, Kirklenton, LE29 4QW*

---

77. Act s 59(2).
78. Act s 59(5)(a).
79. Act s 59(5)(b).

Background:

(1) Samantha and Jacqueline are the daughters of Sharon McPerlin who gave birth to them during an earlier relationship. Sharon and Donald married in July 2000 and they have resided together at the above address since then. Sharon and Donald are the biological parents of Graeme. Donald McPerlin was a 'checker' in the pit, which the writer understands to have been a reasonably well remunerated post, but, like many of the inhabitants of Bruaich, was made redundant in the mid 1980s. He used his redundancy money to set up in business as a car repairer and had some initial success, but the business failed in 2001, only a year or so after the couple got married. He has not worked since and Sharon is now the wage-earner and is hopeful of getting promotion to supervisor in the supermarket where she works.

(2) The writer has the impression that 'playing second fiddle', economically, to a woman ten years younger than himself has had a slightly depressing effect on Donald McPerlin, who was brought up in an ethos of male superiority.

(3) Samantha was born on 15th August 1993, after a difficult birth, with the mother suffering considerable loss of blood. She has attended mainstream schooling in Kirklenton Primary School and is at present in Secondary 2 of Kirklenton High. She was originally a reserved child with only limited interest in games, but, as she advanced in confidence, she has acquired more friends than formerly and is popular among her school mates. Her performance is academically high and she aims to become a social worker. The writer had to prepare a report on Samantha in September 2004 because of her prolonged absence from school in the summer term of that year. It emerged that Samantha had stayed away from school to 'run' the household while Sharon was in hospital for a protracted period leading up to and surrounding the birth of Graeme on 2nd June 2004. No further action was taken, substantially because Samantha had returned to school and was catching up easily.

(4) The family did not come again to the notice of the Department till 13th and 17th January of this year (2006) when Samantha disclosed to the writer that her step-father Donald had been abusing her sexually during the time when the mother was away from the house in the early summer of 2004 – the period when Samantha was absent from school.

(5) Samantha thinks that Donald made some sexual approach towards Jacqueline in the recent Christmas/New Year period but Jacqueline has not confirmed this. Mrs McPerlin is again pregnant and may require another extended stay in hospital. Since Jacqueline is about the same age now as she (Samantha) was in 2004 Samantha is afraid that Donald may try to abuse Jacqueline and that she (Samantha) will not be able to protect her sister.

(6) The sexual abuse of Samantha did not, according to Samantha, go beyond fondling under her night-clothes and she was able to resist

anything further. Samantha, however, is very apprehensive that Donald would go much further with Jacqueline who is not as mature and strong-willed as she is. The writer's assessment of the position, having spoken at length with both girls and discussed the case with other professionals, is that Samantha's fears are well-founded and would go as far as to fear that the potential abuse of Jacqueline might go as far as penetration. Even if it did not the writer and those advising her are convinced that even if the level of sexual interference which was inflicted on Samantha were to be visited on Jacqueline this would have a devastating effect on Jacqueline – far more so than was the case with Samantha, who is a young woman mature beyond her years and has, while obviously damaged by her experiences, coped with them as well as anyone could – better than any other child in a similar position whom the writer has encountered.

(7) On Monday 23rd January 2006 a Child Protection Case Discussion was held, chaired by the writer's Area Manager and attended by representatives of Health, Education, and the Police as well as by the writer and her Senior, Ms Candice Roberts. Amongst the issues discussed was the attitude of Mrs McPerlin. It was noted that, while in other respects a good mother, she was blind to the defects of her husband and would always tend to go against the interests of her children. There had been an incident where Donald had been involved in a serious 'drunk driving' incident for which he had been prosecuted and heavily fined. The children had been in the car at the time but Mrs McPerlin continued to insist that the whole thing was a 'frame-up'. Samantha also had said that her mother would always 'stick up' for Mr McPerlin. It was unanimously decided that applications for Child Protection Orders should be made as soon as possible. The question of including Graeme was specifically discussed and the work of the leading academic experts in the field was referred to. Based on this it was decided that an application should be made in the case of Graeme also and accordingly Applications were prepared and on the afternoon of Thursday 26th January 2006 the writer and Ms Roberts appeared before Sheriff Grey in chambers at Kirklenton and moved for CPOs to be granted in respect of Samantha, Jacqueline, and Graeme.

(8) The applications, as well as requesting CPOs, sought directions in relation to: permission for medical examination of Jacqueline by a suitably qualified paediatrician; permission for routine medical treatment of the children; supervised contact; non-disclosure of the address of the place(s) of safety; service of restricted documents on Jacqueline because of the sensitive nature of the application; and dispensation from service on Graeme because of his age (2 years and 6 months). The sheriff questioned the need for an intimate examination of Jacqueline but ultimately granted it. The sheriff granted permission for routine medical treatment. The sheriff questioned the need for non-disclosure of the address of the place of safety and the restriction of contact to supervised contact. The writer referred to the incident, narrated at paragraph [7] above, as indicative that the mother could not be trusted to protect the children when any issue of misbehaviour by her husband was in question and the sheriff decided to grant only supervised contact and to order non-disclosure of the place of safety. The sheriff questioned the need for a CPO for Graeme and, after

quite prolonged discussion, decided that she was not satisfied on the evidence that Graeme was at significant risk and refused to grant the application in Graeme's case. The sheriff did, however, grant the applications in respect of Samantha and Jacqueline, and also granted the directions sought.

(9) The writer and her seniors have further considered the case of Graeme in the light of the sheriff's decision. There is no ordinary way of challenging the sheriff's decision[80]. The Social Work Department will treat Graeme as a referral to the Department. The health visitor has been advised and will continue to monitor Graeme's situation and will alert the Department if she has any concerns. The department have also referred Graeme's case to the reporter[81].

(10) The mother has not yet seen the girls since the CPOs were granted – the order was only implemented yesterday (Thursday 26th January 2006) evening. The mother has however phoned the writer who is arranging for the girls to come to our contact suite at 4.30 pm today. The girls have been placed with foster-parents who were able, with the assistance of the Department, to get them out to school today. The writer has no reason to think that there has been any material change of circumstances in relation to the necessity for the CPOs and the relative directions.

(11) Both Samantha and Jacqueline have said that they would like to give their views to the hearing but, having regard to the nature of the allegations, they would be too embarrassed to give these views if the parents were present. The writer is satisfied that the girls are sincere in this and that it would therefore be necessary for the parents to be excluded while the children are giving their views – if they were not excluded then the views would not be given. Mr and Mrs McPerlin accept this.

Marcia Drummond

Social Worker

27th January 2006.

Note to the panel members. The Reporter and I agreed that Samantha and Jacqueline should receive copies of the above report, under deletion of paragraph (6). We think it would be detrimental to the girls if said paragraph were explicitly referred to in the course of the hearing.

Marcia Drummond

The above is enclosed with a covering letter in these terms:

---

80. See supra *[14]*.
81. Cf Children (Scotland) Act 1995 s 53(1).

27th January 2006

Dear Laura

Here is my report as promised. I think it covers all 'material' points, but if you have any comments please do not hesitate to tell me.

Although notification of this report to the referred children is not a statutory requirement, it is as you know proper practice, in terms of SCRA's Practice Guidance[82], to give the relevant papers to children over 12 and to children under 12 when the author of the report thinks this is in the child's interests, provided this can be done without causing significant harm and subject to deletion if necessary. Samantha, who is now nearly 12½, is mature beyond her years and should receive a copy of the report, but with deletion of paragraph (6) which I think would cause her unnecessary distress and not add anything to her participation in the proceedings. Jacqueline is two years younger and would on the face of it not be of age to receive a copy – if anything I think she is young for her age. However, since the girls are living together with the foster-parents it is unrealistic to suppose that they would not share information and I therefore think it would be better if we acknowledged this from the start and sent them both a copy of the report, subject to the deletion mentioned. From our previous discussions of this case I thought you would agree with this approach and I have taken the liberty of appending a note to the report conveying to the panel members that the girls will have received the report.

I also enclose a Social Background Report[83] in relation to the baby Graeme as I know you will need this when bringing him into the proceedings.

Yours

Marcia

**Same day, Friday, 27 January 2006 at 2.30 pm –
In Mrs MacDonald's office**

Mr McPerlin has a meeting with Mrs MacDonald, along similar lines to the meeting between Mr Paterson and Mrs McPerlin referred to above, with Mrs MacDonald complying with the 'professional' requirements outlined in paragraph *[21]*. Mrs MacDonald additionally explains that as Mr McPerlin is the person 'accused' his side of the case will be regarded for practical purposes as the principle issue and that therefore, while of course Mr Paterson will prepare the case along with Mrs McPerlin, it will be Mrs MacDonald who will take the lead and, for example, if the matter

---

82. SCRA Practice Guidance Note 24, discussed *infra* Note [24].
83. Not reproduced.

ultimately comes before the sheriff for proof, it will be Mrs MacDonald who will be the first to cross-examine the reporter's witnesses. Mr McPerlin confirms that he would like to await the 2WD hearing and then launch an Application to Recall or Vary. In particular he says he would prefer more contact with the girls.

Mrs MacDonald confirms that she will attend the 2WD hearing, without fee, as a 'representative who may assist the person [she] represents in the discussion of the case'[84].

Mr McPerlin asks about the possibility of a criminal prosecution and Mrs MacDonald advises that the matter will almost certainly have been reported to the procurator fiscal, but that it would be some time before any development would take place in that regard.

Mrs MacDonald says she will send out a 'Terms of Business' letter on the following Monday. She makes out a Legal Aid application form which Mr McPerlin signs. She says she will keep in touch and obtain such further information and instructions as may be necessary. She says she will advise the reporter that she has been instructed. (She does this after the meeting.)

Same day, Friday, 27 January 2006 at 3.45 pm

The case reporter, Laura Cameron, reads the letter from Marcia Drummond and its enclosures and is satisfied that there is nothing further which is 'material to the consideration of the case'[85] which the Panel Members, the relevant persons, and the girls will require for a properly informed hearing to take place – in other words she is satisfied that the report, the copy applications and the copy CPOs are all the paperwork required to enable a properly informed hearing to take place.

The next step is for Miss Cameron to arrange for the relevant documents and notifications which require to be sent to all persons entitled to receive them.

> ### Note [24]   *Provision of papers and notifications – Timescales*
>
> *The reporter has to keep in view the detailed provisions in the rules governing the periods of notice which require to be given in relation to hearings.*
>
> ### *The papers to be provided*
>
> *Rule 5 of the Children's Hearings (Scotland) Rules 1996 contains the provisions as to notification of dates and provision of papers in relation to ordinary children's hearings[86]. Rule 5(1) gives a list of the papers which <u>may</u> be relevant, viz:*

---

84. Children's Hearings (Scotland) Rules 1996, r 11(2).
85. Children's Hearings (Scotland) Rules 1996 r 5(2).
86. As opposed to Business Meetings, which are governed by Children's Hearings (Scotland) Rules 1996 r 4.

a)   a report of a local authority on the child and his social background;

b)   the statement of grounds for the referral of the case to the children's hearing prepared under rule 18;

c)   any judicial remit or reference or any reference by a local authority;

d)   any supervision requirement to which the child is subject;

e)   any report prepared by any safeguarder appointed in the case;

f)   any views of the child given in writing to the Principal Reporter by virtue of rule 15(4).

The Grounds for Referral

The Statement of Grounds is included in the foregoing list of papers to be supplied and special provision is made for their intimation. However where, as here, CPOs have been obtained Ground for Referral are not in existence at this stage. In relation to proceedings commenced by the reporter stating grounds for referral, that is a referral under section 65(1) of the Act – for example the referral of a child (such as, in the present scenario, Graeme[87]) who is not already subject to any order – Rule 18(1) of the Children's Hearings (Scotland) Rules 1996 requires that a copy of the Statement of Grounds must be given to the child and each relevant person (whose whereabouts are known) 'not less than seven days before the date of the hearing'. In the case of a referral of a child who is subject to a Child Protection Order which has been continued by a hearing, that is a referral (such as the present one) under section 65(2) of the Act, the intimation must be given 'not less than three days' before the hearing[88].

When and to whom the papers have to be provided

Rule 5 also prescribes that, subject to the 1996 Regulations[89], a copy of whatever documents <u>are</u> relevant to the child must be given to the panel members and each relevant person and any father of the child who is living with the mother where both are parents of the child. The papers must be delivered 'as soon as is reasonably practicable but <u>not later than three days before the hearing</u> [my underlining]'. The reference is to 'days', not, as in the provisions governing the dates on which post-CPO hearings are to take place[90], 'working days[91]'. The three-day prescription is,

---

87. See below pages 147 et seq.
88. Children's Hearings (Scotland) Rules 1996, r 18(3).
89. The Secure Accommodation (Scotland) Regulations 1996.
90. Children (Scotland) Act 1995 s 59(3), and s 65(2).
91. That is every day except Saturday and Sunday, 25th and 26th December and 1st and 2nd January – Children (Scotland) Act 1995 s 93.

however, mandatory in relation to the documents listed, and failure to observe it, for example by allowing the hearing to consider a document of the type listed which had not been timeously delivered to panel members and parties would be an irregularity which could constitute a prima facie ground of appeal. Where of course it is reasonably practicable to deliver the papers giving a longer period of notice than three days, then this should be done.

When notification of hearings has to be made

The provisions about notification are more flexible in that they have regard to the very tight timescales involved in these hearings. They prescribe that notification must be given 'wherever practic-able [my underlining] at least seven days before the hearing'[92]. 'Practicable' means 'able to be done' and accordingly where time allows this length of notice should be given, but where, as in the fixing of a Second Working Day hearing is involved notifica-tion should be made as soon as the hearing is fixed.

Notification to children

The Rules provide that the child in relation to certain hearings, including Second Working Day Hearings, must be given written notice or, where this is not 'reasonably practicable', oral notice of such hearings, with no timescale prescribed[93]. In relation to other hearings seven days written notice is required[94]. The child must also be told of his entitlement to indicate if he or she wishes to express views that, if so, the opportunity to do so will be provided and that any views given by the child to the reporter will be passed on by the reporter to panel members, relevant persons and any safeguarder[95]. The child must also be notified of his right to attend, even if his duty to attend has been removed under section 45(2) of the Act[96].

Provision of papers to children

The Rules prescribe that the child must, not less than seven days before any hearing at which Grounds for Referral are to be explained, be given a copy of the Grounds[97] – although this does not apply when the child is in a place of safety or secure accommodation, when he must receive the Grounds as soon as reasonably practicable[98]. However neither the Act nor the Rules make any provision for the child to be supplied with any of the other papers. Following the decision in S v Miller 2001 SLT 531

---

92. Children's Hearings (Scotland) Rules 1996 r 5(1).
93. Children's Hearings (Scotland) Rules 1996 r 6(2).
94. Children's Hearings (Scotland) Rules 1996 r 6(1).
95. Children's Hearings (Scotland) Rules 1996 r 6(4).
96. Children's Hearings (Scotland) Rules 1996 r 6(3).
97. Children's Hearings (Scotland) Rules 1996 r 18(1)(b).
98. Children's Hearings (Scotland) Rules 1996 r 18(2).

this anomaly was rectified by the promulgation by SCRA of Practice Guidance Note 24 which provides in effect that a child over the age of 12 is to be supplied with the same papers as are supplied to the panel members and relevant persons unless the information contained or as the case may be the knowledge that the child was receiving the information would cause significant distress or harm to the child or any relevant person or would be likely significantly to hamper any pro-secution[99]. Children under 12 do not receive any report unless requested by or on behalf of the child or where, as here, the writer of the report thinks the child should receive it.

Application of the rules about notification in the present case

Assuming the Initial (or Second Working Day) Hearing (on Monday 30th January 2006) continues the CPOs[100], the 'eighth working day hearing' under s 65(2) of the Act will require (unless there were to be an immediate and successful application for recall or a decision by the reporter not to continue with the CPO) to be held on the eighth working day after the date (Thursday 26th January 2006) when the CPO was implemented – that is Tuesday 7th February 2006. Accordingly notification of this hearing by posting on Monday 30th January (the day of the Second Working Day hearing) would not be in time to meet the seven-day timescale[101] and accordingly Miss Cameron will prepare this notification in advance for handing to parties at the conclusion of the Second Working Day Hearing

She can then send out the other papers, in this case Marcia Drummond's Report of 27th January 2006 (with the omission of paragraph 6 in the copies for the children) any further Social Work Report, any views which either child may have given to the reporter, and the reasons for the decision of the Children's Hearing held on 30th January 2006 at the latest by posting by first class recorded delivery post on Thursday 2nd February 2006. She would require to send out to all parties and the appropriate panel members the Grounds for Referral on the same date.

Monday, 30 January 2006 at 12 noon – In the reporter's office

Laura Cameron hears nothing in the course of the morning. No notice of an application to set aside or vary the CPOs is received at the Reporter's office. Later on in the day Miss Cameron telephones Miss Drummond to check on developments and to find out if anything further needs to be done in preparation for the hearing. Nothing that Miss Drummond says leads the reporter to believe that the CPOs are not essential[102].

---

99.   For fuller discussion see Norrie, op cit, second ed, page 59.
100. If it does not, then each CPO and all orders within it shall cease to have effect – Children (Scotland) Act 1995 s 60(6)(a).
101. Children's Hearings (Scotland) Rules, 1996, SI 96/3261, r 2(1) – definition of 'day'.
102. Cf paragraph *[16]*supra.

Same day, Monday, 30 January 2006 at 2 pm

The three panel members, Mrs Thomasina Young, Mr Robert Pirie and Miss Sandra Robertson, arrive at the reporter's building which also houses the hearings room, into which they are ushered. They discuss who should chair the hearing[103]. Miss Robertson is relatively inexperienced, Mr Pirie is a newly appointed panel member (this is his first hearing) and Mrs Young is a longstanding panel member and is deputy chairman of the Lentonshire Panel[104]. It is agreed that Mrs Young should chair the hearing.

Preliminary procedural discussion

The reporter, Miss Laura Cameron, looks in to check with the panel members that they have received the correct paperwork and they confirm to her that they have. They say that they understand that this is a Second Working Day hearing convened to consider whether or not to confirm the two CPOs. Although aware that the panel members are trained and that Mrs Young is an experienced panel member, the reporter, following good practice, mentions:

- The present position in relation to the CPOs, namely, that Samantha and Jacqueline are with foster-parents, and that no challenge has so far been made against the CPOs.

- That the conditions of the CPOs are:

   - *'That the relevant persons be allowed supervised contact with the children Samantha and Jacqueline at such places and for such periods as the local authority shall in its discretion determine'.*

   - *The applicant is granted the parental right and responsibility of having the child Jacqueline examined by a suitably qualified paediatrician within the Blackmore Memorial Infirmary, Kirklenton.*

   - *The applicant is granted the parental right and responsibility of securing all normal medical and dental treatment of the children Samantha and Jacqueline.*

   - *That the locality of the place of safety should not be disclosed to Mrs Sharon Transom or McPerlin or Mr Donald McPerlin, both of 19 Glenview Cottages, Bruaich, Kirklenton LE29 4QW.*

- That the reporter has taken the view that Mr McPerlin is a relevant person, by virtue of his appearing to be a person who, other than by reason only of his employment, had charge of, or control over, the children[105], but this is something the hearing will require to decide for itself.

---

103. Children (Scotland) Act 1995, s 39(5).
104. Cf Children (Scotland) Act 1995, Schedule 1, paragraph 1.
105. Children (Scotland) Act 1995, s 93(2)(b)(iii)(c), definition of 'relevant person'.

- That the hearing will require to consider appointing a safeguarder[106].

- That the fundamental purpose of the hearing is to decide whether or not to continue the CPOs granted by the sheriff. It will do this by considering all the information before it, written and oral.

- That the hearing will require to consider whether to vary, or alternatively leave undisturbed, the other terms, conditions and directions in the CPOs, including the arrangements for contact set out in the CPOs and consider, depending on what they decide on contact, whether the condition prohibiting disclosure of the foster-carers' address should be varied.

- That the hearing will require to ascertain if the children wish to express a view and, if they do, to give them the chance to do so and, if they decide so to do, to 'have regard to' such views[107]. (In this connection the reporter explains that that means that the hearing does not of course require to follow the children's wishes, but simply treat them as one of the factors in deciding what will best serve their welfare throughout their childhood[108].)

- That the hearing has the power to exclude any parent if satisfied that this is necessary in order to obtain the views of the child or that the presence of such parent would cause significant distress to the child[109] – and that if this power is exercised then the chairman must tell the excluded person the substance of what happened in his absence[110]. In this connection Laura mentions that the children have indicated that they do not wish to see their mother or Donald McPerlin and that consequently, if they were satisfied that the absence was necessary in order to obtain the views of the children or if the adults' presence would cause significant distress to them they could in effect order the hearing to be 'split' with Mr and Mrs McPerlin being heard at the beginning to confirm that they are content to be outwith the hearing room while the children give their views and that if the hearing does decide so to hear the children in the absence of the parents it will have to tell the children that the substance of what they say will be revealed to the parents during the second part of the hearing.

One of the hearing members asks the reporter what would happen if the hearing were to refuse to continue the CPOs and wonders whether it would really be right for the hearing to go against the decision of the sheriff, who has presumably given the matter careful consideration and would not have granted a CPO if it was not necessary. Laura explains that this is the task which the 1995 Act has placed on hearings and that they must of course take their obligations seriously. She says that in practice it is rare for a hearing not to continue a CPO at a Second Working Day

106. Children (Scotland) Act 1995, s 41(1).
107. Children (Scotland) Act 1995, s 16(2)(c).
108. Children (Scotland) Act 1995, s 16(1).
109. Children (Scotland) Act 1995, s 46(1).
110. Children (Scotland) Act 1995. s 46(2).

Hearing, particularly if there has been no significant change since the CPO was granted but that even without such change it is for the hearing members to make up their own minds. She explains that in the event of the hearing not continuing the CPOs then they will cease to have effect[111] with the practical result that the children will go home with their parents.

The same hearing member asks how the hearing can be expected to be satisfied that the conditions for excluding the parents exist without hearing from the children themselves – necessarily in the absence of the parents – is this not a paradox? Laura refers to paragraph (11) of Marcia Drummond's Report dated 27th January 2006 and says that while of course the decision is one for the panel members, they may regard the social worker's opinion as entitling them to exclude the parents. She mentions that, as indicated in paragraph (11), the parents do not object to this course of action, that their consent is not legally necessary, but that it is satisfactory that it has been granted. There would be no harm in checking the position with the children when they arrived at the hearing centre, and if they should indicate that they had changed their minds, then everyone could come in together.

Another hearing member says he would like to be reminded of the next stage in the process in the event of the hearing deciding to continue the order. The experienced panel member, Mrs Young, explains that a decision of this hearing can be made the subject of an Application to the sheriff to recall or vary their decision, that this has to be dealt within three working days[112]. She also mentions that a hearing itself would (unless the sheriff were to recall the orders) have the power to review the position at the Eighth Working Day Hearing[113].

THE SECOND WORKING DAY HEARING

Same day, Monday, 30 January 2006 at 2.30 pm

Preliminary practical discussion

The reporter, Miss Laura Cameron, tells the hearing members that she has checked that the children do not wish to see the McPerlins at this stage and wish to give their views in the absence of the parents and that she believes that the parents are content that the children should give their views without their being present. (She mentions that the girls are at present in a separate waiting room.) The hearing chair observes that this is unusual and will present procedural problems. The reporter agrees. She suggests that the hearing might commence by inviting Mr and Mrs McPerlin, their solicitors and the social worker to come in first in order (a) to determine if Mr McPerlin is a relevant person, and (b) to discuss how

---

111. Children (Scotland) Act 1995, s 60(6)(a).
112. Children (Scotland) Act 1995, s 60(8).
113. Children (Scotland) Act 1995, s 65(2).

the hearing is to be managed. This is agreed and the reporter leaves the hearing room and comes back accompanied by the McPerlins, and their solicitors (Mrs MacDonald, for Mr McPerlin and Miss Robb for Mrs McPerlin) and the social worker, Miss Marcia Drummond.

Preliminary procedural discussion

The Hearing Chair, Mrs Young: Good Afternoon. Mr and Mrs McPerlin?

Mr and Mrs McPerlin: Yes/Hello.

Mrs Young: I think we can now regard this hearing is session. I am Mrs Ina Young. My colleagues this afternoon are Mr Robert Pirie and Miss Sandra Robertson.

Mr Pirie: Good afternoon.

Miss Robertson: Hi.

Mrs Young: The reporter today is?

Miss Cameron: I'm Laura Cameron, the reporter in this case.

Mrs Young: Could the others identify themselves and their interests?

Mrs MacDonald: I am Mrs Mhairi MacDonald. I'm a solicitor and I'm here to help my client Mr McPerlin, whom you have already welcomed.

Mr McPerlin: That's right.

Miss Robb: Dorothy Robb, assistant solicitor with Brodie, Paterson & Co. My senior Mr Paterson would have come but he had a prior engagement which he could not cancel. I am here to help Mrs McPerlin.

Mrs McPerlin: Yes, I am Mrs McPerlin, the girls' mother.

Miss Drummond: I am Marcia Drummond, main grade social worker with Lentonshire Council's Social Work Department. I am the social worker immediately involved with the case of Samantha and Jacqueline. I signed the application for the CPOs.

Mrs Young: Before we do anything else, can I just confirm that this is a hearing about two girls, Samantha McPerlin, whose date of birth is 15th August 1993 and Jacqueline McPerlin, whose date of birth is 10th July 1995 and the normal address of both girls is 19 Glenview Cottages, Bruaich – I think I've got that right?

[General murmurs of assent.]

Mrs Young: Fine. Well the background here, I believe, is that on 26th January of this year the sheriff here granted Child Protection Orders for

Samantha and Jacqueline, with the condition that they should stay with foster-carers, and also making conditions and directions [consulting CPOs]:–

- 'that the locality of the place of safety should not be disclosed to' Mr and Mrs McPerlin;

- that the relevant persons (that is Mr and Mrs McPerlin) be allowed supervised contact with Samantha and Jacqueline at such places and for such periods as the local authority shall in its discretion determine;

- that the applicant (that is in effect the Social Work Department) is granted the parental right and responsibility of having the child Jacqueline examined by a suitably qualified paediatrician within the Blackmore Memorial Infirmary, Kirklenton – this applies to Jacqueline only; and

- that the applicant (once again the Social Work Department) is granted the parental responsibility of securing all normal medical and dental treatment of both girls.

I must make it clear that the purpose of this hearing is (1) to consider whether the grounds for the CPOs, as they are called, still exist[114]; (2) if they do exist, to decide if they should be continued; (3) if they are to be continued, whether the conditions and directions, including the condition about contact which I have mentioned, ought to be continued, discontinued or changed in any way; (4) whether Mr McPerlin is a 'relevant person'; and (5) whether or not to appoint a safeguarder. We can go into more detail later, but is the broad outline clear?

[General murmurs of assent].

Mrs Young: I think the first thing we should consider is whether or not Mr McPerlin is to be regarded as a relevant person. Mr McPerlin, could you tell us what the set-up is, or at least was before the CPOs?

Mr McPerlin: Obviously I've been looking after the girls along with their mother since we got married.

Mrs MacDonald: Miss Robb and I have discussed this and we think there's no possible doubt that Mr McPerlin qualifies as a relevant person.

Miss Drummond: The girls have confirmed what Mr McPerlin has just said and I have explained to them the implications of this and they are quite clear that they expect Mr McPerlin to play his part in these proceedings.

Miss Robertson: I must say it seems pretty obvious.

---

114. Section 59(4) of the Children (Scotland) Act 1995 refers to the hearing being satisfied that the conditions are 'established' – this is rather misleading terminololgy, and Mrs Young avoids it but conveys the meaning of the provision.

Mr Pirie: Same here.

Mrs Young: Very well, that's agreed – not one of our more difficult decisions! Now we must formally decide about hearing from the girls in the absence of their parents and indeed from Mrs and Mr McPerlin in the absence of the girls. I must make it clear that Mr and Mrs McPerlin, like any other person with a right to attend the hearing is entitled to be present throughout the hearing unless and until the hearing makes a decision to exclude them.

Mrs McPerlin: Donald and I have discussed this with each other and with our lawyers. We cannot understand why the girls have taken up this attitude, but <u>we</u> do not want to make difficulties about this or anything else.

Mrs MacDonald: Yes, this has been discussed and there is no objection from my client or my friend's client. [Miss Robb nods in agreement.]

Mrs Young: Well, while the situation is unusual it seems to me that our decision ought to be: we should hear from the girls minus the parents and from the parents without the girls being present?

Mr Pirie and Miss Robertson: Agreed.

Reporter: I should perhaps mention that I have discussed with the McPerlins and their solicitors the possibility of <u>the solicitors</u> being present while the children are participating – that would be perhaps one way whereby they could 'assist' their clients in terms of the rules[115] – but they are happy and indeed say they would prefer the girls to speak to panel members without their solicitors present.

Mrs Young: Very well, that's settled. Miss Drummond, would you perhaps take Mr and Mrs McPerlin and the lawyers to the room where they are to wait and then go and ask the girls to come in?

> *Note [25]   The 'splitting' of the hearing so as to keep children and parents apart presents certain procedural problems for the hearing, which Mrs Young manages deftly. Section 43 of the Children (Scotland) Act 1995 provides for the basic privacy of the proceedings and confers on the chair a wide discretion as to who may attend: he must try to keep the numbers 'to a minimum'[116]. There are however persons who are entitled to attend, viz:*
>
> * *The child – whose <u>obligation</u> to attend may in certain circumstances be dispensed with[117] but whose <u>right</u> to attend cannot be taken away[118];*

---

115. Children's Hearings (Scotland) Rules, 1996, SI 96/3261, r 11(1); cf Children's Hearings (Scotland) Rules, 1996, SI 96/3261, r 13(d).
116. Children (Scotland) Act 1995, s 43(2).
117. Children (Scotland) Act 1995, s 42(2)(a).
118. Children (Scotland) Act 1995, s 45(2).

- *A relevant person – whose obligation to attend may be excused[119] but whose right to attend is secured[120];*

- *The father of a child under consideration who is living with the mother where both father and mother are parents of the child[121];*

- *A safeguarder appointed by a children's hearing[122];*

- *A person to assist each child and relevant person[123];*

- *A member of the Scottish Committee on Tribunals, or of the Scottish Committee of that Council[124];*

- *A bona fide representative of the media (subject to the hearing's power to exclude in certain circumstances to avoid distress to the child)[125];*

- *A social worker for the child[126];*

- *A constable or other person having lawful custody of any person who has to attend a hearing[127];*

- *Any person permitted by the chair of the hearing, including Children's Panel Advisory Committee members, panel members in training, students of the system and 'any other person whose presence at the hearing may in the opinion of the chairman by justified by special circumstances'[128].*

The chair may exclude relevant persons if he is satisfied that this is necessary either to obtain the child's views or where their presence would be likely to cause the child 'significant distress'[129]. The chair must tell any excluded person the substance of what has taken place in his/her absence[130]. A child may not be 'excluded' as such but his/her presence may (if the child agrees) be dispensed with in any case where the hearing think his/her presence would be detrimental to him/her and, in a Schedule 1 offence case, where they are satisfied that the child's presence is unnecessary[131]. The decision to dispense with a child's presence may be taken, as here, at the hearing itself or alternatively at a prior business meeting[132].

---

119. Children (Scotland) Act 1995, s 45(8)(b).
120. Children (Scotland) Act 1995, s 45(8)(a).
121. Children's Hearings (Scotland) Rules, 1996, SI 96/3261, r 12(1).
122. Children's Hearings (Scotland) Rules, 1996, SI 96/3261, r 14(3).
123. Children's Hearings (Scotland) Rules, 1996, SI 96/3261, r 11(1) and (2).
124. Children (Scotland) Act 1995, s 43(3)(a).
125. Children (Scotland) Act 1995, s 43(3)(b) and (4)(a) and (b).
126. Not explicitly stated by but implied in Children's Hearings (Scotland) Rules, 1996, SI 96/3261, r 8.
127. Children's Hearings (Scotland) Rules, 1996, SI 96/3261, r 12(2)
128. Children's Hearings (Scotland) Rules, 1996, SI 96/3261, r 13(a) – (d). In practice teachers, representatives from children's units, family members and the like are commonly allowed to attend.
129. Children Hearings (Scotland) Act 1995, s 46(1)(b).
130. Children (Scotland) Act 1995, s 43(5), s 46(2).
131. Children (Scotland) Act 1995, s 45(2).
132. Children (Scotland) Act 1995, s 64; Children's Hearings (Scotland) Rules 1996, r 4(2)(b). For further discussion of business meeting see below at pages 139, 140.

The hearing discusses the case with the children

[The social worker goes out with the McPerlins and the lawyers and then brings in Samantha and Jacqueline.]

Introductions

Mrs Young: Hello. I guess that you must be Samantha and you are Jacqueline?

[The girls nod, rather shyly.]

Mrs Young: Well, my name is Ina Young, Mrs Young, (Thomasina, I'm afraid) and this is Miss Sandra Robertson and this is Mr Robert Pirie.

Miss Pirie/Mr Robertson: Hi/Hello.

Mrs Young: And you know the reporter, Miss Laura Cameron?

[The girls nod in agreement.}

Mrs Young: The hearing is being arranged in such a way that you do not need to come into direct contact with you mother and Mr McPerlin. I believe this is what you both want. It will be my job to tell your mum and Mr McPerlin what views you have expressed and your mum and Mr McPerlin have said that they are happy for the solicitors not to be here when you give your views.

[The girls smile politely, but still say nothing.]

Mrs Young: I think you will both have a pretty good idea of what we are here for, but the law says that I have to explain it formally and I have to obey the law!

Samantha: Yes, we understand that.

The chair explains the purpose of the hearing to the children

Mrs Young: Can I first check that you are Samantha McPerlin, born 15 August 1993, and that you are Jacqueline McPerlin, born, 10 July 1995, and that you both normally stay at 19 Glenview Cottages, Bruaich, Kirklenton?

Samantha/Jacqueline: Yes/Yes, that's right.

Mrs Young: Good. Well, as you know the sheriff has granted Child Protection Orders for both of you. The purpose of this hearing is to decide whether to continue these orders for the time being and, if they are to be continued, to decide if the conditions attached to these Orders should remain the same or be changed in any way. The whole process is based on what you both have said about Donald. I hope this is not embarrassing but in fairness to everyone I must go into some detail.

Samantha: Yes, we know – don't worry.

Mrs Young: Thank you Samantha. And perhaps you can help me further and tell me if I have got things right. All this procedure was set in motion by you, Samantha, telling Miss Marcia Drummond that Donald had touched you inappropriately – sexually – in the months before Graeme was born in June 2004, which was the time when your mum was in hospital. You also mentioned an incident which Jackie had told you about last Hogmanay when Donald came into her bedroom very drunk and frightened her.

Samantha: Yes.

Mrs Young: And now that your mum is going to have another baby you are afraid that history might repeat itself, but this time with Jackie?

Samantha: Yes that's exactly right.

Mrs Young: Jacqueline, What's your take on this – is Samantha making a mountain out of a molehill?

[Jacqueline bursts out crying.]

Mrs Young: I'm so sorry, that was a clumsy way of putting it.

Jacqueline: [Between sobs.] That's all right. No, I think it was terrible what happened to Samantha.

Mrs Young: Sorry again, but I think I've got the point now. Well, this brings me back to the purpose of today's hearing. There could be more procedure in the sheriff court – your parents might ask the sheriff to cancel the Child Protection Orders but unless that happens the next hearing by a panel must be held on Tuesday 7th February by which time the reporter will have stated in writing the 'Grounds for Referral', in which the information you, Samantha, gave about what Mr McPerlin did to you in the past and also what may have happened to you, Jacqueline, at New Year time. The Grounds for Referral would probably deal mainly with what you, Samantha, said Donald did to you two years ago and state that this was one of the circumstances – technically known as a 'Schedule 1 offence' – which entitles a hearing to take control. In the case of Jacqueline the main ground would be that you are or are likely to become a part of the same household set-up as someone (Samantha) against whom a 'Schedule 1 offence' has been committed. What we have to do today is decide whether to continue CPOs in place or to cancel them. If we decide not to continue the orders then they come to an end right away, so that you would go home to your mum and Donald this afternoon. If we decide to continue the orders then you would return to the Jamiesons' for the time being. If we decide to continue the orders we have the power to make changes such as altering the arrangements for contact between you and mum and Donald.

The children give their views

Samantha: Can I say something?

Mrs Young: Yes, of course, but, as I mentioned I'll have to let your Mum and Mr McPerlin know what you tell us?

Samantha: Yes, I know that. It's just that Jacqueline has said more to me about last Hogmanay, and would like to clear up some things. She would like to speak to you direct.

Mrs Young: That's fine. What do you want to say Jacqueline?

Jacqueline: People call me Jackie.

Mrs Young: OK, what is it, Jackie?

Jacqueline: I've talked about all this with Sam and, you know, about Hogmanay. Daddy, Donald, did come into my room and annoy me, but he didn't touch me or anything. I think he might have wanted to – after what Sam has told me and that – but he was very drunk and mumbled something I didn't hear properly and then fell down on the floor and went to sleep. I didn't know what to do and was frightened. I was ashamed of Daddy, who is normally very nice. I didn't sleep for ages but I must've gone to sleep for when I woke up he was away. I'm sorry. It's all a mess; but I know he didn't touch me. I'm not making this up. I know that he touched Sam. I don't know what to do. I know you want to know my 'views'. I don't know what my views are. Mr and Mrs Jamieson are OK, but they're not the same as Mummy.

Miss Robertson: Do you think you want to go home right away, in spite of everything?

Jacqueline: I don't know [starts crying again].

Samantha: We've talked about this and <u>for the present</u> we'd like to stay with the Jamiesons', to let things cool off, you know, but we must keep in touch with Mummy. We'd like to see Mummy as much as possible, but we certainly don't want to spend the night in a house where Donald is staying.

Jacqueline: Yes, that's right.

Miss Robertson: We shall discuss this with your mum and Donald and work out a form of words and come back to you before fixing it finally. How much have you seen of them since last Thursday?

Samantha: We told Marcia that we wanted to chill out over the week-end and not have any 'contact'.

Miss Drummond: Yes, and actually the parents thought the same.

Miss Robertson: Samantha seems to mean that you both want to see as much as possible of Mum, but not of Donald, and certainly not overnight. Is that about right?

[Jacqueline, between snuffles, nods in agreement].

Mrs Young: And when you are seeing Mum, would you want 'supervision' – in other words would a social worker have to be present?

Samantha: Not if it was only Mum we were seeing.

Mrs Young: [To the other hearing members]: Do you think there is anything more we should discuss with Samantha and Jackie?

Mr Pirie: [To Jacqueline] Would your mum being present not make it unlikely that Donald would do anything bad?

Samantha: We have discussed this a lot and we don't want to have that. It's not that we really think Donald would do anything, it's just that it wouldn't feel right.

Miss Robertson: I think I can understand that.

Mr Pirie: Yes, I think I agree. What do you think Mrs Young?

Mrs Young: Yes, I think that would be the best course.

Miss Robertson: So if that's agreed, is that all we can do for now?

Mrs Young: More or less, but we'd better settle precise times which the girls would like for contact with Donald.

Mr Pirie: Yes of course. [To the girls] I guess you've talked about this already?

Samantha: Yes; and one session a week of about a couple of hours would be what we'd suggest.

Miss Robertson: Fine.

Mr Pirie: Yes that seems all right.

Mrs Young: I think so too.

Miss Robertson: So that's that?

Mrs Young: Just about, but there's another point – should 'contact' with Mr McPerlin be supervised by the Social Work Department?

Miss Robertson: [To Samantha and Jacqueline] What do you two think?

Samantha: We've discussed this and would like the contact to be in neutral territory such as the Social Work suite and, if that's what is meant by supervised contact, then that's what we would like.

Jacqueline: Yes, that's right.

Miss Robertson: Thanks, that's clear. But you know that we still have to check all this out with your Mum and with Donald and see if they have any other ideas?

Samantha/Jacqueline: Yes, we know that/Yes, of course.

Mrs Young: Now one other thing. We have the power to appoint an independent person called a 'safeguarder' to represent your interests. That person would be independent of us and of the Social Work Department, would come and talk to you, and come to hearings to explain your views and tell the hearing what she (and it would almost certainly be a 'she') thought was best for you. Would you like us to appoint a safeguarder?

Samantha: Would this person take our part and tell the hearing what we wanted to happen?

Mrs Young: Not entirely. She would tell the hearing your views, but would not be bound to follow your wishes.

Samantha: What do you think Jackie? – I must say I'd rather speak for myself.

Jacqueline: I agree. I don't like the idea of someone who would be regarded as speaking for us supporting something that we perhaps didn't want.

Mrs Young: I think I've got your views on that. We'll keep in mind what you have said when deciding on this but, as regards this and the other things, we cannot promise to do exactly what you want.

Samantha: Yes, we know that.

Mrs Young: So from all you've said it seems clear that you, Samantha, are standing by what you said to Marcia about what Donald did to you, that you, Jacqueline, are not saying as much as that, that you would both want to stay with the Jamiesons at present, but with as much contact as possible with mum, with two hours supervised contact with Mr McPerlin, and that you don't want a safeguarder?

[The girls nod in agreement]

Mrs Young: Two further points. First – the medical conditions. [To Miss Drummond] I think your department routinely arranges a medical examination to see if there is any attention needed. Has that been done yet?

Miss Drummond: Yes, Dr McLintock saw them on Thursday evening and there was nothing wrong.

[The girls nod in agreement]

Miss Robertson: On the subject of medicals, there's a condition about examination of Jacqueline by a paediatrician, I wonder if we need to leave that in place?

Mrs Young: Yes, that's a good point. I don't think there is any conceivable likelihood on the information before us that there would be physical evidence of any form of 'abuse'. That being so I think it would be quite wrong to subject Jacqueline to an intimate examination.

Samantha: Yes I was wondering about that myself. Jackie, says she cannot see the point of that and certainly doesn't want one.

Jacqueline: Yes, that's right.

Miss Drummond: I agree.

Mrs Young [To the other hearing members]: Is that agreed?

Miss Robertson and Mr Pirie: Most certainly/Yes I think so.

Mrs Young: Now as to 'relevant persons' I think Miss Drummond has already explained to you that for Mr Donald McPerlin to play his part in these proceedings we have to say that he is a 'relevant person' because he normally is in care and control of you. I think you accept that Donald normally did this?

Samantha: Yes, of course.

Mrs Young: Finally, the address of your foster-parents: should that be kept secret from your mum and Mr McPerlin?

Samantha: Jackie and I have discussed this and we don't mind either way – we'd have no real objection.

Mrs Young: Fine, thanks. [To the other hearing members]: Well, unless there are any points you want to raise, I think that we can let the girls go for now?

Miss Robertson and Mr Pirie: Yes.

Mrs Young: Fine. Well, Samantha and Jackie, that's all for now. If you go back into the other room for a while we'll now hear from your Mum and Mr McPerlin and talk things over with them. After that we'll ask you back in again (just yourselves) to tell you what they said to us and to discuss things further with you if necessary. Then we'll tell you what our decision is. [To the social worker] – Marcia, I suppose there's some-one next door to keep the girls company while we get on with the next part of the hearing?

[Miss Drummond nods agreement. She goes out with the girls and after a minute or so Miss Drummond and the lawyers come back with Mr and Mrs McPerlin]

The hearing discusses the case with the relevant persons

Mrs Young: Hello again. Now we have all introduced ourselves and I have already explained the purpose of this hearing. First of all 'relevant persons'. Miss Drummond indicated that the girls had confirmed that Mr McPerlin was normally their carer, along with their mum. We actually mentioned this to the girls direct and they of course confirmed this.

Mr Pirie [To Mr McPerlin]: Yes, so that means we can formally recognise you as a relevant person.

Miss Robb: Yes, my client is aware of the implications of this.

Mrs Young: Very well, that's fine. I have already explained the purpose of this hearing in broad terms and we can go onto the detail in a minute, but first I'd better tell you the essence of what Samantha and Jacqueline said.

The chair explains the substance of what has taken place in the absence of the relevant persons

Mrs Young: Now, first of all, as you know we used our powers to 'exclude' you, Mr and Mrs McPerlin, from the earlier part of the hearing, and I think you have accepted that. We have heard from Samantha and Jacqueline. I must tell you what they said. As to the factual background it was clear that Samantha was sticking to her account of what she said Mr McPerlin did in the past, but Jacqueline was anxious to tell us that there was no 'touching' last Hogmanay, although she said she thought you would have touched her had you not been drunk and fallen asleep. Both girls were reasonably happy to stay with the foster parents at present – they like the foster parents and are obviously being well-treated by them – but they emphasise that this is only for the time being. They want substantial contact with their mother but would only wish contact with you, Mr McPerlin, if the contact were supervised, and that for, say, two hours per week. They do not want to reside in the family home overnight. Do you get the picture?

Mrs McPerlin: Yes, but we do not accept all this about Donald touching Samantha and bothering Jackie.

Mrs Young: Yes, but as I'm sure your lawyers will have told you that's all for the sheriff to decide.

Mr McPerlin: I know, but we just wanted to make our position clear.

Mrs Young: Fine. Now let's get on.

The chair clarifies the purpose of the hearing to the relevant persons

Mrs Young: I have already outlined the purpose of this hearing. I should now get into the detail. As you, Mr and Mrs McPerlin, of course know, the Child Protection Orders were granted by the sheriff on the basis of information given to her by Miss Marcia Drummond here. The purpose of this hearing is (a) to consider whether the grounds on the basis of which the CPOs were granted still exist; (b) to decide whether or not to continue them; and, (c) if we do continue them, to decide whether any of the conditions attached to the CPOs should be changed in any way. But in deciding this we have to approach our task by checking if there were allegations put before the sheriff which, if true, would justify the granting of the orders and that nothing important has changed. We have no power to hear evidence from both sides and choose which side we believe. As I am sure your lawyer will have told you there are procedures whereby the matter can go to the sheriff who has the power to do just that. We have the power to discontinue the orders but we can only do that if we were to come to the conclusion that the best course, in the interests of the girls, was to allow them to go home pending the hearing of evidence by the sheriff.

Mr McPerlin/Mrs McPerlin: Yes/Yes I understand all that.

Mrs Young: One of the things we have to tackle today is whether the conditions attached should be changed in any way. These conditions at present are [reading from one of the CPOs]:

- 'That the relevant persons be allowed supervised contact with the child ... at such places and for such periods as the local authority shall in its discretion determine'.

- The applicant is granted the parental right and responsibility of having the child Jacqueline examined by a suitably qualified paediatrician within the Blackmore Memorial Infirmary, Kirklenton.

- The applicant is granted the parental responsibility of securing all normal medical and dental treatment of the child.

In addition the CPO said:

- The sheriff orders that the locality of the place of safety should not be disclosed to: Mrs Sharon Transom or McPerlin, 19 Glenview Cottages, Bruaich, Kirklenton LE29 4QW, and Mr Donald McPerlin, 19 Glenview Cottages, Bruaich, Kirklenton LE29 4QW.

What I think we should do is deal with these issues in order. Firstly I will ask the social worker, Marcia, about the grounds for making the CPOs. I will then ask you both if you want to say anything about that and we can have such discussion as may be necessary. Then I will ask Marcia what she thinks about changing or not the 'conditions' of the orders in the event that we decide that the orders should continue. Then once again we shall ask you both to join in a discussion on that. Finally we shall discuss whether, (if we decide to continue the orders) what is known as a 'safeguarder' – that is an independent person to work out and put forward what he or she thinks is in the interests of the girls – should be appointed. I can if necessary explain more about all these points as we go along, but is that clear enough so far?

Mr McPerlin, Mrs McPerlin: Yes/Yes, that's quite clear.

Miss Robertson: Yes, that's fine by me.

Mr Pirie: Agreed.

Discussion as to grounds of the CPOs

Mrs Young: Now, Miss Drummond, the parts of your report dealing with the grounds for taking the CPOs are as follows, referring to Report for Second Working Day Hearing]:

- (4)   The family did not come again to the notice of the Department till 13th and 17th January of this year (2006) when Samantha disclosed to the writer that her step-father Donald had been abusing her sexually during the time when the mother was away from the house in the early summer of 2004 – the period when Samantha was absent from school.

- (5)   Samantha thinks that Donald made some sexual approach towards Jacqueline in the recent Christmas/New Year period but Jacqueline has not confirmed this. Mrs McPerlin is again pregnant and may require another extended stay in hospital. Since Jacqueline is about the same age now as she (Samantha) was in 2004 Samantha is afraid that Donald may try to abuse Jacqueline and that she (Samantha) will not be able to protect her sister.

- (6)   The sexual abuse of Samantha did not, according to Samantha, go beyond fondling under her night-clothes and she was able to resist anything further. Samantha, however, is very apprehensive that Donald would go much further with Jacqueline who is not as mature and strong-willed as she is.

That is what Samantha told you on 17th January, which is about three weeks ago. Has anything happened since then which would change that in any way?

Miss Drummond: Nothing as far as Samantha herself is concerned but, as Jackie has already told you, she has now made clear a minute ago as you mentioned, she says she was not touched by Mr McPerlin on the night in question but that he did enter her bedroom, etc.

Mrs Young: Have you spoken to the girls recently?

Miss Drummond: Yes, I had a half hour with them this afternoon. I spoke to them both separately and they told me exactly what they have told you. They are worried that Mrs McPerlin may have to go into hospital at any time and at short notice. They may not be right to have this worry, but that is how things seem to <u>them</u>.

Mrs Young: Thank you. [To the McPerlins and their solicitors] Anyone else want to say anything about the factual grounds?

[No response apart from a shaking of heads and murmurs of 'no'.]

Miss Robertson: It seems to me that at this stage we can hardly say that there is not, at least on the face of things, a foundation for the CPOs. Apart from the slight modification by Jacqueline the girls seemed to be sticking to their account today.

Mr Pirie: I must say I think we should leave things basically as they are. The evidence is ultimately for the sheriff to consider and I would not like to say any more at this stage.

Mrs Young: I agree. The next thing we have to decide is the amount of what is now called 'contact'.

The discussion with the relevant persons as to the appropriate amount of contact

Mrs Young: Marcia, how has contact been getting on since 26th January, i.e. since last Thursday?

Miss Drummond. We thought it was important that contact should not be used as a vehicle for, for example, influencing the girls' account of what had happened but, having discussed this with Mr and Mrs McPerlin and the girls we concluded that this was not likely and decided to have regard to the wishes of the girls to have as much contact as possible with their mother but not, at present at least, contact with Donald McPerlin. We accordingly simply asked the foster parents to allow the girls daytime contact with Mrs McPerlin whenever the girls wanted, subject to practicalities and having regard to the order in the CPO that the foster-carers address was not to be revealed to the McPerlins. In the event the girls said that they wanted to 'chill out' and not see the McPerlins over the week-end. I told Mr and Mrs McPerlin about this and they seemed to understand. As to the future, as the girls told you earlier this afternoon, they want to have substantial contact with Mrs McPerlin but only limited, supervised, contact with Mr McPerlin. May I make a suggestion?

Mrs Young: Yes, of course.

Miss Drummond: The sheriff had ordered, in accordance with our initial request, that the address of the foster parents should not be revealed to the McPerlins. I no longer think that order is appropriate. This is one of these cases in which we can rely on the good sense of all concerned to manage contact in their own way. There is no likelihood in my view, for example, of the McPerlins going to the foster-parents and trying to take the girls away or otherwise cause any trouble.

Mr McPerlin/Mrs McPerlin [Talking over each other]: Of course we wouldn't do that ... that's a ridiculous suggestion.

Mrs Young: Yes, I think Miss Drummond is accepting that.

Miss Drummond: And as to the amount of contact – as we know, the girls are anxious to have as much contact as possible with their mother but only two hours with Mr McPerlin. The girls have also said that they would like the contact with Mr McPerlin to be supervised. As some of you know we have recently set up a well-equipped contact centre in the Department. I have checked that there are slots available on Saturdays from 10 a.m. till 12 midday and from 3 till 5 in the afternoon. Samantha and Jacqueline have indicated their views to me in advance and I was able to talk this over with the McPerlins ...

Miss Robertson: I think Mr McPerlin wants to say something.

Mr McPerlin: Yes I do. Thank you. What I want to say is that while I think it is quite unnecessary for there to be 'supervision' of any sort, I do not want to make difficulties and for that reason I agree to the Saturday morning proposal. I'd like it to be noted that I am doing this in order to keep the peace.

Miss Robertson: I was wondering if supervision was at all necessary, but it would be unusual not to have supervision with allegations like these?

Mr Pirie: I was thinking along these lines too, but I agree.

Mrs Young: Yes, I agree too. Now what about contact with Mrs McPerlin? Isn't there a risk that she might pressurise the children in some way?

Mrs McPerlin: I have no intention of doing any such thing.

Miss Drummond: I would not be too worried about this, particularly since Samantha is so mature for her age.

Mr Pirie: Could we say simply that non-residential contact with the mother should be in accordance with the wishes of the girls and Mrs McPerlin?

Miss Drummond: It may be that the foster-parents would like a time for the girls to be in by, and I think the girls themselves might like to have the security that that would provide.

Mrs Young: A good point, thanks Marcia. Of course we'd have to keep in mind that Bruaich is a good twenty minutes drive from the foster-parents' address.

Mrs McPerlin: I could drive them there if they were having contact at my house and I think about half past nine should be the return time.

Mrs MacDonald: That seems OK.

Mrs Young: Very well. [To the other hearing members] – Is that agreed?

Miss Robertson/Mr Pirie: That's fine/Agreed.

Mrs Young: Fine. Now, as to the 'medical' conditions. The girls have been given a routine medical examination by a GP and there was nothing wrong. The sheriff made it a condition of the CPOs that there should be an examination of Jacqueline by a paediatrician. There is here no sugges-tion of any 'abuse' which would leave physical symptoms, so I think this condition should not be continued.

Miss Drummond: It's certainly been my experience that only when a paediatric examination takes place very soon after will there be any physical symptoms and anyway even if everything Samantha has said is true it is difficult to see what physical symptoms there could ever have been.

Mr McPerlin: I'm not so sure. Wouldn't a negative examination help to clear me?

Mrs MacDonald [to Mr McPerlin]: I see no way how an intimate examination could help you in this case.

[Mr McPerlin indicates reluctant agreement]

Mrs Young: Well, if that's agreed I think we should ask Mr and Mrs McPerlin to go into the waiting room for a minute or two so that we can discuss this with Samantha and Jacqueline and then let them go. We can settle the terms of the order and reasons with the girls present and then go over it with Mr and Mrs McPerlin after that.

Miss Robb: Wouldn't it be better to do the drafting now. The relevant persons might have some suggestion and if the girls were away by that time we could not check the wording with them.

Mrs Young: No, I don't want to go back to the girls with any sort of prepared text, but I see what you mean. I think the answer is to ask them to wait until we get the final wording settled. Is that all right?

[A nodding of heads and murmurs of 'Fine' and 'OK']

Mrs Young: Very well. [To Mr and Mrs McPerlin] – Would you slip into the waiting room for a minute. And Marcia, would you get the girls, please. Miss Robb and Mrs MacDonald, I think the agreement is that you should withdraw also?

[The McPerlins leave and Miss Drummond brings in Samantha and Jacqueline.]

The discussion with the children of the appropriate amount of contact

Mrs Young: We've nearly finished, I hope you haven't been bored waiting?

Samantha/Jacqueline: No, no/That's all right.

Mrs Young: We've been discussing 'contact' with your mum and Donald. You said you'd like as much 'non-residential' contact as possible with your mum but limited contact – and that under supervision – with Donald. We, the panel that is, can make an order saying something like that contact is to be 'as agreed between you on the one hand and mum on the other' and, as to Donald, 'for two hours, under supervision in the Social Services Department's contact centre on Saturdays between 10 am and midday.' Do you think that would work? What would you all actually do?

Samantha: Yes I'm sure it would work all right. We can fix up things by phone. Mummy usually takes us to the baths on Saturday afternoons and that could keep going. Actually it's Mummy rather than Donald who does most with us. Mummy sometimes takes us to the pictures in Kirklenton and I expect that could be managed as well.

Miss Robertson: That might sometimes be in the evening, and that brings me to one point: I think the Jamiesons would like to have a definite time when you were expected back.

Samantha: Yes I see. In fact at home we're supposed to be in by nine at the latest … except perhaps when we are out for the evening, to the pictures, like.

Miss Robertson: Actually we thought half past nine would be about right.

Samantha: Yes, that seems fine. Don't you think so, Jackie?

Jacqueline: OK by me.

Miss Drummond: Oh, I should mention that the girls said they thought that not telling Mum the address of the Jamiesons' was pointless since Mum would be returning them there.

Mrs Young: A good point, I think that should be made clear.

The Reporter drafts the decision

Mrs Young: That's agreed, then. Now so as to make clear that everything is 'above board' the reporter Miss Cameron is going to sketch out our formal order. I shall read it out in a minute.

[After a long pause.]

Mrs Young There will of course be two orders, since there are two children, but they will both be almost the same, as follows [reading from the draft]:–

'The hearing unanimously decided:–

1.   To consider Mr McPerlin, to be a relevant person in relation to the child[133].

2.   To exclude the relevant persons and their representatives from part of the hearing: s 46(1)[134].

3.   To remove the obligations to attend from Samantha McPerlin and Jacqueline McPerlin from part of the hearing: s 45(2)[135].

4.   To continue the Child Protection Orders (s 59(4)) with variations[136]:

   1)   The direction regarding contact is varied to allow as from now non-residential contact between Jacqueline/Samantha and Mrs McPerlin whenever and wherever is agreed between Jacqueline/Samantha and Mrs McPerlin so long as Jacqueline/Samantha return to the foster parents' address no later than 9.30 pm. The direction is also varied to allow Jacqueline/Samantha now to have supervised contact with Mr Donald McPerlin, which is to take place within premises of the Social Work Depart-ment, Kirklenton between 10 am and midday on Satur-days.

   2)   The condition of non-disclosure of the locality of the place of safety is not continued.

   3)   The direction for examination by a paediatrician is not continued.

5.   Not to appoint a safeguarder: s 41.

Mrs Young: The provision about not having an examination by a paediatrician will of course only feature in the order for Jacqueline. Subject to any formal tidying up does that seem right to everyone?

[General indications of approval.]

Mrs Young: While the reporter was writing I was sketching out a summary of our reasons with the help of my colleagues. Subject to any formal tidying up does that seem right to everyone? This is what we might say:

REASONS

•   Everyone agreed that Mr McPerlin routinely looked after the children.

---

133. Children (Scotland) Act 1995, s 93(2)(b), (c).
134. Children (Scotland) Act 1995, s 46(1)
135. Children (Scotland) Act 1995, s 45(2).
136. Children (Scotland) Act 1995, s 59(4).

- The girls had made it clear they did not want to see the relevant persons at this hearing so we thought their presence during that part of the hearing when the children were there would be detrimental to the children. The relevant persons were agreeable to this.

- Serious allegations have been made against Mr McPerlin and there is a real possibility of harm to the girls, particularly Jacqueline, if they were to stay overnight in the family home. There was no indication that these allegations were obviously spurious. We accordingly thought that the conditions as laid before the sheriff who granted the CPOs continued to exist and that therefore we should continue the Child Protection Order with the condition of residence with the foster-parents. This accorded with the wishes of the girls.

- However the possibility of such harm did not seem to the hearing to exist in the context of daytime contact. Samantha and Jacqueline said they wanted as much non-residential contact as possible with Mum but only limited supervised contact with Mr McPerlin. The hearing were confident that the girls on the one hand and Mrs McPerlin on the other hand could be relied upon to come to sensible arrangements. Both the girls and mum agreed that it would be sensible to specify a time for return to the foster-parents' home. The limited contact with Mr McPerlin was acceptable to the girls and, with reluctance, to Mr McPerlin.

- In these circumstances it was obvious that the order not to reveal the foster-carers' address was redundant.

- We thought it was obvious that the condition about ordinary medical care should stay.

- But we thought the condition about a paediatric examination was unnecessary on the alleged facts and, since conducting such intrusive examinations without reasonable cause is objectionable, we cancelled the requirement to do so.

- The girls said they did not want a safeguarder and we thought they were mature enough to participate without a safeguarder, at least for the present.

Note [26]   When two or three panel members are gathered together they sooner or later talk about the proper way to narrate decisions and state reasons. There is no set form. As to narrating decisions, in practice this is done by the reporter, following the decision of the hearing. It is important that all the procedural decisions are recorded – in this case numbers 1, 2, 3 and 5, as well as the substantive decisions. As to reasons, the important thing is to get to the substance of the matter – it would not be good enough to use 'blanket' terminology that is, for example, wording such as:– 'The hearing, having carefully considered all the relevant facts and circumstances decided that it was in the child's best interests to ... ...' – that tells us nothing! On the other hand it is not necessary to go into enormous detail justifying the obvious. As to lay-out, again there is no set formula, but the practice of Mrs

Young in stating a separate reason for each decision in the same order as the decisions themselves is, it is suggested, a sensible one. Mrs Young's practice of going over the reasons in the presence of the parties is not essential, and is by no means universal, but it has the advantage, particularly where, as here, the decision is a complex one and made in the context of a 'split' hearing, of conforming to the principle of open-ness which is inherent to the philosophy of the hearings system. It also tends to eliminate the possibility of mis-remembering[137].

The chair again asks the children about the wording of the decision and the Statement of Reasons

Mrs Young: Do you think that covers it?

Samantha/Jacqueline: That's fine/That's all right.

Mrs Young: Does the reporter's eagle eye spot anything missing?

Reporter: No, it sounds all right to me[138].

Mrs Young: Fine. Assuming Mr and Mrs McPerlin agree then that's what I'll sign as our decision and reasons[139]. I should explain that you[140] have the right to apply to the sheriff to set aside or vary our decision and that if you want to do so you must lodge an Application in the sheriff court on the day after tomorrow at the latest.

Samantha: Yes, Marcia has explained that to us, but as far as we are concerned this decision is OK.

Mrs Young: Very well, would you two go back to the waiting room for a minute so that we can check with your Mum and Donald that what we have said is all right with them. Assuming there is nothing to change I shall then let you know and you can go. So, if we don't see you again, goodbye, and thanks for being so helpful.

---

137. 'Some panel areas in Scotland avoid this [the possible mis-remembering of what has been decided] completely by writing reasons while the child and relevant persons are still present and then reading them back. This is generally a good practice, so long as the family are made aware that it is not an opportunity to reopen the discussion or challenge any decision the hearing members have made.' – Professor Kenneth McK Norrie, *Children's Hearings in Scotland*, second edition, Edinburgh 2005 at footnote 60 on page 125.
138. Note that the usual advice to the parties about the possibility of an appeal to the sheriff is <u>not</u> given here, because the granting of a CPO and the continuing of a CPO by a hearing under s 59(4) of the Act is (like the granting of a CPO by the sheriff) expressly excluded by s 51(15) of the Act. The remedy, as the chair will explain presently, is an Application to Set Aside or Vary.
139. Children's Hearings (Scotland) Rules, 1996, SI 96/3261, r 10(5).
140. Not strictly necessary – Children's Hearings (Scotland) Rules, 1996, SI 96/3261 r 20(5)(c) imposes on the chair in a disposal hearing and a review hearing the obligation to advise of the right of appeal, this is not such a hearing, and an application to set aside or vary is not, strictly speaking an appeal, but the principle is the same and Mrs Young is following good practice.

Miss Robertson/Mr Pirie: Yes, good-bye/Bye-bye, all the best.

Samantha/Jacqueline: Thanks/Good-bye.

[Marcia takes the girls to the waiting room. She then goes to the other waiting room and returns with the McPerlins and their solicitors.]

The chair consults the relevant persons about the wording of the decision and the Statement of Reasons

Mrs Young: Hello again. The reporter has drafted our decision and we have sketched out our reasons. These have been read to Samantha and Jacqueline and they are content. I'll just read out what is here. [Reads the drafts as above.] Any comments?

Mr McPerlin: All this about me is rubbish and we're going to appeal to the sheriff, but I don't suppose there's much we can do now.

Mrs MacDonald: No, this isn't the place to make these points. [To the Chair]: As you will have gathered, my client will be making an application to the sheriff to set aside the CPOs. I have no comment to make on the proposed draft which seems to me to reflect what has been decided and why.

Miss Robb: That goes for Mrs McPerlin too.

Mrs Young: Thank you very much. Well, that's all we can do for the present. Marcia, will you slip out and tell the girls and Mrs Jamieson that they can go now.

[Miss Drummond goes out.]

The chair confirms the final form of the decision and Statement of Reasons

Mrs Young: Well, I have read out what will be our final word. I should explain that you[141] have the right to apply to the sheriff to vary or set aside our decision and that if you want to do so you must lodge an Application in the sheriff court on the day after tomorrow at the latest, but no doubt your lawyer will keep you right on that. The reporter will ensure that our decision and reasons are typed and sent to you both, and to the girls, before the close of business this afternoon[142].

Reporter: Now that the CPO has been continued I can now give the formal notifications for Mr and Mrs McPerlin of the Eighth Working Day hearing. I will give these to the girls before they leave the building this

---

141. Not strictly necessary – see above, footnote 140.
142. Children's Hearings (Scotland) Rules, 1996, SI 96/3261, r 10(5).

afternoon. I will have delivered or posted out any papers, including the Social Work Report, as soon as is practicable, probably tomorrow morning, and the Grounds for Referral will be sent by first class post on Thursday 2nd February 2006 so as to give three clear days notice before the Eighth Working Day hearing on 7th February 2006[143].

[The reporter hands the notifications to the McPerlins.]

Miss Robertson and Mr Pirie: Good-bye.

[Mr and Mrs McPerlin and their solicitors leave the hearing room.]

Mrs Young: Well that concludes this afternoon's business. The reporter will arrange for the formal order to be typed[144] and I'll wait to sign it. We'd better return the papers to you Laura[145].

[Miss Cameron receives the papers from the panel members and goes to the adjoining room to give the notifications to Samantha and Jacqueline.]

Same day, Monday, 30 January 2006 at 4.15 pm

The reporter prepares arranges for the formal orders to be typed. Here is the order for Jacqueline:

Rule 27

FORM 6

SCOTTISH
CHILDREN'S REPORTER
ADMINISTRATION

Continuation under Section 59(4) of the Act
of a Child Protection Order

At 17 Laverock Road, Kirklenton   Date: *30:01:06*

A children's hearing for Lentonshire, in respect of the case of

Name: *Jacqueline McPerlin, d.o.b. 10:07:1995*
       19, Glenview Cottages,
       Bruaich,
       Kirklenton, LE29 4QW.

---

143. See supra Note [24].
144. The decisions and reasons are not always typed – sometimes just handwritten. It is, however, good practice to have them typed.
145. Children's Hearings (Scotland) Rules 1996, r 5(5).

and in exercise of the powers conferred on them by section 59(4) of the Children (Scotland) Act 1995, being satisfied that the conditions for the making of a child protection order under section 57 of the Act are established CONTINUE the Child Protection Order dated 26th January 2006,

a copy of which is attached [and the directions made under section 58 of the Act] until 7th February 2006.

For the duration of the Order the variations of the [Order] [and] [direction[s]] set out below shall have effect:

- The direction regarding contact is varied to allow as from now non-residential contact between Jacqueline and Mrs McPerlin whenever and wherever is agreed between Jacqueline and Mrs McPerlin so long as Jacqueline returns to the foster parents' address no later than 9.30 pm. The direction is also varied to allow Jacqueline as from now to have supervised contact with Mr Donald McPerlin, which is to take place within premises of the Social Work Department, Kirklenton between 10 am and midday on Saturdays.

- The condition of non-disclosure of the locality of the place of safety is not continued.

- The direction for examination by a paediatrician is not continued.

(Sgd) *Thomasina Young*
Chair of the Children's Hearing

Same day, Monday, 30 January 2005 at about 4.30 pm

INFORMAL DISCUSSION AFTER THE 2 WD HEARING

While waiting for the reasons to be typed the reporter, the solicitors for the McPerlins and the social worker have an informal discussion. They remind themselves that there are two working days within which an Application to Recall or Vary the CPOs, as now continued by the hearing, may be made[146], and that consequently such an application would require to be lodged by the evening of Wednesday, 1st February 2006 at the latest. They also recall that if an Application to Set Aside or Vary is lodged on Wednesday 1st February the hearing of that application would require to be determined 'within three working days' of the application being made[147] – that is by Monday 6th February at the latest. The reporter mentions that it is in her experience unlikely that the sheriff would wish to leave the hearing of the Application till the last day and that she would expect it to come before the court on Friday 3rd February 2006.

Miss Robb and Mrs MacDonald state that they have already obtained the client's instructions to lodge an Application to Set Aside or Vary.

---

146. Children (Scotland) Act 1995, s 60(8)(b).
147. Children (Scotland) Act 1995, s 60(8)(b).

The reporter mentions that the 'Eighth Working Day' hearing would be due to be held on Tuesday 7th February 2006[148]. She confirms that she will post the Grounds for Referral 'not later than three days before the date of the hearing'(that is by posting from her office before the close of business on Thursday 2nd February)[149]. Mrs MacDonald remarks jocularly that she will not need to bother since she expects to have the matter thrown out by then and on that note, the solicitors having now received the typed copy of the hearing's decision and reasons, the meeting breaks up.

LEGAL ADVICE ON THE APPLICATION TO SET ASIDE OR VARY CPOs

Tuesday, 31 January 2006 at 2 pm – in Mrs MacDonald's Office

Discussion between Mr McPerlin and his solicitor as to how to approach the Application to Set Aside or Vary Procedure

Initial discussion and instructions

Mr McPerlin arrives to meet with Mrs MacDonald. Mr McPerlin confirms that he wishes to go ahead with an Application to Set Aside or Vary the CPOs[150].

Discussion about contact

Mr McPerlin asks Mrs MacDonald about their chances. She says that in her experience such applications generally have only limited success. She says that sheriffs, while often prepared to vary such matters as provisions for contact, take a lot of persuading, such as by reference to a marked change in circumstances, to set aside CPOs completely.

Mr McPerlin says that while he would like the issue of contact to be pursued his main interest is to get the allegations against him disproved. Mr McPerlin says that he has an older, unmarried brother who lives alone in Bruaich and would be prepared to let him stay with him on week-days for a period, provided it was not too long. This brother lives alone and has a spare bedroom, but would not be able to accommodate him on Saturday and Sunday nights since their elderly mother comes to stay with him then. He has discussed this with his wife and understands she is going to make this the basis for a claim that the girls should be allowed to stay at home

148. Children (Scotland) Act 1995, s 65(2).
149. Ibid.
150. Children (Scotland) Act 1995, s 60(7), Act of Sederunt (Child Care and Maintenance Rules) 1997, SI 1997/291, r 3.33(1) and Schedule 1 Form 52 (which is entitled 'Application to Vary or Recall a Child Protection Order'.)

from Mondays to Fridays. He agrees that Mrs MacDonald may liaise with Mr Paterson about this.

As for himself, he confirms that, as mentioned in 2WD hearing he would 'settle' for two hours contact in the Social Work Department's suite for 2 hours supervised contact on Saturday mornings. He emphasises that this is just for the time being and that if the sheriff were to uphold the Grounds for Referral he would wish to have much more extensive contact. Mrs MacDonald explains that if the Grounds are sustained there will be a full 'dispositive' hearing at which the more long-term arrangements will be put in place. He asks if his accepting a comparatively low amount of contact at present would set a precedent. Mrs MacDonald tells him that one cannot be certain on such matters but that she is inclined to the view that by being 'reasonable' now this may enhance rather than detract from the possibility of greater contact at any dispositive hearing.

Timescales for and outline of the next steps in the procedure

Mrs MacDonald explains that the next big step after the Application to Set Aside or Vary is the Eighth Working Day Hearing[151], which will be on Tuesday 7th February 2006. She explains that that hearing will have before it the Grounds for Referral and will have the duty of ascertaining what the stances of the children and the McPerlins (as 'relevant persons') are in relation to the Grounds for Referral[152], and that unless the Grounds are accepted by the McPerlins the hearing will almost inevitably direct the reporter to make application to the sheriff[153] requesting that a 'proof' be held during which the sheriff will hear evidence and decide whether the grounds are established or not. She advises that it is to be expected that the hearing will grant a warrant for the continued keeping of the girls with the Jamiesons for a period of 22 days[154] in the first instance, that subsequent hearings may require them to be kept there for further periods, with the total period not to exceed 66 days. She adds that, if it is required to keep the girls there for longer before the final disposal, then application has to be made to the sheriff, who has the power to order them to be kept there, pending final disposal, for as long as the sheriff considers necessary[155]. For completeness Mrs MacDonald mentions that the 8 WD hearing has a residual power to discharge the referral[156], but that there is no realistic possibility of this in the present case.

As to times, she explains that the Application to the sheriff to fix a proof must be lodged within 7 days of the direction to make application to the sheriff being made[157], which would mean on or before Monday 13th

---

151. Children (Scotland) Act 1995 s 65(2).
152. Children (Scotland) Act 1995 s 65(4).
153. Children (Scotland) Act 1995 s 65(7)(a).
154. Children (Scotland) Act 1995 s 66(3)(a).
155. Children (Scotland) Act 1995 s 67.
156. Children (Scotland) Act 1995 s 65(7).
157. Act of Sederunt (Child Care and Maintenance Rules) 1997, SI 1997/291 r 3.45(1)

February 2006, but that the practice of the local reporter was to lodge the Application on the day after the direction was made, which would mean that the Application would be lodged on Wednesday 8th February. In that event the case would be bound to call in court within 28 days of the Application being lodged[158] that is on or before Tuesday 7th March. The likelihood was, however, that the sheriff clerk would fix a hearing for some time before 7th March. It would be possible to invite the court to treat this as merely a procedural hearing. Such a procedural hearing would be a formal sitting the court[159], and often enough children and parents, or other relevant persons, attended for it, but no evidence would be heard and a date for the hearing of evidence would be fixed, but in a case such as this all parties were anxious to make rapid progress, and since lawyers had been involved from an early stage it would be practicable for the proof to take place on the first date fixed. For completeness Mrs MacDonald mentions that if all parties were to accept the Grounds for Referral at this time then the sheriff could deem the grounds to be established and refer the matter back to the hearing[160] – but of course that was not going to happen here.

Merits of the McPerlins' position at the Application to Set Aside or Vary Hearing

Mrs MacDonald points out that, as the papers which were before the 2WD hearing reveal, there is evidence which, if believed, would justify the continuation of the Orders and that the sheriff does not 'try' the case at this stage. She says that while the sheriff has the power to set aside the order even without a change of circumstances, it is unlikely that, without such a change, the order would be set aside[161]. She asks her client if he is aware of any matter which might persuade the sheriff. Mrs MacDonald says that the possibility of Mr McPerlin living away from the family home would be an important consideration for the Application to Set Aside or Vary hearing and may persuade the hearing to allow the girls to stay with their mother while he was away. Mr McPerlin says that his brother, Calum, would be happy to have him stay with him, except at week-ends, for a few weeks. She says that Mr Calum McPerlin would be able to give evidence to the sheriff about this. He asks if his brother would have to come to court. She says that it would be possible for his evidence to be conveyed by affidavit but that, if the matter were to be disputed, it would be much more persuasive if he gave the information to the sheriff directly. She mentions that Calum McPerlin would be open to being questioned by the reporter and any other party who was there, for example any safeguarder or curator *ad litem* appointed by the court, and explains that the possibility of such questioning or 'cross-examination' enhances the

---

158. Children (Scotland) Act 1995 s 68(2).
159. *H v Mearns* 1974 SC 152.
160. Children (Scotland) Act 1995 s 68(8).
161. This is the view advanced at paragraph 9.28 of Kearney, B – *Children's Hearings and the Sheriff Court*, second edition, Edinburgh, 2000.

value of the evidence. Mr McPerlin says that he expects to be able to persuade his brother to attend if necessary, but says he would like to use the affidavit procedure if possible. Mrs MacDonald says she would like to be able to lodge an affidavit from the brother with the Application, which will have to be lodged on the following day, 1st February, at the latest. She asks if the brother could come to the office by, say, lunch-time on 1st February. Mr McPerlin replies in the affirmative and says he will, immediately after this present meeting, ask his brother to phone Mrs MacDonald's office right away. He supplies the name and address of the brother.

Persons who must/may attend the Application to Set Aside or Vary hearing – possibility of sheriff seeing the children alone

Mr McPerlin asks if he and his wife and the children will have to attend the Application to Vary or Set Aside. Mrs MacDonald explains that as 'relevant persons' they have no obligation to attend at any sheriff court hearing unless cited by the reporter[162] and that the children must attend any diet to which they have been cited unless this obligation has been dispensed with by the court[163]. Mr McPerlin says that he and his wife will be coming and Mrs MacDonald said that in practice it is almost inevitable that the girls will be present. Mr McPerlin asks if the children will be kept separate from himself and the mother as they were at the 2 WD hearing and points out that by the date of the court hearing there will presumably have been contact visits. Mrs MacDonald says she understands there will be no special 'keeping separate'. She takes this opportunity to say that the sheriff has the power to see the children privately and that the sheriff, unlike the hearing, is entitled to keep confidential what is told to him or her[164].

Final discussions – Legal Aid, etc

Mrs MacDonald outlines the likely course of the Application procedure[165]. She fills out and gets Mr McPerlin to sign Legal Aid papers. The meeting ends.

Mrs MacDonald phones the sheriff clerk's office and advises that an Application to Vary or Set Aside is to be lodged on the following day on behalf of Mr McPerlin (and, she understands, for Mrs McPerlin) and asks

---

162. Act of Sederunt (Child Care and Maintenance Rules) 1997, SI 1997/291 r 3.14(1).
163. Children (Scotland) Act 1995 s 68(4)&(5).
164. Act of Sederunt (Child Care and Maintenance Rules) 1997, SI 1997/291, r 3.5(4). For discussion of the confidentiality provisions see *Dosoo v Dosoo* 1999 SCLR (Notes) 905, *McGrath v McGrath* 1999 SCLR (Notes) 1121 and discussion at Note *[34]* infra and in *Kearney, op cit* at 4.12 to 4.18.
165. She goes over the procedures which follow so her explanation does not need to be reproduced here.

if the sheriff clerk is able to say when on Friday 3rd February will the sheriff be able to hold the hearing. The sheriff clerk checks with Sheriff Grey and reports that the hearing is to be at 11.30 am. Mrs MacDonald informs her client of this. She says that she will now get on with the paper-work including the preparation of short precognitions based on what Mr McPerlin has told her. She confirms with her client that he has no objection to her giving a copy to Mr Paterson and that Mr Paterson will be letting her have a copy of Mrs McPerlin's precognition. She mentions that these will be her 'brief' for taking him through his evidence at the hearing before the sheriff. She concludes by saying that she will not require to hold a further meeting with her client before the hearing but adds that he should phone her at any time if anything occurs to him which he wants to discuss. She suggests that he come to the court about 11 am when she will meet him and cover any last-minute points. Mr McPerlin then leaves.

Tuesday, 31 January 2006 at about the same time –
in Mr Paterson's office

Mrs McPerlin and Mr Paterson have a meeting along similar lines

PREPARATION OF THE APPLICATION TO VARY OR RECALL CPO[166]

Mrs MacDonald and Mr Paterson now prepare the Application Forms, a separate one for each relevant person and for each child. Here is the form, on behalf of Mr Donald McPerlin, for Jacqueline, as finally framed:–

---

166. Children (Scotland) Act 1995 s 60; Act of Sederunt (Child Care and Maintenance Rules) 1997, SI 1997/291 rule 3.33(1), and Schedule 1, Form 52. Form 52 is headed 'Applica-tion to Vary or Recall a Child Protection Order, whereas the empowering statute, at s 60(7), provides for an 'application to the sheriff to set aside or vary a child protection order'. The writer is unaware of the reason for this differing terminology.

Rule 3.33(1)

FORM 52

APPLICATION TO VARY OR RECALL A CHILD PROTECTION ORDER

Section 60 of the Children (Scotland) Act 1995

Case No: 8B 2/06
Date Lodged: 01.02.06

Application to Sheriff at Kirklenton

To vary or recall a Child Protection Order under section 60(7) of the Children (Scotland) Act 1995

Part 1   DETAILS OF APPLICANT AND OTHER PERSONS WHOM THE APPLICANT BELIEVES SHOULD RECEIVE NOTICE OF THE APPLICATION

APPLICANT	*[insert name, address, telephone DX and fax numbers, and details of the capacity of the person making the application]*
	Donald McPerlin, 19 Glenview Cottages, Bruaich, Kirklenton, LE29 4QW, Tel: Tel: 012105 800 511, relevant person, as person ordinarily having charge of the child Jacqueline (Jackie) Transom (also known as Jackie McPerlin), dob 10.07.95;
CHILD	*[insert name, address, gender and date of birth]**
	Jacqueline (Jackie) Transom (also known as Jackie McPerlin), girl, dob 10.07.95.
SAFEGUARDER	**If not applicant** *[insert name, address and telephone number (if known) of any safeguarder appointed by a children's hearing or court in respect of the child]*
	None[167].

---

167. It is submitted that where there is no item in a particular category it is preferable to state this explicitly, rather than write 'Not Applicable' or 'N/A'.

RELEVANT PERSON(S)

If not applicant *[insert name, address and telephone number (if known) and the basis for the person being a relevant person within the meaning of section 93(2)(b) of the Act]*

Sharon Transom or McPerlin, 19 Glenview Cottages, Bruaich, Kirklenton, LE29 4QW. Tel: 012105 800 511, relevant person as mother of the said child.

THE PRINCIPAL REPORTER[168]

Hector Somerville, SCRA, 17 Laverock Road, Kirklenton LE6 7EK.

Telephone: 012104 545 700. Fax: 012104 545 710.

ANY OTHER PERSON WHO SHOULD RECEIVE NOTICE OF THE APPLICATION

[For example, any person who is caring for the child at the time of the application being made: insert name, address and telephone number of person and provide details of their interest in the application and/or child]

Lentonshire Council, per Marcia Drummond, Social Worker, Social Work Services Department, 8 Laverock Road, Kirklenton, LE6 4DV. Tel: 012104 545 554. Fax: 012104 545 555, being the local authority statutorily responsible for looking after the child at present.

*Note: Information to be provided in Part 3 where applicant does not wish to disclose the address or whereabouts of the child or any other person to persons receiving notice of the application.

Part 2   INFORMATION ABOUT THE APPLICATION AND ORDERS

On 26th January 2006 the Sheriff made a Child Protection Order in the following terms [insert full details of order and conditions attaching to it] [Copy original order must be attached in terms of Rule 3.33].

On 30th January 2006 a Second Working Day hearing varied the Conditions to:

---

168. Although Form 52 requests the name of the Principal Reporter it is normal and proper practice to insert the name of the Authority Reporter responsible for handling the case, being of course a person to whom the Principal Reporter has delegated functions by virtue of section 130 of the Local Government (Scotland) Act 1994.

1. The hearing varied the condition as to contact so as to allow non-residential contact between the children and their mother whenever and wherever was agreed between the children and Mrs McPerlin, with it being understood that in the event of contact being exercised the girls would return to the foster-parents no later than 9.30 p.m.

2. The hearing varied the condition as to contact with Donald McPerlin by allowing such contact for two hours per week, to be exercised within the premises of the Social Work Department, Kirklenton between 10 a.m. and midday on Saturdays under supervision of said Department.

3. The hearing thought that the order that the address of the foster-carers should not be revealed to the relevant persons was now unnecessary and inappropriate and therefore recalled that order.

4. The condition about a medical examination by a paediatrician is discontinued.

OTHER APPLICATIONS AND ORDERS WHICH AFFECT THE CHILD JACQUELINE

[insert details of any other applications or orders made which effect or are relevant to the child who is the subject of this application]

None.

ORDER(S) OR CONDITIONS THE VARIATION OR RECALL OF WHICH ARE SOUGHT

[applicant to insert details of order now sought]

The applicant craves the court to recall the Child Protection Order *simpliciter*[169] or, alternatively, to vary said order by adding a condition that the child may reside with her mother, Mrs Sharon McPerlin in the family home each week from Sunday evening at 6 pm till Friday evening at 6 pm provided the applicant does not reside in the family home at such times.

GROUNDS FOR MAKING APPLICATION

[applicant to provide details of grounds for seeking the variation or setting aside]

169. 'Simpliciter' means, roughly, 'in its entirety – without qualification'. It is no longer fashionable to use Latin tags, but this is well recognised by lawyers in Scotland and says in one word that which would otherwise take five. Mrs MacDonald is a traditionalist and uses it.

The applicant denies that he made any sexual approach to the child Jacqueline or her sister Samantha. In any event the applicant is prepared, pending the resolution of this matter by proof before the sheriff, to reside, except at week-ends, with his brother, Calum McPerlin, 6 Potter's Reach, Bruaich and to undertake not to see either of the girls except in terms of the contact arrangements ordered by a children's hearing.

SUPPORTING EVIDENCE

The following supporting evidence –

[list reports, statements or other evidence produced]

Affidavit by Calum More McPerlin dated 1st February 2006.

Part 3 DETAILS OF ORDER SOUGHT AND ANY TERMS, CONDITIONS OR DIRECTIONS

FIRST ORDER

The applicant requests the sheriff to:

a.   Assign a hearing on the application.

*b.   Order the applicant to serve a copy of the application together with the date of hearing on,

     i.   The Principal Reporter.

     ii.   The Local Authority – Lentonshire Council.

     iii.   The child, together with a notice in form 27; and

     iv.   The persons listed in Part 1 of this application, together with a notice in form 35; and

*c.   ~~Dispense with service on the child or any other person for the following reasons [insert details]~~

The applicant, under reference to the Act of Sederunt (Child Care and Maintenance Rules) 1997, r 3.13(2) craves the court to direct that service be effected orally

And thereafter to [enter details of what you want the Sheriff to vary or recall] – *recall or vary the Child Protection Order, as varied, in respect of the child Jacqueline McPerlin dated 26th January 2006, with return of the child to the applicants.*

* delete as appropriate

Signed *Mhairi MacDonald*   Date: *1st February 2006.*

Solicitor for the applicant,
34 Nelson Street, Kirklenton, LE6 9WS, DX KIRKLENTON 2;
Tel: 012104 545 097; e-mail: mhairi.macd@surepost.com

[name, designation and address
telephone, DX and fax numbers]

PREPARATION OF FORM OF INTIMATION ON THE CHILD

Mrs MacDonald now frames the Form of Intimation documents, one for Samantha and one for Jacqueline. This, in final form, is the one for Jacqueline[170]:–

Rule 3.4(1)(b)

FORM 27

NOTICE TO CHILD OF APPLICATION TO VARY OR SET ASIDE CHILD PROTECTION ORDER

Section 60 of the Children (Scotland) Act 1995

CASE NUMBER
8B 2/06

KEEPING YOU SAFE

Dear *[insert name by which child is known]*[171] Jackie,

A Child Protection Order was made on 26th January 2006 to keep you safe from harm. The sheriff (the person who has to decide) made the order, which says you are to continue to live at 103 Gresham Road, Kirklenton, with Mr and Mrs Jamieson at present. On 30th January a hearing changed the conditions of this Order so as (a) to allow non-residential contact between you and your mother whenever you both wished, on the basis that you would always be back at the foster-carers no later than 9.30 pm; and (b) to allow contact with Donald McPerlin for two hours per week, to

---

170. In this Form (as in the immediately foregoing Form) the directions to the drafter contained in the statutory form have been left in position in the interests of accuracy. It is however submitted that in practice they should be omitted on the view that to leave them in would be excessively formalistic and inimical to the informality which should characterise a letter to a child.
171. The instructions in square brackets are left in position here in order accurately to reflect the pro forma – in practice they should be left out.

be exercised on the premises of the Social Work Department, Kirklenton between 10 a.m. and midday on Saturdays under supervision of said Department.

Now the sheriff has been asked to have another look at your situation, *[insert in simple language the person making the application, the reason for making it and the order(s) sought]* at the request of Mr Donald McPerlin who has asked to sheriff to cancel the order or at least to change it by making it a condition of the order by adding a condition that you may stay with your mother in the family home each week from Sunday evening till Friday evening provided that he, Donald, does not reside in the family home at such times. He says in his application that he would be prepared to stay with his brother Calum during week-days for the next few weeks – right up to the time when the sheriff will hear the evidence about what you said Donald did to you. The sheriff would like to hear your views about what you would like to happen before making a decision.

You can tell the sheriff what you think by :–

Going to see the Sheriff

You can take someone like a friend, parent, a teacher or a social worker with you to see the sheriff to support you; or you can ask a lawyer to come with you and tell the court your views.

Not going to see the Sheriff

You can fill in the attached form and send it back in the enclosed stamped addressed envelope **before** the hearing date which is at the end of this letter.

REMEMBER

That someone can help you to fill in this form.

If you return the form it will be given to the sheriff and, if she needs more information, she will ask the Sheriff Clerk who works with her to contact you about this.

IMPORTANT NOTE – You do not have to do any of these things if you would prefer not to; however, it is very important for you to understand that, if you do not do anything, the sheriff might make an order without knowing what your views are.

I should mention that the sheriff will make a written note of any views which you give if you decide to speak to him or her. Whether you speak or write to the sheriff he or she will usually have to tell other people, such as your mother and Mr Donald McPerlin, of your views, but the sheriff has special powers to keep your views confidential and therefore if you want the sheriff to do this you should say so in any letter or at any meeting. However the sheriff is not bound to follow this course of action and even if the sheriff does do this it will sometimes be possible for people to work out what you have said[172].

If you are unsure about what to do you can get free legal advice from a Lawyer or Local Advice Agency or Law Centre about the application and about legal aid.
The Scottish Child Law Centre can refer you to specially trained lawyers who can help you.
They give advice on their free phone no (0131 667 6333) any time between 9.00 am and 5 pm Monday to Friday

---

The hearing to consider the application will be held on **Friday 3rd February 2006 at 11.30 am, in KIRKLENTON SHERIFF COURT, 1 LAVEROCK SQUARE, KIRKLENTON LE6 1AA.**

You will see that, along with this letter, there is a copy of the application to the sheriff, and the sheriff's order fixing the hearing. If you decide to get advice, or to ask someone to go to see the sheriff, make sure you give your advisor a copy of the application, and the sheriff's order.

Signed *Mhairi MacDonald*   Date: *1st February 2006*

Solicitor for the applicant, 34 Nelson Street, Kirklenton, LE6 9WS, DX: KIRKLENTON 2; Tel: 012104 545 097; e-mail: mhairi.macd@surepost.com

---

To the Sheriff Clerk

I would like the Sheriff to know what I have to say before he or she makes a decision.

Write what you want to say here, or you can use a separate sheet of paper.

---

172. This paragraph does not appear in Form 27, but it is suggested that it may properly and usefully be included. See discussion at *[31]* infra. The Children's Hearing does not have the power to keep children's views confidential – hence the warning given by the chair at the Second Working Day Hearing, at page 61 *supra*, under the subheading *The children give their views.*

Name: ....

Address: ....

....

....

Case Reference Number 8B 2/06
(if you know it)

_____

Mrs MacDonald now drafts the Notice to the persons named in the Application. Here, in final form, is the Notice to the Reporter:–

Rule 3.12(1)(b)

FORM 35

NOTICE OF APPLICATION TO VARY OR RECALL CHILD PROTECTION ORDER TO PERSON NAMED IN APPLICATION UNDER SECTION 60 OF THE CHILDREN (SCOTLAND) ACT 1995

_____

CASE NUMBER
8B 2/06

Application to Sheriff Court at *[insert name] Kirklenton*
to vary or recall a Child Protection Order under section 60 of the Children (Scotland) Act 1995

_____

To (insert name and address) *The Principal Reporter per Hector Somerville, SCRA, 17 Laverock Road, Kirklenton LE6 7EK. Telephone: 012104 545 700. Fax: 012104 545 710.*

You are given notice that the court will hear this application –
[applicant to insert details of the date, time and place for hearing]

> The application is to (insert details of purpose of the application) *vary or recall the Child Protection Order granted on 26th January 2006 in respect of the child Jacqueline McPerlin, born 10th July 1995*, with conditions, as varied on 30th January 2006 at Second Working Day hearing to:

1. The hearing varied the condition as to contact so as to allow non-residential contact between the children and their mother whenever and wherever was agreed between the children and Mrs McPerlin, with it being understood that in the event of contact being exercised the girls would return to the foster-parents no later than 9.30 p.m.

2. The hearing varied the condition as to contact with Donald McPerlin by allowing such contact for two hours per week, to be exercised within the premises of the Social Work Department, Kirklenton between 10 a.m. and midday on Saturdays under supervision of said Department.

3. The hearing thought that the order that the address of the foster-carers should not be revealed to the relevant persons was now unnecessary and inappropriate and therefore recalled that order.

4. The condition about a medical examination by a paediatrician is discontinued.

on Friday 3rd February 2006
at 11.30 am
in Kirklenton Sheriff Court, 1 Laverock Square, Kirklenton, LE6 1AA

Along with this notice there is attached a copy of the application and the court's order fixing the hearing.

Signed: *Mhairi MacDonald.*

Solicitor for the applicant, 34 Nelson Street, Kirklenton, LE6 9WS,
DX: KIRKLENTON 2; Tel: 012104 545 097; e-mail:
mhairi.macd@surepost.com

Date: 1st February 2006

WHAT YOU SHOULD DO

YOU SHOULD ATTEND OR BE REPRESENTED AT THE HEARING

If you do not attend or are not represented at the hearing, the court may decide the case in your absence.

YOU SHOULD OBTAIN ADVICE FROM A SOLICITOR OR LOCAL ADVICE AGENCY OR LAW CENTRE. You may be entitled to legal aid. Advice about legal aid is available from any solicitor, advice agency or law centre.

Wednesday, 1 February 2006 at 10 am – in Mrs MacDonald's Office

Mr Calum McPerlin arrives, by arrangement, to swear an affidavit about his willingness to accommodate Donald McPerlin. Mrs MacDonald has a prior engagement at court and has delegated this urgent matter to her assistant, Mr Wynford. Here it is:

Sheriffdom of Lenton and Muirbrachlan at Kirklenton

Case No: 8B 2/06

APPLICATION TO VARY OR RECALL A CHILD PROTECTION ORDER

in respect of the child Jacqueline McPerlin, born 10th July 1995

AFFIDAVIT

by

CALUM MORE McPERLIN (49)

residing at 6 Potter's Reach, Bruaich, Lentonshire.

At Kirklenton the First day of February Two Thousand and Six in the presence of JAMIE GLENDOWER WYNFORD, Solicitor and Notary Public, 34 Nelson Street, Kirklenton, LE6 9WS, COMPEARED: Mr CALUM MORE McPERLIN, residing at 6 Potter's Reach, Bruaich, Lentonshire, who being solemnly sworn, depones as follows:

1.   I am Calum More McPerlin, aged 49, and I live at 6 Potter's Reach, Bruaich, LE29 4SK. I am Manager of the Caremore Supermarket, Main Street, Kirklenton. I am not married.

2.   I am the only brother of Donald McPerlin, one of the Applicants in this Application.

3.   I am on very good terms with my brother and his wife and family. I am a frequent visitor to their house and they come to see me often enough, sometimes as a family, sometimes individually. Mrs McPerlin is a valued employee in Caremore. I sometimes think they are a bit sorry for me, being unmarried. In fact I have plenty to do. My work as manager of the largest supermarket in the district keeps me pretty busy. I am an elder of Bruaich Old Kirk, a member of the Community Council for Bruaich and President of the local Bowling Club.

4.   My house is a semi-detached villa situated at the opposite side of Bruaich from my brother's house. It has two bedrooms, study, dining room, living room and two bathrooms, one of them en suite with the principal bedroom. On a few occasions my brother's family have come to stay with me overnight, generally when Donald and Sharon are going out for the evening and I

would in effect 'baby-sit'. When this has happened Donald and Sharon would occupy the spare bedroom, with the girls in a sofa bed in the living room and Graeme (who was still a baby at the times) accommodated in the study in a travelling cot which I keep for the purpose.

5.   I understand that my brother has been accused of making some sexual advance to Samantha, that a Child Protection Order has been granted and that it is a condition of that Order that Samantha and Jackie should not stay at home overnight but should stay with foster-parents in Kirklenton.

6.   I also understand that it will be argued on behalf of my brother and his wife that the prohibition on the girls' living at home should be re-called or alternatively, varied so as to allow the girls to stay with their mother on week-days. I confirm that I would be glad to have my brother stay with me on week-nights in my house till the proof before the sheriff, which is likely to take place some six to eight weeks or so from now. I cannot accommodate my brother at week-ends, that is on Friday nights and Saturday nights, because our elderly mother, who is in a Nursing Home during the week, comes to stay with me at week-ends.

7.   I should perhaps add that while I find the allegation which has been made difficult to believe I nevertheless recognise why the Order was made in these terms. I would undertake not to do or allow anything which would lead to any condition that my brother should not reside overnight in the family home during the week being breached. Donald has promised me that he would faithfully spend all week-nights in my house and I have told him that if he broke his promise I would alert the authorities immediately.

All of which is truth as the deponent shall answer to God.

Calum M McPerlin   DEPONENT

Jamie G Wynford   NOTARY PUBLIC

**Same day, Wednesday, 1 February 2006 at 2 pm –
in Mrs MacDonald's Office**

Mrs MacDonald has returned from court. She sees the final print of the two Applications to Vary or Recall and the affidavit by Mr Calum McPerlin. She is satisfied with these and sets out for the Sheriff Court with the principal Applications and the relevant documents, namely a copy of the original CPOs and the principal affidavit, which she has attached to the Application in respect of Jacqueline and a copy of it, which she has attached to the Application for Samantha.

Same day, Wednesday, 1 February 2006 at 2.30 pm – in the Sheriff Clerk's Office in Kirklenton Sheriff Court

Mrs MacDonald presents the documents to the sheriff clerk and they recall that they have discussed this already and that Sheriff Grey has indicated that she intends to hold the hearing at 11.30 am on Friday 3rd February 2006. The sheriff clerk says that Sheriff Grey is in the building and will wish, in accordance with her usual practice, to see the papers right away, mainly with a view to confirming the proposed time and date for the hearing and considering whether she should appoint a safeguarder or curator *ad litem*. The sheriff clerk says she thinks the interlocutor fixing the hearing and (probably) appointing a curator *ad litem* will be ready about 3.45 and Mrs MacDonald says that someone from her office will come to collect it about then. The sheriff clerk mentions that Mr Paterson has also lodged Applications on behalf of Mrs McPerlin.

> *Note [27]   By virtue of section 41(1) of the Children (Scotland) Act 1995 the sheriff must at this stage consider appointing a 'person to safeguard the interests of the child in the proceedings'. This does not apply at the stage of granting the CPO. Section 41(2) makes this clear by stating 'Subsection (1) above shall not apply in relation to proceedings under section 57 [i.e. the section governing the granting of CPOs] of this Act', but it seems clear that the various proceedings after a CPO has been granted are not 'proceedings under section 57' – hence, as we have seen, the Second Working Day Hearing required to consider the appointment of a safeguarder.*

Same day, Wednesday, 1 February 2006 at 2.40 pm – in Sheriff Grey's chambers

Sheriff Grey considers the papers which have been presented by the sheriff clerk and confirms that the hearing of the Application will take place at the proposed time and date. She says she will probably appoint a curator *ad litem*[173] and asks the sheriff clerk to tell Mrs MacDonald and Mr Paterson of the diet and that the appointment of a curator *ad litem* is being considered and that this will be confirmed soon. The sheriff clerk returns to the office to advise the agent and then returns to the sheriff's chambers. Sheriff Grey now indicates that she would like a curator *ad litem* appointed. The sheriff clerk has brought the list of solicitors who regularly act as curators *ad litem*. The sheriff indicates that she would like a female curator and the sheriff clerk states that Miss Margaret Wilson, solicitor, of Messrs Harvey and Gillespie, solicitors, 42 Nelson Street, Kirklenton is 'next on the list'.

---

173. See discussion infra at *[28]*.

Same day, Wednesday, 1 February 2006 at 3 pm – in the Sheriff Clerk's office

The sheriff clerk phones Miss Wilson, indicates the general nature of the case, and Miss Wilson says she can take on the task. The sheriff clerk says that the papers will be available before the close of business and Miss Wilson says that someone from her office will collect them. The sheriff clerk drafts an interlocutor for each child's case. Here, in final form, is the interlocutor in Jacqueline's case:–

Case No: 8B 2/06

APPLICATION TO VARY OR RECALL CHILD PROTECTION ORDER –
Jacqueline McPerlin

Rule 3.11

FORM 32

FORM OF FIRST ORDER UNDER THE
CHILDREN (SCOTLAND) ACT 1995

~~SECTION 55 (Application for Child Assessment Order),~~

SECTION 60 (Application to vary or set aside Child Protection Order),

~~SECTION 76 (Application for Exclusion Order)~~

~~SECTION 67 (Application for warrant for further detention of child)~~

[Place and date]
Kirklenton 1st February 2006.

The court assigns *[date]* Friday 3rd February 2006 at *[hour]* 11.30 am within the *[name court]* Sheriff Court of Lenton and Muirbrachlan at Kirklenton in chambers at *[place]* 1 Laverock Square, Kirklenton, LE6 1AA for the hearing of the application;

Appoints the applicant forthwith to give notice to the persons listed in PART I of the application by oral notification and delivery to them as soon as practicable a copy of the application and this order together with notices in Forms *[insert Form Nos]* 27 and 35;

~~Dispenses with notice and service on *[insert name]*~~

~~for the following reasons *[insert reason(s)]*~~

eo die

The court *ex proprio motu* nominates and appoints Margaret Wilson, solicitor, as curator *ad litem* for the child Jacqueline McPerlin and appoints the applicant to give notice of the application to the said Margaret Wilson by oral notification and by delivering to her as soon as practicable a copy of the application and this order together with a notice in Form 35.

[**Note**: *Insert details of any other order granted and in an application under section 76 for an exclusion order insert as appropriate*

~~Meantime grants an interim exclusion order; or interim interdict; or otherwise as the case may be.~~]

Fiona Grey.
*Sheriff ~~or sheriff clerk~~

*delete as appropriate

The sheriff clerk then copies the various papers and leaves them in the office for collection by a representative from Miss Wilson's office. The sheriff clerk phones Mrs MacDonald's and Mr Paterson's offices advising that the papers are now ready for collection and telling of the appointment of Miss Wilson. The other parties will learn of the appointment of the curator *ad litem* when the papers are served.

Note [28]   *Safeguarders and Curators ad litem.*

(a)   *The office of safeguarder was created by sections 66 and 78 of the (English) Children Act, which amended the Social Work (Scotland) Act 1968, but the provisions were not brought until 1985. The current provisions are based upon section 41 of the Children (Scotland) Act 1995. The heading of this section reads, 'Safeguarding child's interests in proceedings'. The terms of s 41 are referred to in paragraph [30] supra. The Act itself does not employ the term 'safeguarder', but it is recognised in the Rules – for example Rule 2, the 'Interpretation' rule of the Children's Hearings (Scotland) Rules 1996, defines 'safeguarder' as 'a person appointed by a children's hearing under section 41(1) of the Act for the purpose of safeguarding the interests of the child in the proceedings'. Oddly enough the Rules governing the procedure in the Sheriff Court – the Act of Sederunt (Child Care and Maintenance Rules) 1997, SI 1997/291 – do not define 'safeguarder', but the safeguarder is referred to in these Rules: for example rule 3.7(1)(a) requires the sheriff to consider the appointment of a safeguarder at the beginning of any proceedings, and rule 3.7(1)(b) empowers the sheriff to appoint a safeguarder at any later time. Rule 3.8(a) provides that the safeguarder is to have 'all the powers and duties at common law of a curator ad litem in respect of the child'. A safeguarder appointed by a hearing has the right to receive the relevant documents, to receive notification of and to attend hearings; he or she must prepare an initial written report and any further report which may be required[174].*

(b)   *Rules about the appointment and management of safeguarders are contained in The Panels of Persons to Safeguard the*

---

174. Children's Hearings (Scotland) Rules, 1996, SI 96/3261, r 14(2)–(5).

*Interests of Children (Scotland) Regulations 2001, SI 2001/476.
Each local authority has the obligation to appoint a 'panel' of
safeguarders after consultation with the chairman of its
children's panel and the sheriff principal of the jurisdiction. No
specific qualifications are enacted, but the local authority, after
consultation with the chairman of the children's panel and the
sheriff principal is to 'determine the experience and standard of
any qualifications' which safeguarders should have*[175]*. Nowadays safeguarders, before taking up any appointment, have
some training under the auspices of the Children's Panel
trainers in the universities. Safeguarders may, and sometimes
do, instruct a solicitor to act for them in court.*

(c)   *In some jurisdictions, including Glasgow, sheriffs, rather
than appointing a safeguarder, tend to appoint a solicitor as
a curator ad litem from an informal list of solicitors known
to have an interest in and experience of children's law.
Curators ad litem may, but are not required to, submit a
written report and in practice generally appear in person and
report verbally on their investigations and conclusions. At
the proof before the sheriff they may, and generally do, act
on behalf of the interests of the child in every way a solicitor
would, by leading evidence if necessary, examining and
cross-examining witnesses, making final submissions to the
court and the like. Both safeguarders and curators ad litem
may be used as a way of communicating the views of the
child to the court. The role of the safeguarder and curator ad
litem is to be distinguished from the role of a solicitor acting
for the child: the solicitor takes the instructions of the child,
whereas the safeguarder or curator ad litem represents what
he or she judges to be the interests of the child. Safeguarders
are entitle to a fee from the local authority. Curators ad
litem are entitled to apply for Legal Aid.*

**Same day, Wednesday, 1 February 2006 at 3.45 pm – in the Sheriff
Clerk's office**

Clerks from Mrs MacDonald's, Mr Paterson's and Miss Wilson's offices
call and collect, for Mrs MacDonald, and Mr Paterson the respective
principal Applications and Warrants, and, for Miss Wilson, copies of these
papers. They return to their respective offices.

**Same day, Wednesday, 1 February 2006 at about 4 pm –
in Mrs MacDonald's and Mr Paterson's offices**

Mrs MacDonald and Mr Paterson must now effect service of the
Applications, and attached affidavit and warrants, on the persons specified

---

175.   *The Panels of Persons to Safeguard the Interests of Children (Scotland) Regulations
2001, SI 2001/476, reg 4(4).*

or referred to in the warrant, that is on: the applicants; the children; the reporter; and Lentonshire Council as the relevant local authority[176]. The children must receive a completed Form 32 (reproduced supra). The others must receive a completed Form 35 (also reproduced supra). Mrs MacDonald must also, as required by the sheriff's order, made ex proprio motu, serve the papers on the curator *ad litem* along with Form 35

> *Note [29]* **Effecting service in relation to the sheriff court procedures.** *The standard modes of effecting service of documents and provisions as to who may effect service, are contained in Rules 3.15 and 3.16 of the Act of Sederunt (Child Care and Maintenance Rules) 1997, SI 1997/291. Modes of service include[177] delivery in person, leaving at house or place of business and at any other place where the recipient may be resident and sending by first class recorded delivery post 'or the nearest equivalent the available postal service permits' to any of these places. Any of these modes may be used by a sheriff officer. Postal citation may be effected by a solicitor, the sheriff clerk, the reporter and an officer of the local authority. If service is personal, then the minimum notice is 48 hours – if service is by post the minimum period of notice is 72 hours[178]. Rule 3.15(3) and Rule 3.16(1)(c) contain the important (and in sheriff court practice unusual) provisions that where service has to be made and there is not sufficient time to employ the foregoing modes, then service may be effected orally 'or in such manner as the sheriff directs' by 'such person as the sheriff directs' – this is competent only in connection with certain procedures, namely: an appeal against a decision to grant a warrant for the detention of a child; a hearing in respect of an exclusion order[179] of a person from the family where an interim exclusion order[180] has been granted; an application for a child assessment order; and, notably for the present purpose, in relation to a hearing on an application to vary or set aside a CPO or any direction given with a CPO.*

Since it is now the late afternoon of Wednesday, 1st February 2006 and the hearing of the Application is fixed for 11.30 a.m. Friday 3rd February, Mrs MacDonald, as the provisions of r 3.13(2)(c) of the Act of Sederunt (Child Care and Maintenance Rules) 1997, SI 1997/291 allow, has applied to the sheriff to direct oral intimation and delivery of the papers as soon as practicable. Mrs MacDonald phones the reporter to intimate.

---

176. Act of Sederunt (Child Care and Maintenance Rules) 1997, SI 1997/291, r 3(4)(1)(b) and r 3(12)(1)(b).
177. There are other modes – see Rule 3.15 for its full terms.
178. Act of Sederunt (Child Care and Maintenance Rules) 1997, SI 1997/291, r 3.13.
179. Children (Scotland) Act 1995 s 76.
180. Children (Scotland) Act 1995 s 76(4); Act of Sederunt (Child Care and Maintenance Rules) 1997, SI 1997/291 r 3.36.

Same day, Wednesday, 1 February 2006 at 4.45 pm – in the office of Messrs Harvey and Gillespie

Miss Margaret Wilson has now read the papers. She rings the foster-carers' number and introduces herself. She explains briefly the function of a curator *ad litem* but does not need greatly to elaborate since the Jamiesons are experienced foster-carers and have dealt with curators *ad litem* and safeguarders before although not, as it happens, with Miss Wilson. The latter asks when it would be convenient to call to see the children, indicating 'the sooner the better' and saying that she would expect be able to come round that very evening. Mrs Jamieson checks with the girls and says that would be fine. Margaret Wilson says she will arrive at 7 p.m. if that is convenient and mentions that she will be accompanied by her secretary, Roisin Glover. Miss Wilson knows she has arranged to go out with her fiancé in the evening but phones up to cancel. Miss Wilson completes an Application Form for Legal Aid and arranges for a member of her staff to take it to the court on the following morning.

> *Note [30]   Curators ad litem are well used to working at top speed and often have to work out of office hours. It is Miss Wilson's practice never to interview a child without someone else being present and she does not want to conduct the interview in the presence of one of the foster-carers since she is conscious of the possibility of the girls' expressed views being affected, even unintentionally, by the presence of the foster-parents. The other advantage of having her secretary present is that the latter can discreetly take notes, thus making is easier for the curator to talk directly to the girls without the need to take notes, which would impart a stilted quality to the interview, and would impair eye-contact. All this is in accordance with good practice, although sometimes the ideal cannot, in practice, be achieved.*

Same day, Wednesday, 1 February 2006 at 7 pm – in the home of the foster-carers

Miss Wilson and her secretary attend and Miss Wilson speaks to the girls. She says she would like to see them together at first and, probably for a comparatively short time, separately. She indicates that she would like to see Jacqueline before Samantha, because she reckons that Jacqueline, although really the primary cause of concern, sees herself as the 'junior partner' in the affair and she (Miss Wilson) wants to try to dispel this by giving Jacqueline the premiere position.

Miss Margaret Wilson explains to both girls her rôle as curator *ad litem*. She discusses the case generally and then explains that at present her primary aim is to obtain their views as to what they wish to happen. She explains that it is her task to convey these views to the sheriff and also, ultimately, to advise the sheriff as to what she, as curator *ad litem*, thinks will be in their best interests. The girls say they understand this. She outlines the procedure in relation to Applications to Vary or Recall. The girls are particularly interested in whether there is any likelihood of the sheriff recalling the CPO. Margaret tells them about the offer by Donald to stay with his brother during week-days and says that this development makes the outcome more difficult to predict. She says that their own views about this will be important, although not of course decisive of the matter. She tells them that she is empowered to convey their views and that, alternatively, the sheriff may speak to them directly in her private room. She says that in her experience Sheriff Grey is inclined to see children directly provided the children wish that. The girls say they would be happy with this.

When seeing each girl separately Miss Wilson explains that if they do give their views in private it is very likely in a case like this that the sheriff would tell the other parties the substance of their views, since it is only where revealing their views would cause real danger to the children that their views could be kept secret[181]. Both Jacqueline and Samantha say they understand this and that this will not bother them. They say they will tell the sheriff in no uncertain terms that they do not wish the CPO to be recalled or varied because they do not consider that Mum would be able to guarantee that Donald kept to his promise to stay away.

> *Note [31]   The sheriff has a wide discretion as to how to take the views of the child[182]. The rules specify, without prejudice to this discretion, four possible methods[183]:*
>
> *'(a)   by the child orally or in writing;*
>
> *(b)   by an advocate or solicitor acting on behalf of the child;*
>
> *(c)   by any safeguarder or curator ad litem appointed by the court; or*
>
> *(d)   by any other person (either orally or in writing), provided that the sheriff is satisfied that that person is a suitable representative and is duly authorised to represent the child.'*
>
> *The rules also require the sheriff, where she takes the views of the child orally, to make a written record of these views[184]. The rules also empower the sheriff (if she think fit) to direct that any written record of the child's views should be placed in a sealed 'confidential' envelope which is only available to the court[185]. The sheriff may use this information and is under no statutory obligation to reveal it, but there are obvious problems, both in*

---

181. 'Before considering whether to depart from that fundamental principle [that all material matters should be disclosed], the court had first to determine whether disclosure of the material would involve a real possibility of significant harm to the child.' – per Sheriff Principal E F Bowen QC in *McGrath v McGrath* 1999 SCCR (Notes) 1121 at 1122D.
182. Act of Sederunt (Child Care and Maintenance Rules) 1997, SI 1997/291 r 3.5(2).
183. Act of Sederunt (Child Care and Maintenance Rules) 1997, SI 1997/291 r 3.5(2)(a)–(d).
184. Act of Sederunt (Child Care and Maintenance Rules) 1997, SI 1997/291 r 3.5(3).
185. Act of Sederunt (Child Care and Maintenance Rules) 1997, SI 1997/291 r 3.5(4).

principle and in practice. Natural justice demands disclosure to interested parties[186], although the interests of the child must be protected[187]. The position is that the sheriff must disclose any material views unless doing so 'would involve a real possibility of significant harm to the child'[188]. The practical difficulty is that if the sheriff 'uses' the confidential material so as to produce a particular result it may be possible to work out what the views expressed by the child were.

Miss Wilson explains that after the hearing on the Application to Recall or Vary and, on the assumption that the CPOs are not recalled, there will be the Eighth Working Day Hearing. She explains that as her appointment as curator *ad litem* relates only to the court proceedings she will not be involved as curator *ad litem* in the 8WD hearing, but she intends to ask the reporter to invite her to attend and expects that she will agree to this[189]. She explains that before that hearing 'Grounds for Referral' will be stated by the reporter and that these Grounds will contain allegations reflecting what the girls have said about Mr McPerlin and say that this means that Mr McPerlin has committed one of the offences listed in Schedule 1 to the Criminal Procedure (Scotland) Act 1995[190]. Miss Wilson explains what is meant by this and tells the girls that at that hearing the Grounds for Referral will be explained by the chair of the hearing and it will be up to the girls and Mr and Mrs McPerlin to say whether they accept them or not. It is clear that Mr and Mrs McPerlin will deny the grounds. The girls confirm that they have understood Miss Wilson's explanation of the grounds and that they will wish to accept them. Miss Wilson then explains that since the McPerlins will be denying the grounds the reporter will be instructed apply to the sheriff for a proof at which evidence will be led. She says it is likely that the sheriff will again appoint her (Miss Wilson) as curator *ad litem* for the proof proceedings and the girls say they would be pleased if this happened. She then asks the girls if they require any 'special measures' to protect them when giving evidence at the proof and she explains the provisions of the Vulnerable Witnesses (Scotland) Act 2004 and Samantha states that she will not require any 'special measures', whereas Jacqueline says she would prefer the use of screens. Miss Wilson explains that this is a matter for the reporter to arrange and says she will report their views on this to the reporter.

Miss Wilson then has a brief word with the girls separately. Jacqueline says she has been thinking about it all and is now more than ever afraid of what Donald might do if the circumstances were right. She says: 'I don't

---

186. Cf *McMichael v United Kingdom* [1995] 29 EHRR 205.
187. Cf Children (Scotland) Act 1995, s 16(1) and (2) and (4)(b)(ii).
188. Per Sheriff Principal E F Bowen QC, applying the House of Lords case *Re D (Minors) (Adoption Reports: Confidentiality)* [1996] AC 593, [1995] 4 AllER 385, in *McGrath v McGrath* 1999 SCCR (Notes) 1121 at 1122D.
189. It will then be open to the chair of the hearing to sanction her presence – Children's Hearings (Scotland) Rules, 1996, r 13(d).
190. It is beyond the scope of this work to define such matters, but see page 126 *infra* for how the chair of the 8WD hearing deals with this.

know what Donald would have done if he hadn't been <u>so</u> drunk. He might get drunk again – he often does – but I would be afraid that this time he might not be 'paralytic' and might do something to me'. Samantha adheres to her previous stance.

> *Note [32]   See paragraph [28] above for discussion of the law and practice affecting safeguarders and curators ad litem. See infra paragraph [38] for discussion of the provisions of and procedures under the Vulnerable Witnesses (Scotland) Act 2004. These procedures concern the giving of <u>evidence</u> by vulnerable witnesses, which by definition includes children, in court. These provisions, it is submitted, have no application to hearings before the sheriff in Applications to Vary or Recall wherein a child may be present in order to give his or her views orally to the sheriff – but this is not giving 'evidence'.*

In conclusion Miss Wilson asks if the girls still want special procedures to be adopted, as at the Second Working Day Hearing, to avoid the chance of their seeing Mum and Donald at the coming procedure or at future hearings. The girls say they no longer require this. Before leaving Miss Wilson speaks to Mr and Mrs Jamieson, with the girls present, and arranges to come to the house at 10.30 a.m. on Friday 3rd February so that she, with Mrs Jamieson and the girls, can go to court together. She concludes by saying that if anyone wishes to contact her they should not hesitate to do so and she gives her office, home, and mobile phone number.

Same day, Wednesday, 1 February 2006 at 3 pm – in reporter's office

Miss Laura Cameron drafts Grounds for Referral for Samantha, Jacqueline and Graeme. The Grounds stated for Jacqueline are as follows:

Form SCRA **F**

SCOTTISH CHILDREN'S REPORTER ADMINISTRATION GROUNDS FOR REFERRAL

The children's reporter has referred the case of Jacqueline (Jackie) Transom, known as Jacqueline (Jackie) McPerlin, (10.07.1995), 19 Glenview Cottages, Bruaich, Kirklenton, LE29 4QW to a children's hearing for Lentonshire Council on the following grounds:

That in terms of Section 52(2)(e) of the Children (Scotland) Act 1995 she is, or is likely to become, a member of the same household as a child in respect of whom any of the offences mentioned in Schedule 1 to the Criminal Procedure (Scotland) Act 1995 (offences against children to which special provisions apply) has been committed.

Statement of Facts

In support of the above it is stated:

1. That Jacqueline McPerlin was born on 10th July 1995 and normally resides with her mother, Mrs Sharon Transom or McPerlin, and her step-father, Mr Donald McPerlin, who is married to Ms McPerlin, at 19 Glenview Cottages, Bruaich, Kirklenton, LE29 4QW.

2. That also resident in the family home are Jacqueline's siblings: Samantha Transom (known as Samantha McPerlin), born 15th August 1993 and Graeme McPerlin, born 2nd June 2004, who is the child of Mrs McPerlin and Mr McPerlin. Ms McPerlin is the mother of Jacqueline and Samantha as a result of a previous relationship.

3. On 13th April 2004 Mrs McPerlin, pregnant with the half-brother Graeme, required to be admitted to the Blackmore Memorial Infirmary because of problems with the pregnancy and she remained there until a week after the birth of Graeme on 2nd June 2004.

4. During the period from Mrs McPerlin's admission to hospital in April 2004 until shortly after the commencement of the new term in September 2004 Jacqueline's sister Samantha was absent from school for approximately 90% of possible attendances. The matter was reported to the Social Work Department and to the reporter but no action was taken because the sister had returned to school in September 2004, was attending regularly, and progressing well.

5. On several dates between 13th April 2004 or thereby and 9th June 2004 or thereby, on Saturday nights, within the family home, Mr McPerlin, the stepfather of Jacqueline and Samantha, did while under the influence of alcohol, use lewd, indecent or libidinous practices or behaviour upon Samantha in that he did enter her bed, fondle her breasts under her night-dress, fondle her private parts under her night dress and attempt to persuade her to fondle his private parts. This is an offence mentioned in Schedule 1(4) to the Criminal Procedure (Scotland) Act 1995 namely an offence involving the use of lewd, indecent or libidinous practice or behaviour towards a child under the age of 17 years.

6. On 31st December 2005 or 1st January 2006 Mr McPerlin, while under the influence of alcohol, entered Jacqueline's bedroom, waking her. He walked some steps towards her bed and then collapsed on the floor in a drunken condition.

7. As a result of the conduct of Mr McPerlin on 31st December 2005 or 1st January 2006 Jacqueline was very frightened. On the night in question she could not sleep for a long time. She has since had difficulty sleeping and refuses to sleep without the light on.

8.   Mrs McPerlin is again pregnant and the new baby is expected to be delivered in early June 2006. It is likely that she will require to be admitted to hospital for some four to six weeks before the birth.

9.   Jacqueline and her sister Samantha are afraid that when Mrs McPerlin is in hospital Mr McPerlin may repeat the conduct of April – June 2004. In particular Samantha is apprehensive that this conduct may be directed towards Jacqueline and that she, Samantha, would not be able to protect Jacqueline.

10.   Jacqueline is or is likely to become a member of the same household as her sister Samantha.

Date: 1st February 2006   (Sgd) Laura Cameron
                                                                              Reporter

---

Notes

The children's hearing will ask the child and relevant persons if they accept the grounds for referral. If the grounds are accepted the children's hearing will discuss with the child and relevant persons what is best for the child. If any of the grounds are not accepted, the hearing may either discharge them or tell the reporter to apply to the sheriff who will decide if any of the grounds are proved.

If the sheriff decides that any of the grounds are proved, the children's hearing will then discuss what is best for the child, as if these grounds had been accepted. If the sheriff decides that no grounds are proved the case will be discharged.

REHABILITATION OF OFFENDERS ACT 1974

If the grounds accepted or established are offences committed by the child, then they will form a record that may have to be disclosed to potential employers. The reporter can give you a leaflet explaining the Act in more detail.

Note [33]   Section 52(1) of the Children (Scotland) Act 1995 provides in effect that a child may only be held to be in need of compulsory measures of supervision where one or more of the 'conditions' listed in section 52(2) exists. The form 'SCRA – F' is not itself enacted in the Act or the Rules. It substantially follows Form 4A of the Children's Hearings (Scotland) Rules of 1986 and, no doubt since the centralised Scottish Children's Reporter Administration is the only body to use the form, it was not thought necessary to re-enact a form.

The first section narrates the particular condition or conditions relied upon. The second section lists the facts on which the reporter relies in order to support the condition. The two sections in conjunction are referred to as 'The Grounds for Referral' but sometimes 'grounds' is used to refer to the conditions only. It is however important in practice to keep the distinction in mind. For example it sometimes happens that a relevant person will accept that all the 'Statements of Fact' are acceptable but is unwilling to accept that these facts 'add up' to the particular condition for referral which the reporter has relied upon.

The condition of referral relied on here is that under section 52(2)(e) of the Children (Scotland) Act 1995 – that the child is, or is likely to become a member of the same household as a child (Samantha) in respect of whom one of the offences mentioned in Schedule 1 to the Criminal Procedure (Scotland) Act 1995 has been committed. The offence is that of 'lewd, indecent or libidinous practice or behaviour towards a child under the age of 17 years – this does not require to be stated in the first section of the Grounds for Referral, but is specified in Statement of Fact 5. The reporter contemplated relying also on the condition enacted in s 52(2)(c) – that the child "is likely – (i) to suffer unnecessarily; or (ii) be impaired seriously in his health or development, due to a lack of parental care" on the basis that the mother's refusing to acknowledge the risk presented by Mr McPerlin's actings had this consequence. However, on reflection, the reporter considered that it would only be if the allegation against Mr McPerlin was accepted or proved that this could be said and that if the allegation against Mr McPerlin were proved then the referral would stand: accordingly the reporter decided that to add the condition under s 52(2)(c) would add nothing to the Grounds and that therefore this condition should not be relied upon. In the writer's view this is good pleading practice and it is understood that it conforms to the guidance to reporters issued by SCRA.

A purist might argue that since the kernal of the Ground was contained in Statements of Fact 5 and 10 it was strictly unnecessary to make the 'background' averments in Statements 6 to 10. The justification for including them is that the reporter would wish to being them out at any proof and is giving the other parties fair notice of this. It is thought that this is a reasonable practice.

Samantha and Graeme. Space does not permit the setting out of the Grounds for Referral in relation to Samantha and Graeme. The Grounds for Graeme are the same as for Jacqueline. In relation to Samantha there will be a difference in that Samantha herself was (she alleges) the target of the stepfather's improper attentions. In consequence of this the reporter in Samantha's case will rely on the condition enacted in section 52(2)(d) of the Act – that which deals with a child in respect of whom a 'Schedule 1 offence' has been committed – as opposed to the position in Jacqueline's case where she relies on the condition in section 52(2)(e). Of course many of the facts will be in common, but in a case involving an assertion that a person is or is likely to become a member of the same household, the reporter must remember to lead evidence on that matter. The concept of what is a 'household' may require exploration[191]. Failure to establish by evidence membership, or likelihood of membership, of a household may be fatal to the reporter's case[192].

Friday, 3 February 2006 at 11 am – in Kirklenton Sheriff Court

Miss McGibbon, sheriff clerk depute, brings the papers in the McPerlin case to Sheriff Grey[193] and tells her that the parties have not yet arrived. She mentions that Margaret Wilson has phoned to say that the children would be happy to give their views directly to the sheriff in chambers and Sheriff Grey indicates that she will probably follow this course and she confirms with Miss McGibbon that she, Miss McGibbon, will be present at the interview. The sheriff clerk also tells the sheriff that Lentonshire Council, as the relevant local authority, will be represented by one of their legal department's solicitors.

Same day, Friday, 3 February 2006 at 11.25 am – in Kirklenton Sheriff Court

The parties have now assembled ready for the hearing. As with all sheriff court proceedings under Chapters 2 and 3 of the Children (Scotland) Act 1995 the hearing is 'in chambers', but where, as in the present situation, there are a relatively large number of parties and representatives, it is not practicable to hold the hearing in the sheriff's room. In Glasgow Sheriff Court there is a 'Children's Referrals Suite' including a fairly large room for hearings, waiting and interview rooms and even a well-equipped crèche supervised by trained child carers. Kirklenton does not possess such luxuries and the proceedings take place in 'the small court', with a 'Closed Court' notice on the door. The solicitors are not wearing the black bar gowns they would wear in normal civil and criminal proceedings.

Same day, Friday 3 February 2006 at 11.30 am – In Kirklenton Sheriff Court

THE HEARING BEFORE THE SHERIFF OF THE APPLICATION TO RECALL OR VARY THE CPOs

The sheriff's bar officer intones, 'Court – all stand please', and all comply. The sheriff, who is not robed or wigged, but wearing her usual sombre suit with white blouse, ascends the bench. The sheriff, and the solicitors and the reporter, exchange formal bows and then all sit down.

---

191. See *Kennedy v R's Curator ad litem* 1993 SLT 295 per Lord President Hope at 299L *et seq.*
192. *Ferguson v S* 1992 SCLR 866.
193. An Application to Set Aside or Vary is not an appeal and there is therefore no constitutional impropriety in the Application being heard by the sheriff who granted the CPO – the matter is discussed in *Kearney* op cit at para 9.23.

The Sheriff Clerk: The case of the McPerlin children.

The Sheriff: Who appears?

Mrs Mhairi MacDonald, solicitor [making to stand up]: Milady ...

The Sheriff: As we are 'in chambers' you may remain seated, and that of course goes for everyone.

Mrs MacDonald: I am obliged. I appear for the applicant, Mr Donald McPerlin, is personally present.

Mr Paterson: I appear for the applicant, Mrs Sharon McPerlin, the children's mother and she is also personally present.

Ms Laura Cameron: I appear for the Principal Reporter, Milady.

Miss Margaret Wilson, solicitor: I appear as curator *ad litem* for the children, Samantha and Jacqueline, who are present in the building. One of the children's foster-carers, Mrs Elizabeth Jamieson, is with them.

Mr Osvaldo d'Annunzio, solicitor: I appear for the local authority, the Lentonshire Council. Present in the witness room are Ms Candice Roberts, Senior Social Worker, who has responsibility for this case, and Ms Marcia Drummond, the main grade social worker most involved with it. Mr Tony Maclagan, Area Manager, Kirklenton, of Lentonshire's Social Work Department is available 'on call' at his office should Your Ladyship require his presence for any purpose.

The Sheriff: Very good. I think we can now get started. [To Mr and Mrs McPerlin] Good morning.

Mr and Mrs McPerlin: Hello/Good morning.

The Sheriff: As you are both being legally advised I do not need to make any very elaborate introductory comments but I would just emphasise that it is not my job today to make a final decision as to the facts of the case – that will probably come later – but what I have to do today is decide if the Child Protection Orders are to continue in place and, if so, whether any of the conditions ought to be changed in any way. Do you see what I mean?

Mrs McPerlin: Yes, we both understand that.

The Sheriff: Mrs MacDonald, Mr Paterson, which of you wishes to open?

Mrs MacDonald: My friend and I have discussed this and have agreed that I should open. Indeed there is substantial common ground in our respective clients' positions.

Mr Paterson: I confirm that I am happy to let Mrs MacDonald make the running – if necessary I can add any observations of my own.

The Sheriff: Fine, please proceed.

Mrs MacDonald: Thank you, Milady. As Your Ladyship is aware this is a case wherein two girls, Samantha, aged 12, and Jacqueline, aged 10, have been removed from the family home by Child Protection Orders dated 26th January 2006, granted indeed by Your Ladyship herself, on ground of concerns by social workers of Lentonshire Council for the safety of both girls. These concerns are founded upon information from Samantha that her step-father, Donald McPerlin, sexually abused her on several occasions some two years ago and that, on the last day of last year he entered Jacqueline's bedroom when intoxicated, leading to the possible inference that he may have intended to molest Jacqueline in some way – the more general inference being that the girls, particularly Jacqueline, are at real risk of sexual assault at the hands of Mr McPerlin, particularly when it appears that the girls' mother may soon require to go to hospital as an in-patient in advance of giving birth to her fourth child, it having been during such a period in 2004 that Samantha says she was molested by Mr McPerlin.

Your Ladyship granted Child Protection Orders and included a condition allowing supervised contact with the relevant persons at the discretion of the Social Work Department. On 30th January 2006 the 'Initial', or 'Second Working Day' hearing took place and the hearing continued Your Ladyship's Orders subject to certain variations including, and this will be a matter for consideration today, the provision for contact, which now reads:–

'The direction regarding contact is varied to allow as from now non-residential contact between Jacqueline/Samantha and Mrs McPerlin whenever and wherever is agreed between Jacqueline/Samantha and Mrs McPerlin so long as Jacqueline/Samantha return to the foster parents' address no later than 9.30 pm. The direction is also varied to allow Jacqueline/Samantha now to have supervised contact with Mr Donald McPerlin, which is to take place within premises of the Social Work Department, Kirklenton between 10 am and midday on Saturdays.'

The children have been living, happily enough as I understand it, with the foster-parents, Mr and Mrs Jamieson, and have been seeing their mother, again happily enough as I understand it, fairly frequently, although it is a bit early for a routine to have been established. I think my friend Miss Wilson can confirm this. Of course the first (supervised) contact with Mr Donald McPerlin will be tomorrow, but I think no problem is anticipated.

Miss Wilson: I'm obliged. Yes, Milady, I can confirm that Samantha and Jacqueline are happy with the foster-carers and that contact is taking place satisfactorily.

The Sheriff: Good, thank you. Now, Mrs MacDonald, would you like to resume?

Mrs MacDonald: Yes. My substantial motion before Your Ladyship is that the Orders be recalled *simpliciter*, alternatively I would ask Your Ladyship to vary the Orders by inserting a condition that, during their currency, Mr Donald McPerlin should not reside overnight in the family home on week-days, thus allowing the girls to reside in the family home on week-days and with the foster parents during week-ends only. Your Ladyship has heard that the non-residential contact is proceeding well. Of course the allegations about Mr McPerlin will no doubt require to be investigated in due course, and I understand that the reporter will be stating Grounds for Referral presently.

Miss Cameron: Yes, that is correct Milady. They are ready for intimation now, if Your Ladyship were minded not to revoke.

Mrs MacDonald: Thank you. It is my submission that the total prohibition of the girls' being in their own home is unreasonable and unnecessary for their protection in the circumstances. I would put my argument under three heads: (1) Assuming, which my client does not of course for a moment accept, that there is any substance in the allegations, it would in any event be unthinkable that Mr McPerlin would make any approach to either of the girls while this matter is pending – that is my main point; (2) Your Ladyship has before her an affidavit by Calum More McPerlin dated 1st February 2006 in which Mr Calum McPerlin depones that he will allow Mr Donald McPerlin to reside with him on week-days until these proceedings are concluded. It appears from the affidavit that Mr Calum McPerlin is a person of standing in the community. He is available and can come to Your Ladyship's court in fifteen minutes should Your Ladyship so require; and (3) I submit that Article 8 of the Convention for the Protection of Human Rights and Fundamental Freedoms comes into play – I do not lay too munch stress on this since I think the same principles are inherent in our own Scots Statute and Common Law

Your Ladyship will be aware that Article 8 provides as follows:–

Right to respect for private and family life

1.   Everyone has the right to respect for his private and family life, his home and his correspondence.

2.   There shall be no interference by a public authority with the exercise of this right except such that is in accordance with the law and is necessary in a democratic society in the interests of national security, public safety or the economic well-being of the country, for the prevention of disorder or crime, for the protection of health or morals, or for the protection of the rights and freedoms of others.

As I have said I do not think this innovates much, if at all, on our own Scots Law but I think it usefully encapsulates the principle of respect for the integrity of the family embodied, for example in sections 11(7)(a) and 16(3) of the Children (Scotland) Act 1995 which provide, in essence, that the state should not step in unless it is clear that by so stepping in the position of the child will be improved. I of course appreciate that my friend the reporter's position must be that the danger posed to the girls is, on its face, enough to justify their being separated from the family, but in my submission such a step is disproportionate to the danger posed, even taking my friend's evidence at its highest.

The only tangible alleged incidents took place in the summer of 2004 – about one and a half years ago – at a time when the mother was in hospital pending the delivery of Graeme. In my submission the pre-condition of these incidents – the absence of the mother in hospital – does not exist at present. The baby Mrs McPerlin is now expecting is not due until June and, while it may be that she will require to be admitted to the hospital some time before this, it is scarcely conceivable that she will require to be admitted at present. If she were to be so admitted then, should your Ladyship recall the existing CPOs, the local authority could then ask for further CPOs. As to the alleged incident involving Jacqueline, if it can be called an incident, it happened, it is said, after much drink had been taken at Hogmanay last. Even taking this as true it must surely be regarded as a 'one-off' and attributable to the over-excitement of the Festive Season. In my submission it is inconceivable that the step-father would act in this way, let alone molest Jacqueline, while the reporter's case is pending. Moreover, as an additional safeguard, Mr McPerlin will be spending five nights out of seven in his brother's house pending the disposal of my friend's proceedings. I respectfully submit that, if these considerations had been before your Ladyship on 26th January, then the Applications might not have been granted in the first place.

The Sheriff: Are you in effect submitting in terms of section 60(11)(a) of the Act that the conditions for granting the Orders no longer exist and that therefore I should recall the Orders under s 60(13) of the Act?

Mrs MacDonald: Your Ladyship has anticipated the line of my principal submission. In all the circumstances, whatever may have been the position as it appeared to Your Ladyship when granting the CPOs, I would maintain that, on the information available at present, it is unnecessary to continue the Orders and that therefore they ought to be recalled, or alternatively that a condition of residence in the family home on week-days, when Mr McPerlin will not be in residence, should be substituted for the present condition.

The Sheriff: But I have to have regard to the concerns of Samantha and Jacqueline, don't I?

Mrs MacDonald: Of course, but Your Ladyship's ruling must be propor-tionate to the needs of the situation and in my submission the Orders are not proportionate to the needs of the situation and in my submission the proposed safeguards should meet the girls' concerns. I accordingly so move Your Ladyship. As to the supervised contact with my client on the Social Work premises on Saturday mornings, my client's view is that this is inadequate and that the provision for supervision is unnecessary but he has expressly instructed that no motion be made to vary it since he is anxious to avoid unnecessary conflict. I think Your Ladyship might regard my client's stance on this matter as indicating good faith.

The Sheriff: Yes, I see. Thank you, that is very clear. Mr Paterson?

Mr Paterson: I'm obliged. I would respectfully adopt my friend's motions and the arguments she has advanced in support of them. On behalf of the mother I would only add that she, the mother, is very concerned that her daughters should in effect be living away from the family – for where one spends the night is where one is effectively 'living' – at such an impressionable age. Of course she would also, on her own account, prefer them to be at home. She makes no bones about that. But she is convinced, and this of course is the relevant consideration, that being deprived of their mother's constant care at this time is highly detrimental to their interests. She would be prepared to testify along these lines but it may be that at this stage Your Ladyship may not think this necessary or appropriate.

The Sheriff: No. I can of course hear witnesses but I don't think in the circumstances of this case it is necessary to take evidence on oath. As for the next step – how to proceed is of course a matter for my discretion. Obviously I shall require to give the reporter and the local authority a right of reply and I should also like to hear from the curator *ad litem*. Madam Reporter, what is your stance in relation to this application?

Ms Cameron: In my submission the Orders should remain in place with their conditions unaltered. Your Ladyship had before her at the original hearing the statement by Samantha dated 17th January 2006 and it is with Your Ladyship's papers today. This is of course not a proof but I think Your Ladyship is entitled to treat it as strong *prima facie* evidence. The main thrust of my friend Mrs MacDonald's argument today is that since Mrs McPerlin is still at home and may not need to go into hospital for some months there is no real risk to the girls, particularly, in the context of my friend's alternative submission, Mr McPerlin is going to be away from the home five nights out of seven. There are two aspects to the latter point, namely the reliability of the brother and the reliability of Mrs McPerlin. I can tell Your Ladyship that my friend Mr d'Annunzio has been able to arrange, at short notice, for a legal assistant in his department to interview Mr Calum McPerlin and that it is this assistant's impression that Mr Calum McPerlin is a trustworthy person, but in my submission it would be asking a lot of human nature to expect a brother to 'police' this agreement to the extent of being ready to 'shop' him in the event of, for example, Mr McPerlin being late in coming to his house on a particular night. As to my friend's main point – that the CPOs are unnecessary because there is no immediate prospect of the mother being admitted to hospital I would only say that the mother's presence did not prevent the incident, or at least the alleged incident, involving Jacqueline at New Year time. My friend said that any such incident was an isolated one, linked to the festive season. Very many people celebrate the New Year by 'having a good drink' without behaving in the way Mr McPerlin is said to have behaved. In my submission the apparently disinhibiting effect of alcohol on Mr McPerlin ought to cause concern and help persuade Your Ladyship that revocation of the CPOs would be inappropriate.

As to my friend's 'Human Rights' point, I of course accept that Mr McPerlin's right to a life in family will be infringed, but would argue that this infringement will be minimal, that is it will only persist until the proof which is likely to take place some six or seven weeks from now, when of course the whole matter will require to be re-visited in the light of the court's decision on the merits of the case. I would respectfully invite Your Ladyship to compare Mr McPerlin's situation with that of a person accused on summary complaint with a 'domestic' assault. Where such a person pleads Not Guilty to such a charge he (and it is generally 'he') is very frequently allowed bail with the 'special condition' that he removes himself entirely from the matrimonial home and makes no attempt to contact his wife and, sometimes, his children. This represents a much more grievous invasion of his private and family life, yet it is granted where the court has before it little more than a bare allegation whereas here Your Ladyship has the statement of Samantha to which I have already referred.

My main point, however, is that the girls are against allowing the CPOs to be recalled. They would feel uneasy at residing permanently with a person – Mr McPerlin – whom they would be giving evidence 'against' in a few weeks' time. I submit that their unease is understandable and that the CPOs, with their present conditions, are far from disproportionate. As to that proposal that the contact conditions be varied so as to allow the girls home during the week when Mr McPerlin was with his brother, I understand the girls would also be uneasy about this. I gather from the curator *ad litem* that the girls would like to convey their views to Your Ladyship orally.

In all the circumstances I would move Your Ladyship to allow the *status quo* to remain unchanged and to refuse my friend's motion.

The Sheriff: Mr d'Annunzio, has the local authority any submission or observation to make at this stage?

Mr d'Annunzio: Your Ladyship will perhaps not be surprised to hear that the local authority associates itself with the stance of the reporter. I can confirm that the foster-parents are willing and able to continue to look after the girls. I can confirm that the Social Workers maintain their stances as set forth in the applications for the CPOs. Beyond that I have nothing to add.

The Sheriff: Miss Wilson?

Miss Wilson: I have discussed this with the girls. I have not seen Mr Calum McPerlin, but would be prepared to accept the report from my friend Mr d'Annunzio's assistant and am content to adopt his stance. As curator *ad litem* I have concluded that it would be in the best interests of the girls to continue living with the foster-parents for the present. If they were to go home and the court were to sustain the reporter's Grounds for Referral, then there would be a lively possibility that they would be removed from the family home. If on the other hand the court were not to sustain the Grounds then of course they would return home. Accordingly, remaining where they are at present allows, foreseeably, for the minimum amount of coming and going. As curator *ad litem* I would regard it as appropriate to tell Your

Ladyship of the views of the girls, but they have indicated to me that they would prefer to speak to Your Ladyship directly if Your Ladyship is prepared to interview them. I have satisfied myself that they would not be excessively intimidated if Your Ladyship were to speak to them in chambers.

The Sheriff: I think this is a case of the type where I should hear directly from the children, and consequently I would propose to do so. Has anyone any observation?

[There is a general shaking of heads from the bar.]

The Sheriff: Very well, I shall see the girls together. I would propose to see them with only my clerk, Miss McGibbon, additionally present. Is that all right with you, Miss Wilson? Or do you think I should see them separately?

Miss Wilson: Yes Milady, and I can say that that is what Samantha and Jacqueline expect and want. In this case I do not think it would be necessary to see them separately.

The Sheriff: Good. I shall rise now. It is ten past twelve. I shall talk with the girls and resume before the lunch adjournment and would hope to be able to give some indication then as to what further procedure is likely to be required.

[The Sheriff's bar officer announces, 'All rise', and all comply. Bows are again exchanged and the Sheriff leaves the court-room.]

> *Note [34]   The foregoing illustrates the blend of formality and informality which characterises this type of proceeding. Note the 'parliamentary language'. In Scottish practice solicitors refer to each other as 'my friend' – if a member of the Faculty of Advocates were appearing it would be 'my learned friend'. The local authority's solicitor feels able to give to the court his assistant's impression of the trustworthiness of a witness whom he has seen. There are not many contexts in which this would be appropriate but it is acceptable in this situation wherein the sheriff has a wide discretion as to how she gathers information – this is not formal 'evidence'. The sheriff would be entitled to ask for evidence to be led if she thought that necessary. It would be open to any party to move the sheriff to hear evidence.*

The sheriff returns to her chambers and arranges for her clerk to go into the room where the girls are waiting and bring them into chambers.

Same day, Friday, 3 February 2006 at 12.15 pm – in Sheriff Grey's chambers

[The sheriff clerk knocks on the door and the sheriff says 'Come in'. Miss McGibbon ushers in Samantha and Jacqueline. The sheriff is not sitting behind her big desk, but has set four chairs in a circle. The sheriff stands up and goes towards the children and shakes each by the hand.]

The Sheriff: Hello, I guess you must be Samantha and you Jacqueline.

Samantha/Jacqueline: Yes, hi.

The Sheriff: Thank you for agreeing to come to see me. I like to deal face to face when I can. As you know I am 'the Sheriff'. Fiona Grey is my name. You have already met my clerk, Anne McGibbon. Please sit down. I want to talk to you directly but the law requires notes to be taken, so I have asked Miss McGibbon to take notes for me so that we can talk more naturally. Do you get the picture?

Samantha/Jacqueline: Yes/Sure.

The Sheriff: What would you like me to call you both? [To Jacqueline] I think I have been told that you are usually called 'Jackie', is that right?

Jacqueline: Yes, I think 'Jacqueline' is too much of a mouthful.

The Sheriff: Very well. And what about you Samantha?

Samantha: Some people shorten it to 'Sam', but I really don't like that.

The Sheriff: OK, I won't do that, Samantha. Right. Now often when I interview children I have to 'break the ice' by talking about football or pop-groups or fashion – all of which I have to mug up on – but I have an idea that you two are old enough to know what's going on?

Samantha: Yes. Jackie and I have discussed this plenty of times. Anyway Margaret Wilson has told us about it.

The Sheriff: Fine – but there are some things I have to make very clear before we begin. In the first place I would like to know what you want to happen. What you want is very important, but it's not the only thing that is important. Other people might want something different and as I'm the judge I have to decide what happens and I can't always please everybody – in other words I may not be able to do what you want, do you see what I mean?

Samantha: Yes, we know that.

The Sheriff: And there's another important thing. Ordinarily the rule, which I shall have to follow here, is that what you say to me in private I have to tell to others – your mother and Mr Donald McPerlin for example – but there is a special exception to that rule which says that you have the right to tell me something which is to be kept strictly to myself, in which case what you want kept secret will be written down and sealed up in an envelope marked 'Confidential'. Do you get the picture so far?

Samantha/Jacqueline: Yes.

The Sheriff: But there's another point – if what you told me contradicted, was different from, everything else I had been told in the case, and if my decision reflected what you told me, then it wouldn't be too difficult for someone to work out what you had said. I could say a bit more about this 'confidential' business, but could I first check with you if there is likely to be anything you wish kept secret?

Samantha: Jackie and I know about this – Margaret told us – and we don't mind in the least. You can pass on anything we say. It's just that we don't like the idea of saying to mummy and Donald face to face that we'd hate to be at home all the time while this case is on. And that's our 'view', isn't it, Jackie?

Jacqueline: Yes, Miss. I'd feel like a cat on eggshells – or whatever it is [giggling nervously] – staying all the time at home knowing that this case was coming up.

The Sheriff: I see. You know that Mr McPerlin has agreed to stay with his brother on week-days and that there is a proposal that you could be with you mum during the week and only stay with the Jamiesons at week-ends?

Samantha: Yes, we know that, but we don't like that idea. We'd always be thinking that somehow Donald would walk in, and with the trial ahead ....

The Sheriff: Do you mean you wouldn't be afraid of Donald 'doing' anything, but simply you'd feel uneasy about staying at home full time knowing that you would soon have to come to court and speak against Donald?

Samantha: Yes, that's exactly it. We could never be <u>sure</u> that Donald would not walk in. Can you imagine what the atmosphere would be like?

The Sheriff: Well, I see what you mean, anyway. There is one thing I'd like to ask you, Samantha. In your statement you say you are concerned about Jackie being molested if your mother was away. What if any do you think would be the likelihood of another approach being made to you?

Samantha: I think I said that I could look after myself.

The Sheriff: Yes.

Samantha: Maybe I should have said that I wouldn't be surprised if an approach was made – that's what I meant.

The Sheriff: Yes, that's what I thought you meant, but I thought I should clear that up. [After a pause.] Well, I wonder if there is much more we need to say. Has either of you got anything else you want to add?

Samantha/Jacqueline: No/No, not really.

The Sheriff: Well, thanks very much. As I have said, I'll have to tell the others what you have told me. Then I shall make my decision, probably after the lunch break. It's up to you whether you come back to the court building after lunch. You may prefer to stay at the Jamiesons'. Miss Margaret Wilson will be representing your interests and I'm sure she will tell you the result right away.

Samantha: And if you decide we have to go home, then I suppose Mummy would come round and collect us?

The Sheriff: I don't know exactly, it might be Marcia, what would you prefer?

Jacqueline: [Sobbing quietly] We'd <u>prefer</u> it not to happen at all.

The Sheriff: Whatever I do will be what I think is best from your point of view.

Samantha: Yes, we know that. Come on Jackie, I'm sure it will be all right.

The Sheriff: Goodbye for now, it's been nice meeting you.

[The interview ends and the Sheriff Clerk goes out of the Sheriff's chambers with the girls. The Sheriff is a bit shaken by the sudden display of emotion and decides not to hear submissions till after lunch. She phones the sheriff clerk and asks her to tell parties that the court will resume at 2 pm prompt.]

> *Note [35]   The Sheriff spoke with the children in the presence of the Sheriff Clerk. Another view is possible, but it is the writer's firm opinion that this is the proper practice and that the sheriff should never see a child without another adult, such as the sheriff clerk, a safeguarder or curator ad litem present. The writer has never interviewed a child without a sheriff clerk present. Sheriff Grey's decision was not to continue the hearing immediately after the interview which, at its conclusion, had upset her. She was right to delay the hearing, even although this would cause some inconvenience to parties: the paramount consideration for a judge is to do the right thing and if the judge thinks she needs time to settle down after an upsetting incident then she is right to act accordingly.*

Same day, Friday, 3 February 2006 at 2 pm – back in the small court

[Preliminaries as before.]

The Sheriff: I am sorry to have kept you waiting, but I needed time to reflect on what the girls told me. I have recorded their views thus: 'Samantha and Jacqueline told the Sheriff in chambers that they would prefer not to reside full-time at home between now and the proof because, while not fearing any molestation by Mr McPerlin, they strongly felt they would feel uneasy about staying overnight in the family home, even for five days out of seven with Mr McPerlin away, while the proof is still pending. They know that it has been agreed that Mr McPerlin should spend nights at his brother's house but their perception was that he 'might walk in at any time'. These views were expressed with some display of emotion. I should add that Samantha made explicit her view, hinted at in her statement, in which she said she could look after herself in the event of an approach being made by Mr McPerlin when her mother was away, that she would not be surprised if an approach were made.

> *Note [36]   The Sheriff, following proper practice, has given an accurate summary of what the children said and an indication of how the views were expressed.*

Mrs MacDonald: I am much obliged to Your Ladyship, and I am sure I speak for my friends.

The Sheriff: Thank you. As to further procedure I am inclined, subject of course to your views, not to require further information from the social workers or indeed to ask for any further information. I am inclined for the purposes of this hearing to accept that Mr Calum McPerlin is a trustworthy person, subject of course to the comment by the reporter that, human nature being what it is, one could not exclude the possibility that, when it came to the point, a brother might be tempted not to inform on his brother, and I am not sure that holding an evidential hearing would enable me to resolve that issue.

Mrs MacDonald: While not necessarily adopting all Your Ladyship has said on this, I would accept that hearing verbal testimony would probably not advance matters.

Mr Paterson: I agree.

The Sheriff: Thank you. That being so I think we can proceed straight to final submissions. Mrs MacDonald?

Mrs MacDonald: From the statement of the children's views it appears that they do not apprehend any molestation by Mr McPerlin even if, which I do not accept, there were any likelihood of his breaching the agreement to stay overnight with his brother. I therefore move Your Ladyship to set aside the CPOs in their entirety. If, however, Your Ladyship's mind is working towards leaving the CPOs in place then I would strongly urge Your Ladyship to vary the conditions so as to let the girls stay in the family home during the week, with my client staying with his brother. I do not think the girls' 'uneasiness' about spending nights in the family home – with only the mother and presumably their brother Graeme also present (and one tends to forget about Graeme, who must surely miss his sisters) – is sufficient cause for breaking up the family pending the proof.

Mr Paterson: I adopt what my friend Mrs MacDonald has submitted. I would also revert to what I said about the interests of the girls to have their mother's support.

Miss Cameron: I can speak for my friend Mr d'Annunzio as well as for myself. In our submission the validity of our position, which we outlined at the outset, is now fortified, and indeed vindicated, by the views of the children as reported by Your Ladyship.

Miss Wilson: I spoke to Samantha and Jacqueline during the lunch interval and they were very pleased that Your Ladyship had spoken to them face to face. Your Ladyship has accurately summed up their views and they have not changed their minds. While accepting that there would be no foreseeable danger of either of the girls being molested in the manner alleged by Samantha in her statement I would submit that their perception that they would feel uncomfortable in the family home is a reasonable one. In any event it is their perception. Children do not lightly want to stay away from their mother. I would move that the Applications be refused and that the Orders, with conditions unchanged, remain in place.

The Sheriff: Thank you. I will rise and give my decision in about twenty minutes.

[The hearing ends with formalities as before.]

The sheriff returns to her chambers and writes out a short opinion. About forty minutes[194] later the court re-convenes, with the usual opening formalities.

The Sheriff: This is an Application under section 60(7) of the Children (Scotland) Act 1995 to set aside or vary Child Protection Orders in relation to the children Samantha and Jacqueline McPerlin granted on 26th January 2006 and confirmed at the second working day hearing on 30th January 2006. While confirming the Orders themselves, with the consequence that the girls remained with foster-parents, the second working day hearing made it a condition that the children should have unlimited daily contact with their mother and two hours supervised contact with their stepfather. I am told that contact is going well with the mother and that no difficulty is expected in relation to contact with the stepfather. The placement with the foster-parents is also satisfactory. The suggestion today is that I should make an order which would result in the girls returning to the family home, either full time or during week-days, when the step-father would stay with his brother.

If I were to recall the CPOs this would of course result in the girls returning home. Alternatively I could leave the CPOs in place but modify the contact arrangements so as to have the girls stay at home but not when

---

194. Not 'twenty minutes' as stated by the sheriff earlier: sheriffs (certainly the writer) sometimes take longer than they predict!

the stepfather was residing there. I will not rehearse the careful arguments addressed to me. The core issue is whether the girls should be required to remain with the foster-parents pending the proof hearing which is to be expected in some six weeks time. My position in law, as I see it, is to consider all the information before me and to decide the matter on the basis of that information. There does not in my view have to be a change of circumstances before I can vary, or indeed recall, a CPO at this stage.

Mrs MacDonald submitted that the CPOs had never been necessary in the first place in that there was and is no <u>immediate</u> likelihood of the mother being admitted to hospital, thus bringing about the circumstances which, according to Samantha, provided the occasion for what she says happened to her. I thought this argument was attractive, but concluded that its attractiveness was superficial only. If there is any truth in Samantha's allegations then a series of serious sexual assaults was committed against her by Mr Donald McPerlin. That in itself is concerning, abstracting from the speciality that it may be more likely that such attacks may be made against Jacqueline in the event of the mother going to hospital again. Samantha still maintains her stance. Jacqueline, while to an extent modifying her position, still sticks by the essence of what she said and, indeed, by somewhat qualifying her position, might be regarded as having enhanced her credibility. There is also the possibility that Mrs McPerlin might be called to the hospital at short notice, before the Social Work Department could be notified, thus producing the scenario which Samantha apprehends. For these reasons I was far from persuaded that the CPOs should never have been granted and should now be recalled.

I think Mrs MacDonald was correct to place more emphasis on her alternative motion to the effect that I should vary the conditions of the Orders, and allow the girls to remain in the family home during week-days on the condition that the step-father absent himself from the family home during week-days and week-nights, thus removing any likelihood of any actings as alleged by Samantha. It was generally accepted that the undertaking by Mr Calum McPerlin to accommodate his brother should be regarded as a genuine one. I accept the qualification, voiced by the reporter, that the latter might be tempted not to report his brother to the authorities in the event of his brother coming home 'late'. However, it is how matters would appear to Mr Donald McPerlin that is more to the point and I am satisfied that it is to the highest degree unlikely that he would risk breaching his undertaking, in the present circumstances, in the hope that his brother would not report this. I must have regard to the principle enunciated in section 16(3) of the Children (Scotland) Act 1995 which in effect says that no requirement should be made unless it benefits the child. Looked at objectively, as the thrust of Mrs MacDonald argument ran, there could be no benefit to the girls in keeping them away from the family home during week-days, when, under the proposed arrangements, any threat presented by the presence of Mr McPerlin in the family home would be removed.

I am of course bound to have regard to (although I am not bound to give effect to) the views of the children. They have made it very clear to me that they would feel under threat that Mr Donald McPerlin might 'walk in at any time' if the condition of residence with the foster-parents changed so as to require them to reside in the family home, even if Mr Donald McPerlin were excluded from it during the week. In my view the risk now presented to the children is one which seems reasonable to them and, that being so, it would harm them to be exposed to it.

There are two main matters for my decision: firstly, as to whether I should recall the CPOs completely; and secondly, as to whether, if I leave them in place, I should vary the conditions more or less along the lines argued for by Mrs MacDonald and Mr Paterson.

I have already indicated, and given my reasons for deciding, that the CPOs should not be set aside in their entirety.

As to whether I should vary the conditions to the CPOs by having the girls stay in family with mother (and for that matter Graeme) from Sunday evening to Friday evening, with Mr McPerlin staying with his brother, I can see that this has some attractions. I have to decide on the basis of what seems to me best to promote the interests and welfare of the children, having regard inter alia to their views. Their views, as I have indicated, are quite clear, but while I have to have regard to them, they are not 'binding' on me. I think there is substance in Mr Paterson's point about girls of that age needing their mother, but I think that 'forcing' them, as it were, would be against their best interests. Also, as pointed out by Miss Wilson, sending them back home today would run the risk, in the event of the Grounds being upheld at proof (with the consequent possibility of a hearing making a supervision requirement involving residing away from the family home), of unnecessary coming and going. They are happy where they are and wish to stay there. As to the 'Human Rights' perspective I would say that in my view the diminution of the Applicants' rights to family life by being denied the presence of the girls overnight is, given the arrangements for contact, not significant enough to affect my decision. I have accordingly decided to refuse the Applications to set aside or vary and accordingly I will leave standing the determination of the Second Working Day Hearing.

Mrs MacDonald: I am obliged to Your Ladyship.

Mr Paterson: As Your Ladyship pleases.

The Sheriff: Thank you. I presume that my decision can be conveyed to Samantha and Jacqueline with the minimum of delay.

Miss Wilson: They decided to come back to court after the lunch break and are still in the building. I shall tell them of Your Ladyship's decision right away. I know from my friend the reporter that she has the Grounds for Referral ready to serve, together with the notification of the Eighth Working Day hearing on Tuesday 7th February at 2.30 pm, so she can give these to the girls before they leave. I have told them to expect them and about what is likely to happen on the Eighth Working Day hearing and at the proof. Of course technically I drop out of the picture at this stage[195], but I understand from Your Ladyship's clerk that in the event of an Application under section 65(7) of the Act that Your Ladyship would be likely to appoint me as curator *ad litem* for the proof proceedings?

The Sheriff: Yes, I would certainly give consideration to that.

Mrs MacDonald: For what it may be worth, my friend Mr Paterson and I would welcome the continued presence of Miss Wilson in any future proceedings.

The Sheriff: Thank you. Well, that is all we can do today.

[The hearing ends with formalities as before.]

Before leaving the court the reporter gives Mrs MacDonald and Mr Paterson the service copies of the Grounds for Referral and the Notifications of the Eighth Working Day Hearing. She then goes into the waiting room with Miss Wilson and gives similar papers to Samantha and Jacqueline.

Same day, Friday, 3 February 2006, late afternoon – in the court.

The sheriff signs the formal interlocutors in each Application. Here is the interlocutor in the Application regarding Jacqueline:

Kirklenton 3rd February, 2006

Act: Ms Cameron, Children's Reporter

Alt: Mrs MacDonald, Solicitor, for Donald McPerlin (personally present)

Mr Paterson, Solicitor, for Sharon McPerlin (personally present)

For the local authority, Lentonshire Council: Mr d'Annunzio, Solicitor

As curator *ad litem* for the child Jacqueline McPerlin: Miss Wilson, solicitor

The sheriff, having considered the Application and heard from the reporter, parties' procurators and the curator *ad litem* thereon, and having had regard to the views, conveyed orally, of the child Jacqueline, REFUSES said Application.

(Signed) Fiona Grey
Sheriff

---

195. Miss Wilson's appointment has been made by the sheriff in connection with the proceedings before her and do not carry over to the subsequent procedure before the children's hearing, but there would be nothing to stop the reporter inviting Miss Wilson to attend the hearing and the chair of the hearing allowing her presence as someone whose presence was justified by special circumstances under Children's Hearings (Scotland) Rules, 1996, r 13(b). This will in fact happen – see infra page 157.

CONSIDERING THE OUTCOME OF THE APPLICATION

Same day, Friday, 3 February 2006 at 3.30 pm –
in the reporter's office.

Laura Cameron now reports on the disposal of the Application to her Authority Reporter, Hector Somerville. The latter, who must always 'keep a continual eye on the situation'[196], applies his mind to whether or not the continuation of the CPOs is justified. He decides, after discussing the matter with Laura Cameron, that it is so justified and accordingly refrains from exercising his powers to bring about the termination of the Orders under section 60(3) of the Children (Scotland) Act 1995.

Miss Cameron suggests that the Reporter's Department should consider asking Miss Wilson if she would like to be invited to attend the 8 WD hearing as a person whom the chair of the hearing could allow to be present under the Children's Hearings (Scotland) Rules, 1996, r 13(d). Mr Somerville agrees and asks Miss Cameron to contact Miss Wilson about this right away. She does so. Miss Wilson agrees and says she will advise the girls.

Stating and Serving Grounds For Referral for Graeme

Same day, Friday, 3 February 2006 – in the Reporter's office – later

Mr Somerville and Miss Cameron discuss the practicalities of bringing Graeme into the procedures and Miss Cameron arranges for a hearing to be fixed for Monday 13th February 2006 at 4.00 pm and then arranges for Grounds for Referral, along with the appropriate Notifications and Miss Drummond's SBR[197] in relation to Graeme to be put into the First Class Recorded Delivery Post to be sent in separate envelopes to Graeme and Mr and Mrs McPerlin.

Miss Cameron must give to the child and relevant persons notification of the hearing which will consider the Grounds for Referral of Graeme. This notification must be given not less than seven days before the hearing[198]. She must also give the hearing members, where it is practicable, the same amount of notice[199]. She must also give to the hearing members[200], and the relevant persons[201], any documents listed in sub-paragraphs (a) to (f) of the Children's Hearings (Scotland) Rules, 1996, rule 5(1) – in the instant case the Grounds for Referral of Graeme, a Social Background Report which the Social Work Department has prepared in relation to Graeme, and the Report for the Second Working Day Hearing.

---

196. The words of *Norrie, op cit*, page 245
197. Referred to supra at page 47.
198. Children's Hearings (Scotland) Rules, 1996, SI 96/3261, rr 6(1) and 7(4).
299. Children's Hearings (Scotland) Rules, 1996, SI 96/3261, r 5(1).
200. Children's Hearings (Scotland) Rules, 1996, SI 96/3261, r 5(1).
201. Children's Hearings (Scotland) Rules, 1996, SI 96/3261, r 5(3).

Same day, Friday, 3 February 2006 at 5 pm –
in Mrs MacDonald's office

Mrs MacDonald has now examined the Grounds for Referral document, which contains no surprises. It is clear that at the Eighth Working Day (8WD) Hearing on Tuesday 7th February 2006 the mother and Mr Donald McPerlin will be 'not admitting' the material averments and that therefore the hearing will direct the reporter to make an application to the sheriff for a finding on the matter[202]. Mrs MacDonald however, in accordance with her careful practice, phones Miss Cameron and both agree that they foresee no difficulty. Miss Cameron mentions that she will be inviting Miss Wilson to attend and that Miss Wilson has agreed to this. Mrs MacDonald then phones Mr McPerlin and confirms that he should attend the 8WD hearing personally and (presumably) maintain his non-acceptance of the grounds. Had he been less articulate she would have offered that either she or her assistant Mr Wynford should attend and act without fee. She suggests that he should phone her office on the following day. Mr McPerlin has no difficulty in agreeing to this. Mrs MacDonald concludes by saying that once (and this seems inevitable now) the matter is referred to the sheriff for proof she will arrange to prepare the case fully, which will involve, most notably, taking a full precognition from Mr McPerlin.

Same day, Friday, 3 February 2006 at 5 pm – in Mr Paterson's office

Mr Paterson makes parallel phone calls as Mrs MacDonald has done, as above.

The days leading up to the Eighth Working Day Hearing

Preparations for this hearing include discussions between the reporter and the other parties, including arranging the practicalities of arranging for the children to attend the hearing.

THE EIGHTH WORKING DAY HEARING

Tuesday, 7 February 2006 at 2.30 pm – In the Hearings suite in the Reporter's premises in Kirklenton

The persons present at the hearing are: Mrs Theresa Kelly, an experienced panel member; Mr James Hamilton, also an experienced panel member; and the less experienced Miss Sandra Robertson (who was present at the 2WD hearing); Samantha and Jacqueline (who have indicated that they no longer require the hearing to be 'split'); Mr McPerlin, Mrs McPerlin; Miss

---

202. Children (Scotland) Act 1995 s 65(7) – in theory the hearing, in terms of this sub-section, could still 'discharge the referral' but it is inconceivable in the circumstances of this case that the hearing would do so at this stage.

Laura Cameron, as reporter; Miss Wilson, who has been invited by the reporter to attend, and social worker Miss Marcia Drummond. The panel members have agreed that Miss Robertson (who has just undergone her 'chairing' course, organised by the Children's Panel Advisory Committee) should chair the session.

> *Note [37]   The presence of Miss Robertson gives a measure of continuity. This is not a statutory necessity but there is a view (not held by all) that in some cases it may be appropriate. The chair of the Lentonshire panel does, however, take this view – hence Miss Robertson. She is not 'very experienced' but, having recently done her 'chairing' course, is eligible to chair the meeting, and as this is likely to be a fairly formal hearing, it will be a good opportunity for her to get experience, with other hearing members who are very experienced.*

Miss Robertson: Hello, good afternoon. I think I have met most of you already since I was one of the hearing members at the Second Working Day Hearing on Monday 26th January. We thought it would be good if there was at least one familiar face on the panel. Just to remind you, and for the benefit of Miss Wilson, who was not at that hearing, my name is Sandra Robertson. Today my colleagues are Mrs Theresa Kelly and Mr James Hamilton. Hello again, Samantha and Jacqueline.

[Samantha and Jacqueline nod in acknowledgement]

Mrs Kelly, Mr Hamilton: Hello/Good afternoon.

Miss Robertson. Could I first of all go round the table and ask everyone to identify him or herself?

[This is done, as before[203], with the addition that Miss Robertson identifies Miss Wilson as a solicitor who was curator *ad litem* for the girls at the Motion to Set Aside or Vary stage and has been invited to attend by the reporter as a person who, by her knowledge of the case and the fact that she has the confidence of the girls, is being allowed by her, as Chair of the hearing, to be present[204]]

Miss Robertson: This is a hearing about the two girls who are here, Samantha and Jacqueline McPerlin, who usually stay at 19 Glenview Cottages, Bruaich. Samantha's date of birth is 15th August 1993 and Jacqueline's 10th July 1995.

The background is that on 26th January of this year the sheriff granted Child Protection Orders for Samantha and Jacqueline, with the condition that they should stay with foster-carers, and also making conditions as to contact with Mr and Mrs McPerlin. The Second Working Day Hearing to

---

203. *Supra* p 55.
204. Children's Hearings (Scotland) Rules, 1996, r 13(d).

which I have referred continued the Orders but made some changes to the conditions regarding contact. Mr and Mrs McPerlin then applied to the Sheriff to set aside or vary the orders but the Sheriff refused to do so with the result that they still stand, subject to the conditions set by the Second Working Day Hearing. The reporter has now stated Grounds for Referral. This is the Eighth Working Day Hearing and the purpose of this hearing is (a) to find out which of the Grounds for Referral, if any, are accepted by the children and the relevant persons (Mr and Mrs McPerlin) and which Grounds, if any, are not accepted by the children and relevant persons; (b) in the event of all the Grounds being accepted, to consider (i) whether we should continue the case to a further hearing hearing for further inquiry, (ii) whether we should discharge the referral or, if we do not decide to do either of these things, then we can (iii) discuss the case here and now and make a supervision requirement of some kind[205]. We may also wish to consider granting a warrant to continue the keeping of Samantha and Jacqueline with the foster-parents[206].

Alternatively, if not all the Grounds are accepted but some of them are accepted, we could think about going ahead on the basis of the Grounds so accepted. However, if we decide we cannot go ahead on that basis (and if we decide we should not use our residual power to discharge the referral) then we would have to direct the reporter to make application to the sheriff who will decide which of the grounds, if any, which have not been accepted are in the sheriff's opinion established by the evidence which will be laid before the sheriff[207].

We also have to decide whether or not to appoint a safeguarder. I realise that was rather a long story, but no doubt it has been explained to the girls by Miss Wilson and to Mr and Mrs McPerlin by their solicitors?

[General assent]

Miss Robertson: I should also make clear that what you say here about whether you accept Grounds is very important and will be noted, but that if the matter goes before the sheriff to 'try' the case and anyone changes his or her mind as to accepting or not accepting grounds, then that person is entitled to do so and tell the sheriff about the change[208].

Miss Robertson: I know we would normally leave this to later on, once the Grounds for Referral have been discussed, but since Miss Wilson has been mentioned I thought we might now consider the issue of a safeguarder?

Samantha: As we have said before we are not in favour of a safeguarder – the more so since Miss Wilson is present.

Miss Robertson: So we won't appoint a safeguarder?

---

205. Children (Scotland) Act 1995, s 65(6).
206. Children (Scotland) Act 1995, s 66.
207. Children (Scotland) Act 1995, s 65(7).
208. *Kennedy v R* 1992 SCLR (Notes) 564; sub nom *Kennedy v R's curator ad litem* 1993 SLT 295.

[General assent]

Miss Robertson: Now, Jacqueline and Samantha, Mr and Mrs McPerlin, I expect you will already have some idea of the meaning of the Grounds for Referral, but to keep matters right I propose to go through them carefully, explain their meaning, and find out what is accepted and not accepted by each of you. It's a bit laborious, but I think the safest course is to plod through them one by one, checking as we go along who accepts or does not accept what. Do you see what I mean? If you don't understand anything just say.

[General assent]

Miss Robertson: Now you've all got the Grounds for Referral document there[209], and you can see that it's in two main parts, the bit above the 'Statement of Facts' and the numbered paragraphs making up the Statement of Facts. The bit above contains the particular provision or 'condition', as I shall call it, of the Children (Scotland) Act 1995 which the reporter says exist, thus entitling a Children's Hearing to consider a child's case. There are similarities between the Grounds for Samantha and Jacqueline, but there are also important differences, and I will explain them separately, starting with Jacqueline.

I'd like to go first to what I have called the 'Condition of Referral', set out towards the top of the document. This is the legal foundation for the case being dealt with under the hearings procedures. The facts relied on are the allegations contained in Statements 5 and 10. The 'charge', if I may use that term, against Mr McPerlin is that he did the things alleged in Statement 5. The exact wording of the 'Condition' is: 'That in terms of Section 52(2)(e) of the Children (Scotland) Act 1995 she is, or is likely to become, a member of the same household as a child in respect of whom any of the offences mentioned in Schedule 1 to the Criminal Procedure (Scotland) Act 1995 (offences against children to which special provisions apply) has been committed.' This also needs a bit of explanation. As is said Statement of Fact 5 the 'offence involving the use of lewd, indecent or libidinous practice or behaviour towards a child under the age of 17 years' is one of the offences mentioned in Schedule 1 of the Criminal Procedure (Scotland) Act 1995. It is therefore an offence which, if admitted or proved in relation to one child, may allow a children's hearing to step in and make decisions about that child and indeed any child who is or is likely to become a member of the same household as that child. I'll say more about the definition of this offence when we come to Statement 5, but is what I have said so far quite clear?

[General assent]

Miss Robertson: I'll now go the Statements of Fact. Now Statement of Fact 1 says: 'That Jacqueline McPerlin was born on 10th July 1995 and

---

209. *Supra* pp 102, 103.

normally resides with her mother, Mrs Sharon Transom or McPerlin, and her step-father, Mr Donald McPerlin, who is married to the mother, at 19, Glenview Cottages, Bruaich, Kirklenton, LE29 4QW.' I hardly need to explain that beyond perhaps saying the 'normally' means 'in the ordinary way', meaning, in this instance, if there were not any CPO involved. Jacqueline what do you think about this Statement of Fact?

Jacqueline: Yes, that's right[210].

Miss Robertson: Mr McPerlin?

Mr McPerlin: Yes, of course.

Miss Robertson: Mrs McPerlin?

Mrs McPerlin: Yes, that's correct.

Miss Robertson: Statement of Fact 2 states: 'That also resident in the family home are Jacqueline's siblings: Samantha Transom (known as Samantha McPerlin), born 15th August 1993 and Graeme McPerlin, born 2nd June 2004, who is the child of Mrs McPerlin and Mr McPerlin. Mrs McPerlin is the mother of Jacqueline and Samantha as a result of a previous relationship.' Once again I don't think this needs much explaining – I think everyone knows that 'siblings' means 'brothers or sisters'. What to you say to this Statement of Fact?

[Jacqueline and the McPerlins, individually, indicate agreement as before.]

Miss Robertson: Statement of Fact 3 says: 'On 13th April 2004 Mrs McPerlin, pregnant with the half-brother Graeme, required to be admitted to the Blackmore Memorial Infirmary because of problems with the pregnancy and she remained there until a week after the birth of Graeme on 2nd June 2004.' What about this one?

[Jacqueline and the McPerlins, individually, indicate agreement as before.]

Miss Robertson: Statement 4 says: 'During the period from Mrs McPerlin's admission to hospital in April 2004 until shortly after the commencement of the new term in September 2004 Jacqueline's sister Samantha was absent from school for approximately 90% of possible attendances. The matter was reported to the Social Work Department and to the reporter but no action was taken because the sister had returned to school in September 2004, was attending regularly, and progressing well.' That's quite a lot of detail, but, unless there's anything you want to clarify?

[The girls and the McPerlins, individually, indicate agreement as before.]

---

210.   Since this is about Jacqueline's Grounds Samantha is not invited to comment.

Miss Robertson: Statement of Fact 5 states: 'On several dates between 13th April 2004 or thereby and 9th June 2004 or thereby, on Saturday nights, within the family home, Mr McPerlin, the stepfather of Jacqueline and Samantha, did while under the influence of alcohol, use lewd, indecent or libidinous practices or behaviour upon Samantha in that he did enter her bed, fondle her breasts under her night-dress, fondle her private parts under her night dress and attempt to persuade her to fondle his private parts. This is an offence mentioned in Schedule 1(4) to the Criminal Procedure (Scotland) Act 1995 namely an offence involving the use of lewd, indecent or libidinous practice or behaviour towards a child under the age of 17 years.' Now this <u>does</u> require some explanation. Schedule 1 of the Criminal Procedure (Scotland) Act 1995 lists a number of offences, which are, as the Act puts it, 'offences against children to which special provisions apply'. Is that clear so far?

[Indications that this is understood]

Miss Robertson: Fine. Now one of these offences is that which the law describes as 'an offence involving the use of lewd, indecent or libidinous practice or behaviour towards a child under the age of 17 years'. The description 'lewd and libidinous practices' is an antiquated one. It means any form of sexual abuse of a child carried out with the purpose of achieving some sort of sexual satisfaction for the abuser. It includes the activities mentioned in Statement 5 and if it were proved that Mr McPerlin, carried out these actions then that would amount to the commission of that offence. It is also said that Mr McPerlin was the stepfather of Samantha at the time and that the offence was carried out in the family home – these elements are not part of the offence but they are important background features. I hope I have made that clear. I will now ask Jacqueline and Mr and Mrs McPerlin if they have understood my explanation. I do not want you to tell me at this stage whether you agree with the allegation, I simply want to make sure you have understood what I have said and we can come in a minute to the question of whether this statement of fact is accepted or not.

Jacqueline: Yes, we both understand this. Margaret – Miss Wilson, has explained the technical side, but we understood about 'touching up' anyway.

Miss Robertson: Fine. Mr McPerlin?

Mr McPerlin: Yes I have understood your explanation perfectly.

Mrs McPerlin: So have I.

Miss Robertson: Good. I will now move on to finding out whether these allegations are accepted or not. Jacqueline?

Jacqueline: [*Becoming upset*] I believe her. I think everything that is said here is right.

Miss Robertson: Mr McPerlin?

Mr McPerlin: Of course I deny all this. I don't know what has got into these girls. I blame this so-called sex education they get at school I think ....

Miss Robertson: I don't think we can go into that here, but I am noting you as not accepting this ground?

Mr McPerlin: That's exactly right.

Miss Robertson: Mrs McPerlin?

Mrs McPerlin: I am denying this too.

Miss Robertson: Very well. Statement of Fact 6 states: 'On 31st December 2005 or 1st January 2006 Mr McPerlin, while under the influence of alcohol, entered Jacqueline's bedroom, waking her. He walked some steps towards her bed and then collapsed on the floor in a drunken condition.' Jacqueline?

Jacqueline: All true.

Miss Robertson: Mr and Mrs McPerlin?

Mr McPerlin: Totally denied.

Mrs McPerlin: Yes, denied.

Miss Robertson: Statement of Fact 7: 'As a result of the conduct of Mr McPerlin on 31st December 2005 or 1st January 2006 Jacqueline was very frightened. On the night in question she could not sleep for a long time. She has since had difficulty sleeping and refuses to sleep without the light on.' Jacqueline?

Jacqueline: Quite true.

Miss Robertson: Mr and Mrs McPerlin?

Mr McPerlin: Denied.

Mrs McPerlin: Not true at all.

Miss Robertson: Statement 8: 'Mrs McPerlin is again pregnant and the new baby is expected to be delivered in early June 2006. It is likely that she will require to be admitted to hospital for some four to six weeks before the birth.'

Miss Robertson: Jacqueline?

Jacqueline: Yes.

Miss Robertson: Mr and Mrs McPerlin?

Mrs McPerlin: Yes, that's what I've been told.

Mr McPerlin: That's right.

Miss Robertson: Statement 9: 'Jacqueline and her sister Samantha are afraid that when Mrs McPerlin is in hospital Mr McPerlin may repeat the conduct of April – June 2004. In particular Samantha is apprehensive that this conduct may be directed towards Jacqueline and that she, Samantha, would not be able to protect Jacqueline.' Jacqueline?

Jacqueline: Yes, that's what I think, anyway.

Miss Robertson: Mr McPerlin?

Mr McPerlin: It's a bit like 'When did you stop beating your wife?' I don't accept the basis of all this so you can take me as denying.

Mrs McPerlin: That's what I think too.

Miss Robertson: Now for the last Statement of Fact, No 10: 'Jacqueline is or is likely to become a member of the same household as her sister Samantha.' I should explain that 'household' means a family unit, a group of people who are held together by some kind of tie and normally live together[211]. The importance of this concept here is that if it should be admitted or proved that Mr McPerlin did do what he is alleged to have done with Samantha then the hearings system would be entitled to 'step in' as I have put it not only with Samantha, but also in relation to any other child, in this case Jacqueline, who is or is likely to become a member of the same household as Samantha. If that is clear I will check on what your views are. Jacqueline?

Jacqueline: Yes that's quite clear, and I think the answer is obvious – yes.

Miss Robertson: Mr and Mrs McPerlin?

Mr McPerlin: Yes, agreed.

Mrs McPerlin: Yes, that's clearly right.

Miss Robertson: I'd now like to turn back to what I have called the 'Condition of Referral', set out towards the top of the document. The reporter is saying in effect that if the 'Statement of Fact' exist then it follows that the 'Condition' also exists ...

Mr McPerlin [interrupting]: Yes, my wife and I understand that perfectly and we think it is nonsense.

---

211. Cf *McGregor v H*, 1983 SLT 626 per Lord President Emslie at 628.

Miss Robertson: You've answered my next question and it will be noted that you both do not accept this aspect of the Grounds for Referral. Jacqueline?

Jacqueline: Yes we have both understood your explanation – Miss Wilson has discussed this already with both of us – and we have to say that we do accept this.

Miss Robertson: Okay. [*Turning to the other hearing members*]: Is there anything you'd like to say at this stage?

Mrs Kelly: No, nothing. I think the situation is quite clear.

Mr Hamilton: No thank you; there's nothing I want to raise.

Miss Robertson: Miss Wilson?

Miss Wilson: No, except to confirm that I believe Jacqueline and indeed Samantha understand what is going on in these proceedings and know what may happen next.

[Miss Robertson now goes through the Grounds for Referral for Samantha asking everyone to state what is accepted and what is not. She does not need to repeat the definitions already supplied but highlights the only difference, viz that Samantha's case rests on <u>her</u> being the target of the alleged behaviour with the condition of referral being that 'she is a child in respect of whom any of the offences mentioned in Schedule 1 to the Criminal Procedure (Scotland) Act 1995 (offences against children to which special provisions apply) has been committed.' (There is therefore no parallel to Statement of Fact 10.) The girls and Mr and Mrs McPerlin reply along the same lines as before.]

Miss Robertson: Well, that seems pretty clear. Samantha and Jacqueline are accepting the entire Grounds for Referral. Mr and Mrs McPerlin, while accepting what might be termed the 'formal' Statements of Fact, that is 1 to 4 and, importantly in Jacqueline's case, No 10, are not accepting the substantial grounds. Any thoughts?

Mrs Kelly: Yes, I think that sums matters up perfectly.

Mr Hamilton: Agreed. And that means we can now, as the Act tells us, proceed on the facts as accepted, discharge the referral or send the matter to the sheriff for proof[212]. And it seems to me that we couldn't really 'proceed on the facts as accepted' since nothing except fairly formal things have been accepted by Mr and Mrs McPerlin?

Miss Robertson: Yes that's right. Of course it's our decision but I'll just check on people's views. Samantha and Jacqueline? Mr and Mrs McPerlin?

---

212. Children (Scotland) Act 1995 s 65(7).

Samantha: We want the matter cleared up – proof.

Jacqueline: Yes.

Mr McPerlin: Of course I want this cleared up – proof. Our solicitors say they will be ready within a few weeks.

Mrs McPerlin: I agree.

Miss Drummond: I think it is essential that these serious allegations should be decided on the evidence.

Miss Robertson [*To the other hearing members*]: It is of course a decision for all three of us, but I think it is obvious in the interests of the girls, and for that matter in the interests of Mr and Mrs McPerlin, that these matters be cleared up by evidence.

Mrs Kelly: Yes, that's obvious.

Mr Hamilton: Oh yes, I entirely agree.

Miss Robertson: Very well – our decision will be, in accordance with section 65(7) of the Children (Scotland) Act 1995, to direct the reporter to make an application to the sheriff for a finding as to whether the grounds which have not been accepted are established. Now we must think about the warrants. The continuation of the CPOs at the Second Working Day Hearing expires today and I think we should now decide whether or not it is necessary for us to grant warrants requiring the girls to remain with the foster parents.

Miss Robertson: But are they really necessary?

Mr Hamilton: I think we should hear what Samantha and Jacqueline have to say about this.

Samantha: We think we should like the present position to continue, with us staying with the Jamiesons at nights, being able to see Mummy during the day and Mr McPerlin for two hours at the week-end. We would be very uneasy about anything else.

Jacqueline: Definitely.

Mr Hamilton: But is there anything much to justify this unease?

Miss Drummond: On a recent visit to Mr and Mrs McPerlin, Mr McPerlin had been drinking and said that for two pins he'd go and pick up the girls in the car if he felt like it.

Mr McPerlin: That's a libel. I said no such thing.

Miss Drummond: [To the panel members] I don't want to get into an argument but I am, as professional social worker stating what happened.

Mr McPerlin: I stick by what I said but my solicitor has advised me not to oppose the warrant and I don't want to make waves. I hope my reasonableness will be noted.

Miss Robertson: What do you think, Mrs McPerlin?

Mrs McPerlin: I go along with everything Donald has said.

Mr Hamilton: We have to decide that the warrant is necessary in order to safeguard or promote the welfare of the girls[213]. They have given their views, and while these views are not binding on us, we must take account of them and there does seem to be some information that Mr McPerlin may possibly act in an unpredictable way. I therefore think that warrants should be issued. What so you think, Miss Drummond?

Miss Drummond: The department thinks warrant should be in position.

Mr Hamilton[214]: And is that your own view?

Miss Drummond: Yes, I stand by what I said a minute ago.

Mr Hamilton: Thank you. Miss Wilson, do you have anything to say on this in the interests of the girls?

Miss Wilson: No, indeed this is what they themselves want.

Mr Hamilton: [Turning to the other panel members] What do you think?

Mrs Kelly: I agree.

Miss Robertson: So do I. Well, that seems to be that. Just to sum up. Our decision is that as the substantial Grounds for Referral are not accepted by the relevant persons, the hearing directs the reporter to make application, or rather two applications, to the sheriff for a finding as to the disputed grounds, in terms of section 65(7) of the Children (Scotland) Act 1995. It will be noted on the Grounds for Referral documents that the relevant persons do not admit the Condition of Referral, and that they do not accept what I have called the substantial Statements of Fact, ie Statements 5 to 7 and 9, but that they accept Statements 1 to 4, inclusive, Statement 8, and also, and this applies only in the Grounds for Jacqueline, Statement 10. It will be noted that Samantha and Jacqueline admit the Condition of Referral and all of the Statements of Fact. We do not appoint a safeguarder.

The rules provide that the reporter must lodge the applications to the sheriff within seven days[215], but I think, Miss Cameron, that the Application will be lodged well within that time?

---

213. Children (Scotland) Act 1995 s 66(2)(b).
214. Who, like the author, likes to get at the professional opinion of the individual social worker.
215. Act of Sederunt (Child Care and Maintenance Rules) 1997, SI 1997/291 r 3.45(1).

Miss Cameron: Tomorrow or the day after.

Miss Robertson: Good. Once the Applications are lodged the court will fix a date, within 28 days of the date of lodging, for the case to be heard by the sheriff[216]. The reporter will notify all parties of the date, time and place fixed for this hearing. Mr and Mrs McPerlin, I understand you have already instructed solicitors and are aware of the possibility of free Legal Aid, but could I underline the importance of keeping in touch with your lawyers and fully instructing them so that there is no unnecessary delay in getting on with the case?

Mr McPerlin: Yes we both understand that and are as anxious as anyone to get this cleared up.

Miss Robertson: I must also advise you that you have the right to appeal to the sheriff against our decision to grant a warrant[217] – any such appeal must be lodged with the sheriff court within three weeks, counting from today's date[218]. If an appeal is lodged, then it must be disposed of by the sheriff within three days[219].

Mrs McPerlin: Yes, our lawyers told us that. There will be no appeal.

Miss Robertson: Samantha, Jacqueline, I know Margaret Wilson may be continuing to act as your curator *ad litem* but I have to tell you that it would be open to you both to instruct a lawyer and that you would be entitled to apply for free Legal Aid for the court proceedings.

Samantha: Yes, we both know that, but we do not want a lawyer.

Jacqueline: Yes, that's right.

Miss Robertson: Very good: that concludes this hearing. The formal decision, with our reasons, including the granting of the warrant for 22 days, that is until Tuesday 28th February 2006, will be sent out to-morrow.

[General assent]

Miss Robertson: That's very kind of you. Well that concludes this hearing. [To Miss Cameron] We'll just return the papers to you now[220].

[The hearing members give their papers to Miss Cameron and the hearing breaks up.]

---

216. Children (Scotland) Act 1995 s 68(2)
217. There can be no appeal against the decisions not to discharge the referral and to direct application to the sheriff for proof – *H and H v McGregor* 1973 SC 95, 1973 SLT 110.
218. Children (Scotland) Act 1995 s 51(1).
219. Children (Scotland) Act 1995 s 51(8).
220. Children's Hearings (Scotland) Rules, 1996, SI 96/3261, r 5(5).

THE FORMAL WARRANT under Section 66(1) OF THE 1995 ACT

Here is the warrant for Jacqueline:

Rule 27

FORM 12

WARRANT UNDER SECTION 66(1) OF THE ACT FOR KEEPING A CHILD IN A PLACE OF SAFETY

17 Laverock Road, KIRKLENTON, 7th February 2006.

A children's hearing for Lentonshire in respect of the case of Jacqueline McPerlin (d.o.b. 10.07.95), 19, Glenview Cottages, Bruaich, Kirklenton, LE29 4QW, being unable to dispose of the case and in the exercise of the powers conferred on them by section 63(5) of the Act, being satisfied [that it is necessary in order to safeguard or promote his/her welfare]* [the child may not attend at any hearing of his/her case]* [there is reason to believe that the child may fail to comply with a requirement under section 69(3) of the Act]* [there is reason to believe that the child may not attend at any hearing of his/her case], grant warrant to (insert name and address and where appropriate full designation of applicant) The Chief Social Work Officer of Lentonshire Council, of 8 Laverock Road, Kirllenton, [to find and keep the child in (name of place or places) a place of safety chosen by the Chief Social Work Officer of Lentonshire Council for a period from (insert period not exceeding 22 days) 7th February 2006 to 28th February 2006, both dates inclusive [and for the bringing of that child before a children's hearing at (insert time and/or date) at a date and time to be notified].

[For the duration of this warrant the child shall be subject to the conditions noted below]*

[The children's hearing in granting this warrant order that the place where (the child) is to reside in accordance with the warrant shall not be disclosed to (person or class of persons)]*

[CONDITIONS REFERRED TO IN THE FOREGOING WARRANT

1. (Insert conditions)]* The child Jacqueline is entitled to have such daytime contact as she shall wish with Mrs McPerlin before 9.30 pm and shall be returned to the place of safety not later than 9.30 pm on any day.

2. Jacqueline to have contact with her stepfather, Mr Donald McPerlin, for two hours per week, to be exercised within the Kirklenton premises of the Lentonshire Social Work Department, between 10 a.m. and midday on Saturdays under supervision of said Department.

(Sgd) Sandra Robertson

....

Chair of the Children's Hearing

*Delete as appropriate

LODGING AND SERVING THE APPLICATIONS FOR THE s 68 PROOF

Wednesday, 8 February 2006 – in the Reporter's office at 10 am

Miss Cameron has to lodge and serve Applications for the s 68 proof for Samantha and Jacqueline.

Reckoning that it would be helpful to know the date of the proof as soon as possible she takes the two Applications to the sheriff clerk's office for a diet for the proof to be assigned and warrant to cite witnesses and havers to be granted.

Same day, Wednesday, 8 February 2006 at 11.30 am – in the Sheriff Clerk's office

Miss Cameron, in passing the Applications to the sheriff clerk, mentions that she is about to have a hearing where Grounds will be put in connection with Graeme and therefore would be glad if the diet of proof, at which Graeme's case would be likely to be conjoined, could be nearer the end than the beginning of the 28 day period prescribed by section 68(2) of the Children (Scotland) Act 1995 and in any event not before 23rd February 2006. The sheriff clerk takes the papers to Sheriff Grey, who, although in the middle of a civil proof, is available in chambers having allowed parties an adjournment in order to agree certain matters. The sheriff clerk asks if the sheriff wishes to appoint a curator *ad litem*. Sheriff Grey remembers that she was involved in the hearing of the Application to Recall or Vary and decides to appoint Miss Wilson as curator *ad litem*. Here is the completed document for Jacqueline[221]:

---

221. The formal style is set out as Form 60 of the Act of Sederunt (Child Care and Maintenance Rules) 1997, SI 1997/291, to which the reader is referred. The instructions in the statutory form have been left in place.

Rule 3.45(1)

FORM 60

APPLICATION TO SHERIFF UNDER SECTION 65 OF THE CHILDREN (SCOTLAND) ACT 1995

SHERIFF COURT AT [insert place] KIRKLENTON

APPLICANT:
[insert name, address and designation of applicant]

> *The Principal Reporter, per Hector Somerville, Authority Reporter, Scottish Children's Reporter Administration, 17 Laverock Road, Kirklenton LE6 7EK. Tel: 012104 545 700. Fax: 012104 545 710*

in the case of

[insert name and address of child]

> *Jacqueline (Jackie) Transom, known as Jackie McPerlin, (10.07.1995), 19 Glenview Cottages, Bruaich, Kirklenton, LE29 4QW*

1. On [date] 7th February 2006 a children's hearing for *[local authority]* Lentonshire gave a direction to the Principal Reporter under section *65(7) or 65(9)* of the Children (Scotland) Act 1995 in respect of *[insert name of child]* Jacqueline McPerlin (10.07.1995). ~~The hearing appointed *[insert name and designation]* as a safeguarder~~. No safeguarder was appointed.

2. A copy of the statement by the Principal Reporter of the grounds for referral of the case of the said *[insert name of child]* Jacqueline McPerlin to the children's hearing is attached ~~together with any report of the safeguarder appointed for the purpose of safeguarding the interests of the child in the proceedings.~~

*3. The said *[insert name of child]* or *[insert name and address and status of the relevant person or persons]* Donald McPerlin, 19, Glenview Cottages, Bruaich, Kirklenton, LE29 4QW, Tel: Tel: 012105 800 511, relevant person, as person ordinarily having charge of the said child, and Sharon Transom or McPerlin, 19, Glenview Cottages, Bruaich, Kirklenton, LE29 4QW, Tel: Tel: 012105 800 511, relevant person, as mother of the child Jacqueline, did not accept the ground of referral so far as relating to *[specify conditions /statements not accepted]* the Condition of referral and Statements 5 to 7 inclusive and Statement 9 of the Statement of Facts of the Principal Reporter.

OR

~~*4. The children's hearing were satisfied that the said *[insert name of child]* will not be capable of understanding or has not understood the explanation of the grounds of referral given under section 65(4) of the Act.~~

5. The Principal Reporter therefore makes application to the sheriff to find whether the grounds of referral not accepted by *~~[insert name of child]~~* ~~or~~ *[insert name of relevant person]* Mr Donald McPerlin and Mrs Sharon McPerlin *~~or not understood by said child~~* are established.

~~6. The Principal Reporter requests the sheriff to remove the obligation on the child to attend the hearing in view of [state reason(s)]. And to dispense with service on [insert name and give reasons][222].~~ *

Hector Somerville
HECTOR SOMERVILLE
Authority Reporter
SCRA, 17 Laverock Road,
Kirklenton LE6 7EK,
Tel: 012104 545 700,
Fax: 012104 545 710.
Date: 8th February 2006.

*delete as appropriate

[Place and Date] Kirklenton, 8th February 2006.

The court assigns *[date]* Monday 6th March 2006 at *[hour]* 10 am within *[name court]* Kirklenton Sheriff Court in chambers at *[place]* 1 Laverock Square, Kirklenton LE6 1AA for the hearing of the application; appoints the Principal Reporter forthwith*

a.   to serve a copy of the application and relative statement of grounds of referral and this warrant on,

   i.   the child, together with a notice in form 31 or orders service of the following documents only *[insert details of documents to be served on child, eg, notice in form 31 only]*; and

   ii.   *[insert name of relevant person or persons]* Sharon Transom or McPerlin, and Donald McPerlin, together with a notice in form 39.

   iii.   the ~~safeguarder~~/curator *ad litem [insert name and designation]* Miss Margaret Wilson, solicitor, appointed by the sheriff.*

~~*b.   Orders that the address of [insert name] should not be disclosed in the application.~~

~~*c.   Dispenses with service on the child or any other person for the following reasons [insert details].~~

---

222.   By s 68(5) of the Children (Scotland) Act 1995 the sheriff may, in relation to a number of specified Conditions of Referral, including where, as here, a Schedule 1 offence is involved, and in any case wherein the child's presence would be detrimental to the child's interests, dispense with the attendance of the child. In the instant case the age and manifest maturity of Samantha and Jacqueline render such dispensation inappropriate.

*d.   ~~Dispenses with the obligation on the child to attend the hearing in view of [insert details] and grants warrant to cite witnesses and havers.~~

Anne McGibbon
~~Sheriff or~~ Sheriff Clerk

*delete as appropriate.

Same day, Wednesday, 8 February 2006 at 2 pm –
in the Reporter's office

Service of Application to the Sheriff for the proof hearing

Miss Cameron serves, by First Class Recorded Delivery Post, the papers specified by paragraph (a) of the above on the persons named in the sub-paragraphs of paragraph (a).

Deciding about the attendance of Graeme at hearings

BUSINESS MEETINGS

> *Note [38]   Before the Children (Scotland) Act 1995 preliminary issues such as whether or not the presence of a child at a hearing could be dispensed with[223] were in practice sometimes dealt with at 'preliminary hearings'[224] or 'business meetings'. This proce-dure was non-statutory but received the approval of the Court of Session in Sloan v B, 1991 SLT 530 at 540F.*

> *Section 64 of the Children (Scotland) Act 1995 put business meetings on a statutory basis, providing that such meetings might give the reporter any direction and guidance as to the conduct of the proceedings at the hearing[225], and rule on procedural matters, ie: whether a particular person qualified as a relevant person by reason of ordinarily (apart from owing to employment) having charge of or control over a child and as such had to be notified of a hearing; whether a child was to be excused attendance at a hearing; and whether a particular relevant person's presence was necessary for the proper consideration of the case[226]. Such meetings may be held at any time before a hearing. In practice they should take place over a week before the projected hearing since the decision of the business meeting may affect the persons whom the reporter will require to give notification of the hearing and the notification period for most hearings is seven days*

223. Under the statutory provisions then in force, viz, s 41(2) of the Social Work (Scotland) Act 1968.
224. Cf Kearney, *Children's Hearings and the Sheriff Court*, first edition, page 85 *et seq.*
225. Children's Hearings (Scotland) Rules, 1996, SI 96/3261 r 4(1)(b).
226. Children's Hearings (Scotland) Rules 1996, r 4(2).

minimum[227]. The <u>date</u> *of the business meeting must be notified not later than four working days before its date to: the panel members who are to comprise the meeting, the child or children, the relevant person or persons and any safeguarder. The notification must be accompanied by: (a) notice of the matters to be considered at the meeting; (b) a copy of any documents or information relevant to these matters; and (c) a copy of the Grounds for Referral*[228]. *It informs the parties of their entitlement to make their views known to the reporter who will convey such views to the meeting for consideration by it*[229]. *The reporter must record any views in writing*[230]*and send copies to the panel members and to the others who have received notice of the meeting*[231]. *Where such views are laid before a meeting that meeting must take account of these views before coming to a decision*[232]. *In relation to the panel members the notification must also advise of the time and place of the business meeting but this information is not imparted to the others*[233]. *A business meeting cannot appoint a safeguarder since it is not a full hearing. The only persons present at a business meeting are the hearing members and the reporter.*

Miss Cameron has regard to the terms of s 45 of the Children (Scotland) Act 1995 which provides:

'(1) Where a child has been notified in accordance with rules made under subsection (1) of section 42 of this Act by virtue of subsection (2)(b) of that section that his case has been referred to a children's hearing he shall –

a)   have the right to attend at all stages of the hearing; and

b)   subject to subsection (2) below, be under an obligation to attend those stages in accordance with the notice.

(2) Without prejudice to subsection (1)(a) above, and section 65(4) of this Act, where a children's hearing are satisfied –

a)   in a case concerned with an offence mentioned in Schedule 1 to the Criminal Procedure (Scotland) Act 1995, that the attendance of the child is not necessary for the just hearing of that case; or

b)   in any case, that it would be detrimental to the interests of the child for him to be present at the hearing of his case, they may release the child from the obligation imposed by subsection 1(b) above.'

---

227.   Children's Hearings (Scotland) Rules 1996, rr 6 (1) and 7(4).
228.   Children's Hearings (Scotland) Rules 1996, r 4(3).
229.   Children's Hearings (Scotland) Rules, 1996, r 4(4).
230.   Children's Hearings (Scotland) Rules, 1996, r 4(5).
231.   Children's Hearings (Scotland) Rules, 1996, r 4(6).
232.   Children's Hearings (Scotland) Rules, 1996, r 4(7)
233.   Children's Hearings (Scotland) Rules 1996, r 4(3).

She decides that it could not be detrimental to Graeme to come to this or any subsequent hearing and that while his attendance will not be necessary it would not in all the circumstances be appropriate to hold business meetings formally to release him from his obligations.

PREPARING FOR THE PROOF – THE VULNERABLE WITNESS PROCEDURE

Note [39]   (i) *It is now time for parties to prepare for the proof before the sheriff. The reporter must first of all serve the completed Form 60 (pp 137–139 above) on all parties. The reporter decides that she should take formal precognitions from the girls. She does not delegate this to a precognition-taker[234] but sees the children herself, separately, by arrangement with the foster-carers. It is normal practice for the reporter not to precognosce the persons blamed by a child and the reporter adheres to this practice[235]. The reporter decides to cite the relevant persons – it is not generally appropriate to cite a witness whom one has not precognosced[236], but this is an exception to that rule[237].*

(ii) The reporter, in addition to serving the foregoing on the children, wishes to cite them as witnesses and accordingly the provisions of the Vulnerable Witnesses (Scotland) Act 2004 come into play. Sections 11 to 23 of this Act introduce the concept of providing 'special measures' for 'vulnerable' witnesses. Section 11(1) enacts that a person shall be regarded as 'vulnerable' if

'(a)   *that person is under the age of 16 on the date of the commencement of the proceedings ......, or*

(b)   *where the person is not a child witness, there is a significant risk that the quality of the evidence to be given by the person will be diminished by reason of –*

(i) *mental disorder (within the meaning of section 328 of the Mental Health (Care and Treatment) (Scotland) Act) 2003 (asp 130), or*

(ii) *fear or distress in connection with giving evidence in the proceedings.'*

---

234. Cf Kearney, *Children's Hearings and the Sheriff Court*, second ed, para 30.30. It would be in order to delegate this task to someone who, though not a reporter or solicitor, was trained in interviewing children, but generally, in a case such as this, the reporter prefers to take the precognition herself.
235. See Kearney, *op cit* paragraphs 30.24 to 30.46, for a discussion of the issues surrounding the precognition of witnesses (before the enactment of the Vulnerable Witnesses (Scotland) Act 2004).
236. Or at least this is the professional practice which the writer was brought up to observe – whether it is universally observed nowadays he would not like to say.
237. See Kearney, *op cit*, paragraph 30.26.

(iii) The operative enactment is in section 12 of the Act and its terms are mandatory: 'Where a child witness is to give evidence in or for the purposes of any civil proceedings, the court must, <u>before</u> the proof or other hearing at which the child is to give evidence [my emphases] ...' make the appropriate order[238]. (There would therefore appear to be no scope, within the statutory scheme at least, for a motion for a section 12 order, written or verbal, being lodged at the bar during the course of a hearing.) The Act provides that where a child is to give evidence the court must issue an order authorising the use of special measure(s) <u>or</u> certifying that the child is to give evidence without any special measure[239]. The person citing the vulnerable witness must lodge with the court a 'child witness notice' specifying the special measure desiderated or stating that no special measure is considered necessary[240]. The order may authorise the use of the most appropriate 'special measure or measures'[241] for the purpose of taking the evidence of a child witness.

(iv) The 'special measures' at present enacted are: the taking of evidence by a commissioner; the use of live television link; the use of a screen (coupled with camera facilities to enable the parties to be able to see the witness, although the witness cannot see the parties); and the presence of an individual known as a 'supporter'[242].

(v) The relevant rules now governing the procedures under the Vulnerable Witnesses (Scotland) Act 2004 are contained in the Act of Sederunt (Child Care and Maintenance Rules) (Amendment) (Vulnerable Witnesses (Scotland) Act 2004) 2005, SSI 2005/190. This amends the Act of Sederunt (Child Care and Main-tenance Rules) 1997, SI 1997/291 by adding rules 3.65 to 3.81and Forms 75 to 80. These provide inter alia that the sheriff, on receiving such a notice, may make an order without holding a hearing, or require further information from parties, or fix a hearing which shall be intimated to parties[243]. It is submitted that it is good practice for the sheriff to ask the sheriff clerk to ascertain if any party wishes to be heard and to fix a hearing if any party does so wish. There are elaborate provisions for review of any order under the 2004 Act[244]. (The Act of Sederunt (Child Care and Maintenance Rules) Amendment (Vulnerable Witnesses (Scotland) Act 2004) 2006, SSI 2006/75 which came into force on 1st April 2006, enacts rules in respect of vulnerable witnesses other than children.)

---

238. Vulnerable Witnesses (Scotland) Act 2004, s12(1).
239. Vulnerable Witnesses (Scotland) Act 2004 s 12(1).
240. Vulnerable Witnesses (Scotland) Act 2004 s 12(2).
241. Vulnerable Witnesses (Scotland) Act 2004, s 12(1)(a).
242. Vulnerable Witnesses (Scotland) Act 2004 s 18.
243. Act of Sederunt (Child Care and Maintenance Rules) 1997, SI 1997/291, as amended r 3.69(1).
244. Act of Sederunt (Child Care and Maintenance Rules) 1997, SI 1997/291, as amended r 3.70 to 3.72.

(vi) It should be noted that, in view of section 11(1)(a), quoted above, <u>all</u> persons under the age of 16 are by definition 'vulnerable' and therefore even a mature 12 year old such as Samantha, who has said she does not wish a safeguarder to be appointed must be dealt with under the vulnerable witness procedures. The reporter has discussed the matter with Samantha and Jacqueline. Jacqueline has said she would like a 'supporter', while Samantha has said she would prefer to have no 'special measure'. The reporter accordingly prepares to cite the girls and processes the necessary documents. It is good practice to cite witnesses in good time – if possible three weeks before the proof.

(vii) Where special measures are required the party adducing the witness should make sure that the technical equipment is available at the appropriate place and time.

The reporter cites Samantha and Jacqueline in the usual way and prepares the appropriate Certificates of Execution of Citation[245]. She then prepares two Child Witness Notices – separate Notices are prepared for Samantha and Jacqueline – and takes them to the Sheriff Clerk's office.

The sheriff clerk phones the reporter's office and is told that the solicitor for Mr McPerlin will be objecting to the Notice in respect of Jacqueline and would like a hearing. Here is the form in relation to Jacqueline, after it has been submitted to the sheriff clerk:

Rule 3.67

FORM 75

VULNERABLE WITNESSES (SCOTLAND) ACT 2004
Section 12

Received the *13th day of February 2006*
(Date of receipt of this notice)

(Sgd) *Anne McGibbon*
Sheriff Clerk

CHILD WITNESS NOTICE

Sheriff Court: *Lenton and Muirbrachlan at Kirklenton*   *13th February 2006*
Court Ref. No: 8B 2/06

1.   The applicant, Laura Cameron, Reporter to the Children's Panel of Lentonshire, is a party to an application under section 65(7) of the Children (Scotland) Act 1995.

---

245. Using Forms 41 and 42 in Schedule 1 of the Act of Sederunt (Child Care and Maintenance Rules) 1997, SI 1997/291.

2.   The applicant has cited Jacqueline McPerlin (d.o.b.10.07.95) as a witness to the proof in relation to her Application regarding the said child and her sister Samantha under s 65 of the Children (Scotland) Act 1995 fixed for 6th March 2006 at 10 a.m. within this court.

3.   Jacqueline McPerlin is a child witness under section 11 of the Vulnerable Witnesses (Scotland) Act 2004 and was under the age of sixteen on the date of the commencement of proceedings.

4.   The applicant considers that the following special measures are the most appropriate for the purpose of taking the evidence of Jacqueline McPerlin:– The use of a screen in accordance with section 21 of the Vulnerable Witnesses (Scotland) Act 2004 while Jacqueline McPerlin gives her evidence

5.   The reasons this special measure is considered the most appropriate are as follows:– In the Grounds for Referral it is alleged that Jacqueline's sister Samantha was the victim of an indecent assault by one of the relevant persons, namely her stepfather, Mr Donald McPerlin, who, it is anticipated, will be present during the proof hearing of the application under section 65(7) of the said Act. There is also an averment in the Statement of Facts that Mr Donald McPerlin entered Jacqueline's bedroom while drunk. Jacqueline's mother has not accepted the Grounds for Referral and, that being so, her presence at the proof hearing would not re-assure Jacqueline. Her biological father, Rorie McLansing, no longer lives in the district and has had no contact with Jacqueline for many years.

6.   Jacqueline McPerlin has expressed the view that, while not afraid to 'confront' her stepfather while giving evidence, she would feel uncomfortable in giving evidence without the 'special measure', in the form of a screen. The curator *ad litem*, Miss Margaret Wilson, solicitor, has discussed this with the applicant, and she, Miss Wilson, agrees that this 'special measure' would be appropriate.

7.   Other information considered relevant to this application is as follows:– None.

8.   The applicant asks the court:

     a)   to consider this child witness notice;

     b)   to make an order authorising the special measure sought.

Laura Cameron
LAURA CAMERON
Children's Reporter
SCRA, 17 Laverock Road,
Kirklenton LE6 7EK,
Tel: 012104 545 700,
Fax: 012104 545 710.
Date: 13th February 2006.

NOTE: This form should be suitably adapted where section 16 of the Act of 2004[246] applies.

The text of the Child Witness Notice for Samantha is in these terms:–

1.   The applicant, Laura Cameron, Reporter to the Children's Panel of Lentonshire, is a party to an application under section 65(7) of the Children (Scotland) Act 1995.

2.   The applicant has cited Samantha McPerlin (d.o.b.15.08.93)) as a witness to the proof of her Application in relation to her Application regarding the said child and her sister Jacqueline under s 65 of the Children (Scotland) Act 1995 fixed for 6th March 2006 at 10 a.m. within this court

3.   Samantha McPerlin was under the age of sixteen on the date of the commencement of proceedings and is consequently a child witness under section 11 of the Vulnerable Witnesses (Scotland) Act 2004.

4.   Samantha McPerlin, is now aged some 12 years and 6 months. She it was who effectively initiated this referral by reporting matters to the Applicant and has throughout the procedures of this case impressed the Social Work Services Department as being mature and sensible. She has expressed the wish that no safeguarder need be appointed. She has told the Applicant that she does not wish any 'special measure' taken in relation to her giving evidence before the sheriff.

5.   The Applicant accordingly considers that no special measure need be taken in relation to the child Samantha McPerlin. Miss Margaret Wilson, the curator *ad litem* appointed by the court, is of the same view.

6.   Other information considered relevant to this application is as follows:– None.

7.   The applicant asks the court:

     a)   to consider this child witness notice;

     b)   to make an order in terms of s 12(1)(b) of the Vulnerable Witnesses (Scotland) Act 2004 certifying that the child Samantha McPerlin is to give evidence without the benefit of any special measure.

---

246.   This section substantially provides that where the child who is a party to the proceedings is to give evidence that child is to be regarded as a 'witness' and therefore subject to the provisions of the Vulnerable Witnesses (Scotland) Act 2004.

Monday, 13 February 2006 at 2.30 pm – In the Sheriff Clerk's office

The reporter lodges both notices with the sheriff clerk who books them and takes them to one of the sheriffs for signature. Sheriff Grey is not available. Sheriff Thomson asks the sheriff clerk to phone parties' agents and the curator *ad litem* to find if a hearing is sought. Mr Paterson, after consulting his client by phone, states that no hearing is required in respect of either application, and that his client is consenting to both. Mrs MacDonald, after advising her client and obtaining his instructions, indicates that she is instructed to ask for a hearing in relation to the Application for Jacqueline (who alone wishes special measures). The following interlocutor is granted in respect of the Notice for Jacqueline:

Children: Samantha and Jacqueline McPerlin   8B 2/06

Witness: Jacqueline McPerlin

Kirklenton 13th February 2006

Before: Sheriff Ralph Thomson

The sheriff, having considered the foregoing application fixes 17th February 2006 at 9.45 am within the Sheriff Court, 1 Laverock Square, Kirklenton LE6 1AA, as a hearing on the application, and APPOINTS the sheriff clerk to intimate said diet to parties forthwith.

Ralph Thomson
Sheriff

In relation to the Application for Samantha, the sheriff decides that it is unnecessary to hold a hearing, and, using his powers under r 3.69(1)(a) of the Act of Sederunt (Child Care and Maintenance Rules) 1997, SI 1997/291, as now amended, pronounces the following:

The sheriff, having considered the foregoing application GRANTS same and, in terms of s 12(1)(b) of the Vulnerable Witnesses (Scotland) Act 2004, ORDERS that the child Samantha McPerlin is to give evidence at the proof on 6th March 2006 or any adjournment therefor without the benefit of any special measure under said Act. APPOINTS the sheriff clerk to intimate this interlocutor to parties forthwith.

Ralph Thomson
Sheriff

The reporter has waited in the sheriff clerk's office and is able to collect copies of the interlocutors. The sheriff clerk intimates the interlocutors to the other parties and attaches to the principal Applications a certificate in these terms:–

Kirklenton 13th February 2006. I hereby certify the foregoing application and interlocutor was this day duly notified by me by first class recorded delivery post to: Mhairi MacDonald, solicitor, 34 Nelson Street, Kirklenton, LE6 9WS, David Paterson, solicitor, 33 Wallace Street, Kirklenton LE17 9EZ, Miss Margaret Wilson, solicitor, 42 Nelson Street, Kirklenton LE10 WS; and was collected by the Reporter to the Children's Panel.

Anne McGibbon
Sheriff Clerk

[The relative recorded delivery slips are affixed.]

INITIAL HEARING IN THE CASE OF GRAEME McPERLIN

Monday, 13 February 2006 at 4.00 pm – In the Hearings room in the Reporter's premises

At the initial hearing to consider the case of Graeme, there are present: the reporter, Mrs McPerlin, and Miss Drummond. The hearing considers the report by Miss Drummond, are satisfied that the child will not be capable of understanding the Grounds for Referral because of his age and directs the reporter to make an Application to the sheriff for a finding as to whether the grounds are established[247]. The hearing also decides that a Warrant is not necessary and that a safeguarder is not to be appointed.

The reporter later prepares a Form 60, founding on section 65(9) of the Act, obtains a warrant from the Sheriff Clerk, giving the same date for the proof before the sheriff as that which was fixed for Samantha and Jacqueline, and serves same on all appropriate parties.

THE HEARING BEFORE THE SHERIFF IN RELATION TO THE VULNERABLE WITNESS APPLICATION ON BEHALF OF JACQUELINE

Friday, 17 February 2006 at 9.45 am – in Kirklenton Sheriff Court

The reporter, Mrs MacDonald[248] and Miss Wilson (without relevant persons or the girls) appear before Sheriff Grey in chambers. No evidence is led[249]. Sheriff Grey indicates that she thinks it appropriate for her to deal with the application because of her knowledge of the background. The parties concur in this.

---

247. Children (Scotland) Act 1995 s 65(9).
248. Mr Paterson, since his client does not oppose the motion, does not appear.
249. Although it is thought, having regard to the nature of the various relevant considerations set out in s 11(2) of the Act, that the leading of evidence would be competent.

Mrs MacDonald submits that no independent or professional evidence, psychological or otherwise, has been led to support the proposition that there is a significant risk that the quality of the child's evidence will be diminished in the absence of the special measure proposed. She draws attention to the consideration that the Application makes no mention of Mr McPerlin who, as a parent, is entitled to have his views taken into account[250]. She argues that Jacqueline, being under the age of twelve, enjoys no presumption in favour of being of sufficient age and maturity to form a view[251]. She submits that there has been no independent evidence produced to support the proposition that 'there is a significant risk that the quality of evidence to be given will be diminished by reason of … … fear or distress in connection with the proceedings and that therefore the answer "none" to the question asking for further information is fatal to the Application.

The reporter submits that the provision[252] enjoining the taking account of the views of the parent must be regarded as less persuasive when the parents are the blamed persons and reminds the sheriff of the provision[253] that where the views expressed by the witness are inconsistent with any views expressed by the parent, then the views of the witness are to be given 'greater weight'. She accepts that there has been no expert evidence but contends that this is unnecessary in a field where common-sense and common knowledge tells us that a child would be embarrassed in such a situation and that therefore the quality of her evidence would be impaired.

Miss Wilson concurs with the reporter and says that in her view the granting of the application is in the interests of Jacqueline.

The sheriff observes that the point about the parent's views would have been stronger if objection had been made by the parent, Mrs McPerlin. In giving her decision she says she thinks it is inappropriate to go into detail at this stage, but she rejects the argument that it is necessary in all the circumstances, particularly when all that is being asked for is 'screens', for expert evidence to be led. She says that she considers that she is able to assess the position in the light of the undisputed facts, namely that a 10½ year old is being asked to give sensitive evidence against her step-parent, and concludes by stating that on balance she thinks the application in relation to Jacqueline should be granted. Sheriff Grey indicates that the proof will be heard by Sheriff Ralph Thomson.

> *Note [40]   Which sheriff should deal with what? In principle there is no impropriety in the same sheriff dealing with all stages of a case such as this – indeed in the smaller courts this is routine. However, where a sheriff has dealt with the CPO and the Motion to Recall or Vary that sheriff may feel that the parties ought to have a fresh mind brought to bear on the matter and that, where, as here, it is practicable to do so, then another sheriff may hear the full proof.*

---

250. Vulnerable Witnesses (Scotland) Act 2004 s 15(2)(b)(ii).
251. Vulnerable Witnesses (Scotland) Act 2004 s 15(3)(a).
252. Vulnerable Witnesses (Scotland) Act 2004 s 15(2)(b)(ii).
253. Vulnerable Witnesses (Scotland) Act 2004 s 15(3)(b).

APPLICATION TO A HEARING TO EXTEND THE WARRANT

The warrant granted at the 8 WD hearing on 7th February 2006 is due to expire on 28th February 2006. Since it will not be possible for the case to be determined by a hearing for some weeks, the reporter is under the necessity of applying for an extension of the warrant. A hearing's powers to extend are governed by section 66 of the Children (Scotland) Act 1995. This provides that a warrant granted by a hearing may be extended for a period nor exceeding 22 days[254] and that a child shall not be kept in a place of safety for a period exceeding 66 days 'from the day when he was first taken to a place of safety under a warrant granted under subsection (1) [of section 66].'[255] Although the girls were taken to the Place of Safety, in the form of the Jamiesons' house, on 26th January 2006, this was by virtue of the Child Protection Order granted by the sheriff. This order was continued at the Second Working Day Hearing on 30th January 2006 and it was only at the Eighth Working Day Hearing on 7th February 2006 that the hearing itself granted warrant. Accordingly hearings have power to detain the girls for a period not exceeding 66 days in all from the Eighth Working Day hearing, that is, in this case, (counting that hearing's date, 7th February 2006, as 'day one') until 13th April 2006.

The reporter arranges for a hearing on Tuesday 28th February 2006 and intimates this to parties. The reporter recognises that if the sheriff sustains the Grounds of Referral at the proof on 6th March 2006, a hearing can be fixed for on or about Monday 20th March 2006. She nevertheless, in case the extra day should be needed, applies for the full 22 day extension which is competent under the Act, namely until 21st March 2006.

Mrs MacDonald and Mr Paterson advise their clients that they should not oppose the application for an extension since the proof is only five days away and if they 'win' at the proof on 6th March then the warrant will fall and if they 'lose' at the proof then, even if the warrant had been recalled now, it would almost certainly be granted anew by a subsequent hearing. The McPerlins accept this advice. Mrs MacDonald and Mr Paterson write to the reporter stating that they have no objection to the warrant being extended by the hearing and stating that their clients will be attending the hearing. The reporter notifies the children. A hearing takes place and grants the extension till 21st March 2006.

THE SECTION 68 PROOF BEFORE THE SHERIFF[256]

Monday, 6 March 2006 at 10 am – In Kirklenton Sheriff Court

One of the small courts is deemed to be the sheriff's chambers. In theory all the parties, ie the relevant persons and the girls, have the right, as

---

254. Children (Scotland) Act 1995 s 66(5).
255. Children (Scotland) Act 1995 s 66(8).
256. A more detailed description of the course of a proof is contained in Part Two of this book.

parties, to be present throughout the proof proceedings. However, as the girls are plainly going to be witnesses 'against' the relevant persons the principle that a witness should not generally sit through the evidence of another witness has to be regarded and it has been agreed by the reporter, Mrs MacDonald, Mr Paterson and the curator *ad litem* that evidence of Jacqueline should come first, with Samantha absent, and that Samantha's evidence shall follow. The relevant persons, as parties, are entitled to hear the whole proceedings, even although that will mean that one will hear the evidence of the other. This is strictly illogical, but the law bends over backwards to be fair to persons who are accused.

Graeme, aged 1 year and 8 months, has had his attendance excused by the sheriff when the diet of proof was fixed[257]. The three cases were also formally 'conjoined' at that diet.

The reporter, Mrs MacDonald and Mr Paterson, with their clients Mr and Mrs McPerlin, and Miss Wilson, assemble in the small court. A police officer is present, as is usual at any substantive hearing at which persons other than professional representatives are present[258]. The sheriff clerk depute, Miss McGibbon is at the table with the Grounds for Referral and the other parts of the process[259]. The Sheriff's bar officer enters and, having checked that all is in order, goes into the side-room where the sheriff is waiting and brings the sheriff into the room and says 'Court. All stand, please'. Sheriff Thomson comes in and all stand. The solicitors, the reporter, the curator *ad litem* and the sheriff clerk bow formal to the sheriff, who bows to them. The parties' representatives formally introduce themselves and say whom they are representing. The sheriff acknowledges the presence of Mr and Mrs McPerlin and says 'Good Morning' to them. He says that he has read the Grounds for Referral. He refers to that part of the Applications which state that Mr and Mrs McPerlin are not accepting the substantial Grounds and asks their agents if this is still the position[260]. Mrs MacDonald and Mr Paterson reply in the affirmative. The sheriff then invites the reporter to start.

The reporter adduces Jacqueline as her first witness. Screens are in position but the sheriff makes no comment on this aspect. Jacqueline gives her

---

257. Children (Scotland) Act 1995 s 68(5)(a); Act of Sederunt (Child Care and Maintenance Rules) 1997, SI 1997/291, Form 33.
258. It is a universal practice, and considered by the Scottish judiciary to be a necessary one, that there should be police presence in all criminal courts. Cases arising out of Children's Hearing are of course, in the words of Lord President Emslie in *McGregor v D*, 1977 SLT 182 at 185, 'civil proceedings *sui generis*', but sheriffs generally insist on a police presence in substantive diets because of the sensitive nature of the subject matter.
259. 'Process' is the term for the whole material in a civil case, including all the documentation and all 'productions', ie items, documentary or otherwise which have been lodged in process so that they may be referred to by witnesses.
260. This is not a statutory requirement, but it is good practice – if it should turn out that Grounds are now accepted the sheriff may dispense with hearing evidence and hold the grounds to be established (Children (Scotland) Act 1995 s 68(8). For discussion see *Kearney, op cit* paragraph 36.09, and *Norrie, op cit*, p 101.

evidence, and then Samantha (in Samantha's case without the screens). Being under the age of 14 they are simply 'admonished' by the sheriff to tell the truth. The sheriff does this by saying to each girl: 'The reporter and others will be asking you some questions. I have to tell you that you must say exactly what happened – no fibs, no imaginings, just answer all the questions truthfully – Miss Cameron, what is your first question?'

> *Note [41]   The former requirement on the sheriff to 'examine'*
> *child witnesses and decide whether they knew the difference*
> *between truth and falsehood and understood the necessity of*
> *telling the truth*[261] *has been abolished by section 24(2) of the*
> *Vulnerable Witnesses (Scotland) Act 2004 which is in these*
> *peremptory terms: 'Accordingly, the court must not, <u>at any time</u>*
> *<u>before the witness gives evidence</u> [my underlining], take any step*
> *intended to establish whether the witness understands these*
> *matters'. It follows that the sheriff must be careful to avoid ending*
> *his 'admonition' of the witness by any such expression as 'Do you*
> *understand?' (which, it must be said, it is almost second nature for*
> *a judge to say in such circumstances). Hence the sheriff here does*
> *not allow the child any opportunity to open up a dialogue as to*
> *the meaning of the 'admonition'. It is thought, having regard to*
> *the words 'at any time before the witness gives evidence' would*
> *leave it open to any of the pleaders to address questions to the*
> *witness as to his or her knowledge of the difference between*
> *falsehood and the necessity of telling the truth and that in this*
> *event the sheriff would be entitled to use his or her usual powers*
> *to ask questions 'provided this is done with caution'*[262].

Samantha and Jacqueline substantially confirm what they have said already. The reporter is of course the first questioner: she 'examines in chief'. The curator *ad litem* comes first to cross-examine. Mr Paterson cross-examines next and Mrs MacDonald, as the substantial contradictor, questions last[263]. The reporter re-examines in order to pick up and clarify any matters which have arisen during cross-examination.

> *Note [42]   Mr and Mrs McPerlin could have been called as*
> *witnesses by the reporter, but it would be unusual for a reporter*
> *to call them in a case like this.*

Mr and Mrs McPerlin give evidence by answering questions put to them by their respective solicitors and are cross-examined and re-examined. The sheriff warns them that they do not require to answer any question if they thought the answer would tend to suggest that they were guilty of any

---

261. Discussed in *Kearney, op cit*, at 37.06
262. Cf *Thomson v Glasgow Corporation* 1962 SC(HL) 36 per Lord Justice-Clerk Thomson at 51, 52
263. The order of questioning is within the discretion of the presiding sheriff. Practices vary, and the same sheriff may adapt his or her practice to the circumstances of the case. It is submitted that the practice adopted here is appropriate in the circumstances.

crime[264]. Mr McPerlin denies all the allegations. Mrs McPerlin gives evidence tending to support her husband. The reporter, Mr Paterson and Mrs MacDonald and the curator *ad litem* address the sheriff, who states that he will give his decision after the lunch break.

Monday, 6 March 2006 at 2 pm – In Kirklenton Sheriff Court

> *Note [43]   The rules provide that the sheriff shall give his decision orally at the end of the proof and <u>may</u>, on so doing or within seven days thereafter, issue a note giving reasons for his decision[265]. The issues in this proof, while weighty from the point of view of the parties, are uncomplicated for an experienced sheriff and Sheriff Thomson here, rather than adopting the common enough procedure of using his power to adjourn the proof[266] to give himself more time to write a considered judgement on the day which will constitute the end of the proof, decides that he need not delay matters and will be able to write out a considered decision in the hour and a half of the lunch interval.*

Same day, Monday, 6 March 2006 at 2 pm – in Kirklenton Sheriff Court

Parties assemble in the same small court as before. The sheriff comes in and reads his written judgement. In this he summarises briefly the evidence and the submissions which have been made to him. He discusses the arguments in the light of the evidence and states that the pivotal issue is the credibility and reliability of the witnesses. He says he prefers the evidence of Jacqueline and Samantha to that of Mr and Mrs McPerlin and gives his reasons for this. He concludes:

Sheriff Thomson: '... I have therefore decided that the averments in the Statements of Facts are true and that they support the Condition of Referral. I accordingly find that the grounds for the referral to which this application relates have been established and I accordingly remit the cases of Samantha, Jacqueline and Graeme to the reporter to make arrangements for a children's hearing to consider and determine their cases.'

Miss Cameron/Mrs MacDonald/Mr Paterson/Miss Wilson: Much obliged M'Lord.

Sheriff Thomson [addressing himself to the girls and Mr and Mrs McPerlin]: As I am sure your advisers will have told you, it is now for a children's hearing, and not for me, to decide what is to happen. You

---

264. For discussion of this see Kearney, *op cit*, paragraph 37.12.
265. Act of Sederunt (Child Care and Maintenance Rules) 1997, SI 1997/291 r 3.51(1) and (3).
266. Act of Sederunt (Child Care and Maintenance Rules) 1997, SI 1997/291 r 3.49.

should go to the hearing and say to it what you want to say and it will decide what it thinks is in the best interests of Samantha, Jacqueline and Graeme. Madam Reporter you will be sending out notification of the date and place for the hearing?

Miss Cameron: Yes, indeed, very soon M'Lord.

Sheriff Thomson: Thank you. The sheriff clerk will distribute copies of my decision presently. Thank you all for your help. That concludes today's proceedings.

PREPARATIONS FOR THE DISPOSITIVE HEARING

On the granting of the CPOs on 26th January 2006 Samantha and Jacqueline became children 'looked after' by the local authority in terms of section 17(6) of the Children (Scotland) Act 1995. On this happening the local authority attracted to itself the obligations under s 17(1) of that Act. The reader is referred to this for its full terms, but substantially they amount to safeguarding and promoting the interests of such children by making use of such services as seem reasonable and promoting so far as appropriate contact with parents and those with parental responsibilities. The local authority also has the duty to 'make a care plan to address the immediate and longer-term needs of the child with a view to safeguarding and promotion of his welfare'[267].

While the foregoing proceedings have been going on the Social Work Department has been making further inquiries and drafting such a plan. Now that a dispositive hearing before panel members is in prospect it becomes important to crystallise this in a report and, in modern practice, a 'Full Assessment and Care Plan' is prepared and it will be amongst the papers submitted to and considered by the hearing. Local Authorities have devised elaborate forms designed to try to ensure that all material matters are covered. In Lentonshire, following the practice of Glasgow City Council, there is a section headed 'Assessment & Evaluation of Risk' which tries to sum up the Department's view of what will be in the bests interests of the child or children concerned. In the case of Samantha and Jacqueline this section includes:

> The birth of Samantha (15.08.93) was difficult, with mother suffering considerable loss of blood. Samantha attended Kirklenton Primary School and is at present in Secondary 2 of Kirklenton High. Her performance is academically high and she aims to become a social worker. In 2004 she had a prolonged absence from school in the summer term of that year. It emerged that Samantha had stayed away from school to 'run' the household while her mother was in hospital for the period leading up to the birth of Graeme

---

267. The Arrangements to Look after Children (Scotland) Regulations, SI 1996/3262 reg 3(1).

(02.06.2004). This was referred to the reporter and marked 'No further formal proceedings' (as recommended by the Depart-ment), because Samantha had returned to school and was doing well.

On 17.01.2006 Samantha disclosed to the writer that step-father Donald McPerlin had been abusing her sexually during the time when the mother was away from the home during the above period. This did not, according to Samantha, go beyond fondling under her night-clothes and she was able to resist anything further. Mum is pregnant again with the new baby expected in June of this year. Samantha is afraid that when her mother is absent Donald McPerlin will molest Jacqueline, who is now about the same age as she, Samantha, was on the earlier occasion and reckons that he would go much further with Jacqueline. Jacqueline says that on Hogmanay of last year – some two months ago – Donald McPerlin entered her bedroom when very drunk and collapsed on the floor in a drunken condition.

Child Protection Orders were applied for in respect of all three children and on 26th January 2006. CPOs were granted in respect of Samantha and Jacqueline but refused in respect of Graeme. The girls were placed with foster parents and Graeme remained in the family home. Grounds for referral of both girls were stated by the reporter based on the Schedule 1 offence of lewd and libidinous practices alleged to have been committed against Samantha. Similar Grounds were stated in respect of Graeme. These were denied by step-father and mother but sustained by the sheriff on 6th March 2006.

The writer, having spoken at length with both girls and discussed the case with other professionals, considers that Samantha's fears are well-founded and that the potential abuse of Jacqueline by Donald McPerlin might go as far as penetration. Even if it did not any sexual abuse would have a devastating effect on Jacqueline – far more so than was the case with Samantha, who is very mature.

The writer has also spoken with the mother of the girls, Mrs Sharon McPerlin. She refuses, even after the findings of the sheriff, to accept that her husband molested Samantha in any way or that there will be any danger to either girl in the event of her requiring to be away from the family home for any period of time as a result of her present pregnancy. The writer put to Mrs McPerlin information, obtained from the health visitor and the police, that about eighteen months ago Donald McPerlin was convicted of drunk driving and heavily fined and disqualified. At first Mrs McPerlin seemed to want to deny that this had happened but when pressed she said she meant that there had been a conviction but that Mr McPerlin had been wrongly convicted because of false police evidence. It appears that Samantha and Jacqueline were in the car at the time. The writer is concerned that the mother should so consistently side with her husband.

A risk assessment tool, Level of Services Inventory – Revised (LSI-R), which is a validated risk assessment device, was employed and this indicates that Donald McPerlin poses a medium to high risk of re-offending, and that consequently the girls would be exposed to that degree of risk if left to live in family with him. The Department has commissioned a full risk assessment from Dr Alexander Jardine-Smith MB ChB PhD FRCPsych of the Muirbrachlan Royal Hospital and expect this will be available in under three months' time.

Samantha and Jacqueline have now been accommodated by foster parents since 26th January 2006 and they are happy and well-cared for with them. The mother is allowed unlimited non-residential contact with the girls and this has been exercised frequently and with apparent success on both sides. Mr McPerlin is entitled to supervised contact with the girls for two hours per week within the Department's premises and this has been exercised successfully. Mr McPerlin has said that he would be willing to stay overnight with his brother during the week but not at week-ends, and suggested that the girls might therefore be able to stay at home throughout the week, but the department does not consider this to be a practical solution on any long-term basis, particularly as the mother may have to spend time in hospital on account of her pregnancy.

The Department has carried out the procedures required by regulation 15 of the Fostering of Children (Scotland) Regulations 1996 in relation to the possible placement of Samantha and Jacqueline with the present foster parents and are satisfied that all the conditions of regulation 12(1) and (2) of these Regulations are in place. The department therefore recommends that a supervision requirement be made in respect of Samantha and Jacqueline with a condition of residence with the present foster-parents, who are willing and able to continue to accommodate them. The present contact arrangements should continue.

Note [44]   The foregoing information is supplied having regard to the requirement that a hearing may not make a supervision requirement requiring a child to reside other than at home without having information that the needs of the child will be met in the proposed accommodation[268].

The department also recommends that a review hearing should be fixed four months from now, at which Dr Jardine-Smith's report and the department's long-term plans in the light of Dr Jardine-Smith's report may be considered.

In relation to the male child Graeme, now aged 1 year and 9 months, the department considers that the risk to him is not so great as to outweigh the upset which would be caused to him if he were removed from the family home at this time. The department thinks that a 'Home Supervision Requirement' be made for Graeme and

---

268. Children's Hearings (Scotland) Rules, 1996, SI 96/3261, r 20(6).

that his position be reviewed once Dr Jardine-Smith's report becomes available.

The section in this document headed 'Child(ren)/Young Person's Views (including attitude to grounds of referral if relevant)' contains the following:

> Both Samantha and Jacqueline wish to stay with the present foster-parents, at least until the new baby is born and Mrs McPerlin returns with him or her to the family home, when they would like to have the chance of re-considering their position.

Tuesday, 7 March 2006

The reporter receives from the department the 'Assessment & Evaluation of Risk'. The reporter arranges a hearing for Tuesday 21 March 2006 at 2.30 p.m. within 17 Laverock Road, Kirklenton LE6 7EK.

On the same day the reporter notifies all the parties of this[269] by first class recorded delivery post and sends to parties a document setting out the 'Grounds for Referral as Established by the Sheriff' and a copy of the said 'Assessment & Evaluation of Risk'. The notification to the girls and relevant persons tells them that they must attend the hearing.

THE DISPOSITIVE HEARING ON 21 MARCH 2006

Tuesday, 21 March 2006 at 2.30 pm – in the Hearings suite in the Reporter's premises in Kirklenton

The hearing members are Mrs Muriel Maxwell, Mr Robert Shaw and Miss Amanda McCracken[270]. All are experienced panel members. The hearing members have decided that Mrs Maxwell should take the chair. The children are still not worried about being confronted by Mr and Mrs McPerlin, so the hearing does not require to be 'split'. Those appearing are: Samantha and Jacqueline; Miss Wilson, as a person assisting the girls; Mr McPerlin; Mrs Mhairi MacDonald, as his solicitor; Mrs McPerlin; Mr Paterson, as her solicitor; Mrs Jamieson, one of the foster-parents[271], Miss Laura Cameron, as reporter; and social worker Miss Marcia Drummond[272].

---

269. Well complying with the minimum seven days prescribed by Children's Hearings (Scotland) Rules 1996 r 7(4).
270. It has not been practicable to obtain the services of any of the previous panel members.
271. Foster carers by virtue of a supervision requirement are now to be treated as relevant persons – *S v N* 2002 SLT 589, 2002 Fam LR 40, Ex Div, sub nom *JS and TK v MN* 2002 GWD 9-275 – but the Jamiesons are not, at this time, in that category and would, accordingly, not be entitled to attend as a matter of right, but, as the chair of the hearing indicates, she has decided that the presence of Mrs Jamieson 'would be justified by special circumstances' – see Children's Hearings (Scotland) Rules, 1996, SI 96/3261, r 13. It is not uncommon, for obvious reasons, for only one of the foster carers to come.
272. Ten people! – It is not uncommon to have quite a large number of persons present at a hearing.

Mrs Maxwell: I am Mrs Muriel Maxwell. This is Mr Robert Shaw. This is Miss Amanda McCracken.

Mr Shaw/Miss McCracken: Hello.

Those appearing: Good afternoon/Hello etc.

[Mrs Maxwell then quickly 'goes round' those present making sure, so far as is necessary, that everybody knows who is who. In particular Samantha and Jacqueline are identified as the children concerned in this hearing.]

Mrs Maxwell: This is a hearing to consider the cases of Samantha McPerlin, born 15th August 1993, Jacqueline McPerlin, born 10th July 1995 and Graeme McPerlin, born 2nd June 2004. I think both Samantha and Jacqueline and Mr and Mrs McPerlin will already have been told of the purpose of this hearing by, in the case of the McPerlins, their solicitors and in the case of the girls, by Miss Wilson, the curator *ad litem* who was appointed by the sheriff and whom Samantha and Jacqueline have indicated they would like to be present to assist them today, but the law provides that I myself must explain the purpose of this hearing[273] and I, like everyone else in this room, must obey the law! The first thing I'd better do is an important formality. As I have mentioned, Miss Wilson was appointed by the sheriff as curator *ad litem* for the girls and appears with them this afternoon in order to assist them[274]. In the circumstances do you think we should appoint a safeguarder for all the children – Samantha, Jacqueline and Graeme? I should explain that if a safeguarder is appointed, whether it be Miss Wilson or someone else, then the safeguarder would require to prepare a written report[275], which would mean that this hearing will have to be continued for that report to be considered at the continued hearing. Samantha and Jacqueline, what do you think?

Samantha: We have discussed this with Miss Wilson and are happy that she just 'helps' us today.

Miss Wilson: I am certainly happy to carry on without being appointed as safeguarder.

Mr Shaw: That means that we only have to think about Graeme. I must say I can't see what a safeguarder would add at this stage. I think we should press on.

Mrs Maxwell: [To Mr and Mrs McPerlin] What do you both think?

Mr McPerlin: I'd prefer to get this over today.

Mrs McPerlin: So would I.

---

273. Children's Hearings (Scotland) Rules, 1996, SI 96/3261 r 20(2).
274. Children's Hearings (Scotland) Rules, 1996, SI 96/3261 r 11(1).
275. Children's Hearings (Scotland) Rules, 1996, SI 96/3261 r 14(1).

Mrs Maxwell: Very well. [To Miss McCracken] What do you think?

Miss McCracken: I think we should proceed now. Graeme could not express a view and the social worker can tell us about Graeme's home set-up if necessary.

Miss Drummond: Yes, I am well aware of that.

Mrs Maxwell: Fine. I shall take it that the decision has been made not to appoint a safeguarder at present. If things look differently at the end of this hearing we can think about this again. I shall now explain briefly the purpose of this hearing. As you know the sheriff has decided that the Grounds of Referral exist. We must then take that as a 'given' background. You have all got a copy of the 'Grounds for Referral as Established by the Sheriff'. I know that Mr and Mrs McPerlin may not agree with this but we in the hearing today must accept the sheriff's ruling. Now the whole idea of a hearing such as this is to let everyone who has anything they want to say to have the chance to say it. I will therefore ask you all first of all if you understand the position. First of all, Samantha and Jacqueline?

Samantha: Yes Jackie and I understand this. [Jacqueline, over-awed, nods her head.]

Mrs Maxwell: OK. Mr and Mrs McPerlin?

Mr McPerlin: Well, since you have said that we can have our say I want to say that our 'say' is that we think the sheriff's decision was a disaster. How can one child's evidence count against two decent adults? I know the law and there must be two witnesses to a crime. I wanted to appeal but Mrs MacDonald says there is no prospect of a successful appeal. I'd like to take this to the Human Rights Court. Can't I do that now?

Mrs Maxwell: I am sure Mrs MacDonald and Mr Paterson will have advised you that there was a legal possibility of an appeal against the sheriff's decision and as to the chances of success of such an appeal. I cannot give you legal advice, but I suspect your lawyers will also have advised you as to whether you can go to the European Court.

Mrs MacDonald/Mr Paterson: Yes.

Mr McPerlin: I know, but I just wanted to make our view clear for the record.

Mrs Maxwell: Very well; as I have said, we cannot interfere with the sheriff's decision about the facts. What we have to decide this afternoon is what, if anything, requires to be done in the long-term best interests of the children. I should emphasise at the outset that our overriding concern is the interests of Samantha, Jacqueline and Graeme as opposed to anyone else's. We have to consider the documentation provided. In particular we have all seen the Grounds for Referral as established, to which I have already referred, and I repeat that we today must treat that as 'given'. We also have the document, prepared by Social Work, headed 'Assessment & Evaluation of Risk'. This says in substance that the girls would be at 'medium to high' risk if left to live in family with Mr McPerlin, that the girls do not want to live in family with him, and that they are happy with the foster-parents. The report also tells us that the Department are obtaining a full risk assessment by a psychiatrist which should be available in about three months time. As to Graeme, the department thinks there is no significant risk at present and that what is known as a 'Home Supervision Requirement' should be put in place pending the receipt of the full Risk assessment. We have to give the girls a chance to give their own ideas. We are of course not obliged to follow their wishes, but we must listen to them and have regard to what they say, taking into account their age and degree of maturity as we see it. We must also only order what in our opinion is necessary to advance their welfare and not do anything that we are not convinced would do some real good[276]. Now, can we get the discussion going? Samantha, what would you like to happen?

Mrs McPerlin: I'm their mother, isn't it the law that it's the parent who has rights and responsibilities?

Mrs Maxwell: Yes, but as your lawyer will I am sure have told you in these proceedings we have to give children the chance to give their views direct. You will have your chance in a moment. Samantha?

Samantha: [Giggles nervously] Well ...

[Jacqueline begins to sob.]

Mrs Maxwell: I think you had both indicated that it was all right to have your mother and Mr McPerlin present all through the hearing. Do you want to change your mind? As I think you know I can ask them to leave while you are speaking, though I'd have to tell them what you said[277].

Samantha [composing herself.]: No, we'll just carry on. Are you all right Jackie?

[Jacqueline nods.]

Samantha: We're both fond of Mum and Mr McPerlin but I just don't think I should feel it was safe for Jackie to be in the house with Donald as the only adult.

Mrs Maxwell: What about after the new baby arrived?

Samantha: I can't think that far ahead. It might be all right. I just don't know.

---

276. The chairman explains in ordinary language the relevant provisions of s 16 of the Children (Scotland) Act 1995 which govern the hearing's powers.
277. Children (Scotland) Act 1995 s 46.

Mrs Maxwell: Jackie?

Jacqueline: Yes, that's right.

Mr Shaw: What if Mr McPerlin were to stay with his brother, your Uncle Calum?

Samantha: That just wouldn't work, what would happen when Mum went to hospital?

Mr Shaw: Thank you.

Mrs Maxwell: Mrs McPerlin, Mr McPerlin?

Mrs McPerlin: I think we are at cross-purposes, because we don't for a minute accept what's being said. If what is being said were true, then I think we'd agree to them being away, but the point is we don't and it's not fair to ask us on the basis that it is true.

Mr McPerlin: Exactly.

Mrs Maxwell: Miss Drummond, we have of course got here the department's recommendation that the girls remain with the foster-parents meantime and that we fix a review, as of course we have the power to[278]. Would there be any advantage in making a home supervision requirement for the present, provided that Mr McPerlin was not there and that when the mother has to go to hospital the girls will be transferred to the Jamiesons?

Miss Drummond: Subject to any comment the reporter might have as to the legal possibility of such a disposal I would still be in favour of the department's proposal. I think our proposals would provide more protection for the girls and in any case they are clear about what they want. I don't believe they would adopt that position without good reason.

Miss Cameron: I think it <u>might</u> be possible to frame a supervision requirement along the lines suggested; I should like to think about it[279].

Mr Shaw: I must say I think there are attractions in this line of thought.

Mrs Maxwell [looking towards the other hearing member, Miss McCracken]: Any thoughts?

Miss McCracken: No, I think that looks clever but I doubt if it would work out well. Anyway Samantha and Jackie don't want that.

---

278. Children (Scotland) Act 1995 s 70(7).
279. Section 70(3) of the Children (Scotland) Act 1995 provides that a supervision requirement may require the child to reside at a specified place and to comply with any condition. A supervision requirement cannot place conditions on an adult – hence the reporter's hesitation. However in *C v Kennedy*. Court of Session, 4 July 1986 (unreported but referred to in *Kearney, op cit*, at 25.26) a condition under s 44(1)(a) of the Social Work (Scotland) Act 1968 requiring a child to reside with the mother but not under the same roof as the father was upheld.

Mr Shaw: Yes but we are not bound by their views.

Miss McCracken: I know, but where these views are so strong I think it would be regarded by the girls as us letting them down if we went down this road. Has Miss Wilson got any thoughts on this?

Miss Wilson: I think Miss McCracken has hit the nail on the head. You can see that they are already looking concerned. I am clearly of the view that anything short of the department's proposals would not be in their best interests.

Mrs Maxwell: Mr and Mrs McPerlin, would something along these lines be acceptable to you?

Mrs MacDonald: I've discussed this possibility with Mr McPerlin. As you will have gathered from what he has said he does not want to compromise his position of denying the grounds, but I have explained to them that agreeing to some such proposal would not amount to compromising this position and if this is being seriously considered we could get down to settling the precise details.

Mr Paterson: That is the mother's position also.

Mrs Maxwell: Very well, I think what we have to decide is, first of all, if some form of supervision is required or whether we should exercise our power to discharge the referral. If I may say so I don't think, standing the decision of the sheriff, that the option of discharging the referral[280] is a realistic one. Is that agreed?

Mrs MacDonald: While not making any formal concession on the matter, I would not wish to argue that point in the circumstances.

Mr Paterson: Agreed.

Miss Wilson: I think it is clear that the hearing should not discharge the referral.

Mrs Maxwell: Very well. Then we had better consider if we want to follow the department's advice or whether we are in favour of working out some half-way house along the lines now being suggested.

Miss Drummond: I must emphasise that the department is still firmly of the view that the children should reside with the foster-parents at present. We would have the gravest reservations about the viability of supervising any 'half-way house' arrangement effectively. We have actually discussed this possibility and rejected it.

Mrs Maxwell: There's no mention of such a discussion in your report.

---

280.   Children (Scotland) Act 1995 s 69(12).

Miss Drummond: No, because we did not think this a practicable option.

Mrs Maxwell: Well, do we want to discuss this further, or indeed continue this hearing for further investigation?[281]

Miss Drummond: Of course that is a matter for the panel, but I don't think there is anything here to investigate.

Miss McCracken: Neither do I. The girls have given their views and it would be a slap in the face to them if we were to ignore their views in these circumstances. They seem to be well-settled with the foster carers and I don't like the idea of chopping and changing. What do you think Mrs Jamieson?

Mrs Jamieson: I don't know if I should express an opinion on the basic point, but I can certainly confirm that the girls are well settled with us.

Mrs Maxwell: [Turns to Mr Shaw.] What do you think?

Mr Shaw: I think we should continue for investigation.

Mrs Maxwell: I must say I am inclined to agree with Miss McCracken. I think it's perhaps a pity that the discussions the social workers had on this matter were not mentioned in the report, but I don't see any advantage in delaying. The report is well argued and I think its conclusion is a reasonable one. Also, and this is what clinches it for me, it represents what these obviously sensible girls want. Mr Shaw, are you still for continuing for further investigation?

Mr Shaw: Yes.

Mrs Maxwell: Anyone got anything to add on this point?

[A general shaking of heads and murmurs of 'No'.]

Mrs Maxwell: Now can we talk about contact? First of all could we discuss the arrangements in relation to Mrs McPerlin.

Mrs McPerlin: I should hope there would be no change. Everything is going fine, but Mr McPerlin would like more contact. Isn't that right Donald?

Mr McPerlin: Yes, two hours in the artificial atmosphere of the Social Work Department is totally inadequate. I'd like some time in the more normal atmosphere of the home.

Miss Drummond: I'm sorry to have to go on about this, but we must remember that as a result of the sheriff's decision it has been held that Mr

---

281.   Children (Scotland) Act 1995 s 69(2).

McPerlin is now a Schedule 1 offender. An argument could be made out for terminating Mr McPerlin's contact and even for limiting Mrs McPerlin's contact. However, as the matter of risk is to be looked into by a psychiatrist I would be content that the present arrangements stand, but I should be against any increase in the contact with Mr McPerlin.

Miss Wilson: That is what Samantha and Jacqueline would like.

Mr McPerlin: As I have said before, I have no wish to make unnecessary difficulties and I will not press this today, but I'm sure that when the psychiatrist's report comes out it will favour me so I shall wait till then to argue my point. And I hope everyone will note that I am trying to be reasonable.

Mrs Maxwell: I'm sure they will. [To Mr Shaw and Mr Hamilton] It looks as if we should leave contact arrangements as they are?

Mr Shaw/Mr Hamilton: Yes/Agreed.

Mrs Young: Now we must consider the position of Graeme.

Mr Shaw: If Mr and Mrs McPerlin do not present any danger to Graeme, why is a supervision requirement necessary at all?

Mrs MacDonald: Mr Paterson and I have explained the concept of what is known as a 'Home Supervision Requirement'[282] to our clients and while they do not think this is necessary they have accepted this in order to be reasonable and not obstructive.

Mr Paterson: Yes, that's right.

Mrs Maxwell: Thank you very much. Mr Shaw, I think, in view of Mr McPerlin's status as a Schedule 1 offender, that a supervision requirement would be appropriate for Graeme.

Mr Shaw: I don't think that follows. The offence was one against a 10 year old girl not against a male baby who is his own son. I think I'd have to maintain my disagreement.

Mrs Maxwell: And are you still in favour of continuing for further investigation?

Mr Shaw: Yes.

Mrs Maxwell: Miss McCracken, what do you think about a supervision requirement for Graeme?

Miss McCracken: I agree with your position. I think there should be a home supervision requirement for Graeme.

---

282. A convenient and self-explanatory term which does not appear in the Act.

Mrs Maxwell: Very well. The decision will be along these lines:

The relevant persons continued not to accept the substantive Grounds for Referral.

By a majority[283] a supervision requirement to be made in respect of Samantha and Jacqueline with a condition of residence with the present foster-parents, with the present contact arrangements to continue. The hearing decided by a majority[284] that a supervision requirement be made for Graeme. A full risk assessment from psychiatrist Dr Alexander Jardine-Smith of the Muirbrachlan Royal Hospital to be carried out and made available in three months' time. A review hearing to take place four months from now.

No safeguarder appointed.

We shall write this down immediately after the hearing, along with our reasons. Miss McCracken, I would suggest that our reasons will be along theses lines:

'We thought the fears of the children that the stepfather might molest Jacqueline if they resided in the family home were valid and supported by the contents of the 'Assessment & Evaluation of Risk' laid before the hearing by the Social Work Department, and that in any event the views of the children, who struck us as mature and sensible enough to express views which we should take into account, were in favour of remaining with the foster-carers at present, with the contact arrangements un-changed. As to Graeme our reason is that although there is no immediate danger to him at present, we thought it was essential that he be subject to supervision because Mr McPerlin has been held to be a Schedule 1 offender and noted that Mr and Mrs McPerlin did not object.'

Miss McCracken: Yes that sounds fine.

Mrs Maxwell: And of course it will be recorded that this was a majority decision.

Mr Shaw: Yes – and I should make clear that I think that there should be a supervision requirement but with the condition that Samantha and Jacqueline reside in the family home until the mother has to go to hospital. I say this because I believe that families should be together except where there is real risk to the children and I do not think it has been established that there is such a risk while the mother is at home. I do not agree that the children are mature enough to express views which should be given as much weight as the majority seems to think. I still think we should continue for investigation. But in view of the fact that the majority is

---

283. Mr Shaw wanted the matter continued for investigation and therefore is not with the majority in favour of an immediate supervision requirement.
284. Because Mr Shaw was in favour of continuing for further investigation.

against this I agree that a full risk assessment should be obtained and that a review should be held in four months time.

Mrs Maxwell: Thank you. However, the majority view of course prevails. I shall arrange for a written copy of our decision and the reasons for it to be sent out to you all in a few days[285]. I should explain that as a consequence of our decision all the children are now children 'looked after' by the local authority and that therefore Lentonshire Council have an overriding duty to safeguard and promote their welfare and to formulate a care plan for them[286]. I must also make it clear that Mr and Mrs McPerlin and indeed Samantha, Jacqueline and Graeme have the right to appeal to the sheriff against our decision. Any appeal must be lodged within three weeks counting from today[287]. Your lawyers will keep you right on the details, but I should tell you that you may be eligible for free Legal Aid. If there is an appeal then the person appealing has the right to ask a children's hearing to suspend the supervision requirement pending the determination of the appeal[288]. I should also say something about how our decision today may be subject to review – that is may be changed, or extended, or both, by a future hearing.

Mr McPerlin, Mrs McPerlin, Samantha, Jacqueline and indeed Graeme each has the right, at any time after three months have passed from today, to apply to a hearing to have the decision we have made today reviewed[289]. In any event the reporter must arrange a review within a year of today's date[290]. In other words in a situation wherein there has been no review arranged there is bound to be what is called the 'Annual Review' on or before 20th March 2007. But of course we have ordered a review four months from now so that the psychiatrist's report can be considered. The local authority may ask for a review at any time[291]. I should also say that in the event of a supervision requirement being still being in force at the end of a person's 'childhood' that it expires automatically at the end of the day before that child's eighteenth birthday[292].

We shall be returning the papers in connection with this hearing to the reporter[293]. I appreciate that Mrs MacDonald, Mr Paterson and Miss Wilson will require to retain the papers in the meantime, but I am sure I do not need to emphasise that they must be kept confidential. That is all for today.

---

285. Children's Hearings (Scotland) Rules, 1996, SI 96/3261, r 21.
286. Children (Scotland) Act 1995 s 17(1) and (6); Arrangements to Look After Children (Scotland) Regulations, SI 1996 No. 3262 reg 3(1).
287. Children (Scotland) Act 1995 s 51(1)(a).
288. Children (Scotland) Act 1995 s 51(9).
289. Children (Scotland) Act 1995 s 73(4) and 73(6).
290. Children (Scotland) Act 1995 s 73(8)(a)(v).
291. Children (Scotland) Act 1995 s 73(4).
292. Children (Scotland) Act 1995 s 73(3).
293. Children's Hearings (Scotland) Rules, 1996, SI 96/3261 r 5(5).

Part II

The Case of William Brown

The Case of William Brown

Chronological table

Thursday, 3 November 2005, morning

It is discovered that someone has spray-painted in red the words 'F***
Boozer Black' on a classroom door in Kirklenton High School. (The head
teacher is Mr Black and that is the unflattering and wholly defamatory
nickname of the teetotal Mr Black). William Brown is accused of the
'crime' on the basis that another pupil, Stephen Green, has implicated him.
Mr Black interviews both boys. William protests his innocence, says he
had an alibi witness, that Stephen had always been an 'enemy', and points
out that he had not been found to be in possession of spray paint. Mr
Black, who has always regarded William as a trouble-maker, makes no
further investigation, accepts Stephen's word, and imposes detention for
the following afternoon.

Friday, 4 November 2005, evening

William, having served out his detention meets Stephen in the street and
knocks him down, causing bruising to his chest. This is observed by
passing police officers, PCs Wilfred MacTaggart and Margaret Myles, who
apprehend him and take him home. At William's home, in the presence of
his parents, the police caution William and charge him with assaulting
Stephen to his injury. William replies: 'The grassing little bastard had it
coming to him'. The police leave William with his parents and say that a
report will be sent to the children's reporter. They report that Stephen's
parents and Stephen himself have told them that they are not greatly
bothered about what has happened, Stephen's parents regarding it as part
of the rough and tumble of school life in an area where petty assaults and
other crimes are common enough. Stephen said little but PC Myles
thought he muttered something to the effect that he would 'get even' in his
own way.

Saturday, 5 November 2005, late evening

A small outhouse in Kirklenton High School is damaged by fire. The fire is
put out by the janitor. It is attributed to a misdirected Guy Fawkes' night
firework and no formal investigation takes place.

Monday, 7 November 2005

PC Wilfred MacTaggart, the reporting officer in relation to the alleged
assault on Stephen Green, takes the view that this offence does not fall
within *The Lord Advocate's Directions as to the Prosecution of Children*[1],

---

1.   Reproduced in Kearney, *Children's Hearings and the Sheriff Court*, ed 2, para 1.26.

and sends a report to the children's reporter. The report states that the police saw the punching incident briefly but that they had to drive up the road and turn the car to come back to the locus so that the boys were out of view after the punch and therefore they could not speak to any kicking incident. The police officers did not see any obvious evidence of injury to Stephen Green's head.

Friday, 11 November 2005

The reporter, having read and considered the police report, and, having in mind his obligations under section 56(1) of the Children (Scotland) Act 1995, commissions an Initial Assessment Report (IAR) from the Social Work Department of the relevant local authority, Lentonshire Council. The reporter writes to William and to Mr and Mrs Brown to say that a referral has been received, and outlines its contents.

Friday, 25 November 2005

The reporter receives an IAR from the local authority. This report indicates that there is good family support for William, and that, although regarded as a bit wild at school, his behaviour is well within acceptable parameters. It states that William accepts that he punched Stephen Green on 4 November 2005 because Stephen Green had taunted him, but that he denies emphatically having kicked him. It states that William Brown reports that Stephen Green has no visible signs of a kicking to the head and that neither Stephen nor his parents regard the matter as particularly serious. The report mentions the 'spray painting' allegation and notes that William still protests his innocence and now, having obtained his own revenge on Stephen, is more resentful of the school's unfair and off-hand (as he sees it) handling of his case than of Stephen's having caused him to be detained[2]. It concludes that no social work intervention is required.

Monday, 28 November 2005

The reporter considers the Report with a view to deciding which of the courses open to him under section 56(4) and (6) of the Children (Scotland) Act 1995 he should take. The basic question is whether or not a hearing should be arranged. In essence this decision turns on two separate issues, namely whether or not there is evidence capable of establishing whether any ground of referral exists and if there is such evidence, are compulsory measures of supervision 'necessary in respect of the child'[3].

> Note [1]   *The first task is an entirely 'legal' one, in the sense that it involves weighing the evidence. The second issue, whether compulsory measures of supervision are necessary, is a wider one,*

---

2.   This report is not reproduced here, since its contents are substantially rehearsed in the IER dated 19th December 2005, reproduced in the entry *infra* of that date.
3.   Children (Scotland) Act 1995 s 56(6).

involving primarily the interests of the child. In the instant case the 'obvious' ground of referral is that the child has committed an offence, but the reporter should consider all the information available to him, including that contained in the IAR. Having examined the Police Report the reporter concludes that there is sufficient evidence to establish the ground of referral under s 52(2)(i) of the Act[4]. The reporter examines the whole circumstances in the light of the IAR and considers whether any other ground, such as being beyond control[5], falling into bad associations[6], or even lack of parental care[7] may be relevant. If it seemed, on the face of it, that further investigation was required then the reporter may make further investigations as part of his initial investigations under s 56(1). In the instant case the reporter is satisfied (a) that there is ample evidence supporting a ground under s 52(2)(i) of the Act and (b) that there is no evidence, either actual or potential, supporting any other ground (and that therefore no further investigation is required).

Note [2]   The second task involves consideration of the interests of the child. If a hearing is to be convened to consider the disposal of the child's case they will require to have regard to the relevant provisions of section 16 of the Children (Scotland) Act 1995[8]. This section is not specifically enacted as binding on the reporter but since any hearing will be bound by it, it follows that the reporter must take account of its provisions at this stage. The main section 16 principle is that a hearing, where considering any matter with respect to a child, shall treat 'the welfare of the child throughout his childhood' as their paramount consideration (the 'paramountcy principle')[9]. The other principles require the hearing, having regard to the age and maturity of the child, to give him a chance to give his views and to have regard to any such views (the 'consulting the child principle')[10]; and also, before deciding to make any requirement, to be satisfied that making the requirement will be better for the child than making no requirement at all (the 'no non-beneficial order principle')[11]. There is also a slight derogation from the 'paramountcy' principle in that section 16(5) provides in effect that in the event that the application of this principle would not be consistent with 'protecting members of the public from serious [my emphasis] harm (whether or not physical

---

4. '[that the child] has committed an offence'.
5. '[that the child] is beyond the control of any relevant person' – Children (Scotland) Act 1995 s 52(2)(a).
6. '[that the child] is falling into bad associations or is exposed to moral danger' – Children (Scotland) Act 1995 s 52(2)(b).
7. '[that the child] is likely – (i) to suffer unnecessarily, or (ii) be impaired seriously in his health or development, due to a lack of parental care' – Children (Scotland) Act 1995 s 52(2)(c).
8. Reproduced as Appendix 1.
9. Children (Scotland) Act 1995 s 16(1).
10. Children (Scotland) Act 1995 s 16(2).
11. Children (Scotland) Act 1995 s 16(3).

harm)' then the hearing (or, as the case may be, the sheriff) may make a decision which does not observe the paramountcy principle.

*Note [3] **The reporter's decision**[12]. In practice reporters in 'alleged offence by the child' cases have regard principally to:*

- *the seriousness or otherwise of the offence;*

- *the child's prior offending, if any;*

- *the attitude of the family – e.g. how seriously the family are concerned by the allegation of the offence;*

- *the attitude of the child;*

- *the presence or otherwise of addiction and/or aggression;*

- *the age of the child;*

- *the presence or absence of risk to the child;*

- *the state of relationships within the family; and*

- *how the child is regarded/is getting on in school.*

The reporter will also be influenced by his/her assessment of the value of the advice of the social worker and, of course, have regard to the no non-beneficial order principle enacted by s 16(3) of the Act, referred to above. In relation to 'the seriousness or otherwise of the offence' reporters, while primarily concerned with the child's needs, must also concern themselves with the child's deeds in that it is a 'need' of the child to be encouraged to feel responsible for the actions which he or she has taken. This reflects the reality that was also recognised by the court in Humphries v S[13], wherein a decision to hold a child in secure accommodation was sustained on the basis that it was in the child's interests to be restrained from further offending.

Reporters and hearings, as public authorities under section 6 of the Human Rights Act, 1998, require to comply with those provisions of the European Convention on Human Rights which that Act incorporates into our law such as Article 6 ('Right to a fair trial') and Article 7 (No punishment without law') and Article 8 ('Right to respect for private and family life)[14]. Reporters must accordingly have regard to these provisions of the Convention.

In relation to the present case the reporter, having regard to the considerations set out above, and principally influenced by the relatively

---

12. As mentioned in relation to para *[2]* of Part one of this book, the Scottish Children's Reporter Administration ('SCRA') has issued a 'Framework for Decision Making for Reporters', available on SCRA's website (at www.scra.gov.uk). What appears here, while broadly consistent with the SCRA 'Framework', represents the writer's interpretation of the rôle of the reporter at this stage.

13. 1986 SLT 683.

14. For the texts of these Articles see Appendix 2.

minor nature of the offence, the attitude of Stephen and his parents, the lack of previous offending, the stable situation at home – concerned and supportive parents – the relatively good report from the school, and the conclusion of the social worker that no social work intervention is required decides that compulsory measures of supervision are not necessary and also that it would not be appropriate to use his power under s 56(4)(b) of the Act to refer William to the local authority 'with a view to their making arrangements for the advice, guidance and assistance of the child and his family in accordance with Chapter 1 of this Part of this Act'

Tuesday, 29 November 2005

The reporter accordingly writes to the child and parents (who are the 'relevant persons' under s 56(4)[15]) informing them that he has decided, in terms of section 56(4) of the Act that a children's hearing does not require to be arranged. The reporter also, as required by said s 56(4), advises the police in their capacity as 'the person who has brought the case to his notice' of his decision. He also, and having regard to the recognised importance of keeping alleged victims informed[16], advises Stephen Green and his parents of his decision.

Monday, 5 December 2005

The head teacher, Mr Black, receives an anonymous letter stating that he will find something of interest connected with the fire in a cupboard in the changing room of the gym. He goes to investigate and finds an empty tin which seems to have contained petrol and, just beside it, a tin of red spray paint. Mr Black, recalling the spray-painting incident for which William was blamed, now suspects that William may have set fire to the outhouse. He questions William about both incidents and presses him to name the alibi witness he mentioned in relation to the spray paint incident. William refuses to say anything and becomes abusive. After the interview with William Mr Black calls the police.

6 to 9 December 2005

The police carry out investigations, including obtaining a statement from Mr Black and report from the Assistant Chief Fire Officer, and, having regard to the consideration that this is a case prima facie falling within the Lord Advocate's Directions (which include 'fire-raising', which is normally prosecuted on indictment, i.e. by the procedure involving trial by jury)

---

15. For the definition of 'relevant person', see Part One of this book, para [1].
16. Section 53 of the Criminal Justice (Scotland) Act 2003 contains detailed provisions empowering the reporter to convey information to persons (and, in the case of children, the relevant persons) against whom an offence appears to have been committed. Other persons who may be informed are listed in The Children's Hearings (Provision of Information by Principal Reporter) (Prescribed Persons) (Scotland) Order 2003, SI 2003/424.

sends a report to the procurator fiscal[17], with a copy to the reporter[18], with the evidence implicating William in the setting fire to the outhouse. The police go to William Brown's house and question him under caution[19] and in the presence of his mother about the alleged fire-raising. William says he has nothing to say.

Monday, 12 December 2005

The procurator fiscal and the reporter have each considered the case. The procurator fiscal has come to the view that the case of causing some damage to a shed by setting fire to it, while of course a serious matter and within the Lord Advocate's categories, is one which she would be happy to have dealt within the hearings system. She recalls that some very serious cases have been dealt with in the hearings system, including a few cases of culpable homicide.

Tuesday, 13 December 2005

The reporter phones the procurator fiscal to discuss this case. He indicates his attitude which, as already mentioned, concurs with that of the procurator fiscal. The procurator fiscal asks if the reporter is going to use only the fire-raising as the ground of referral and the reporter indicates that he will also found on the spray-painting incident, partly in order to keep open the possibility of arguing that the case of *Moorov v HM Advocate* 1930 JC 68 may apply and thus assist in establishing the grounds in any Application to the sheriff. The procurator fiscal confirms that she does not intend to prosecute at this time.

> *Note [4]   The discussion between the reporter and the procurator fiscal is typical of the good working relationship which exists. There is nothing improper in these two public officials discussing the case in this way and in effect doing a 'deal'. The two systems are meant to run side by side and they could not satisfactorily do so unless such discussions took place. Technically the procurator fiscal has the last word – if the procurator fiscal decides to prosecute then stating grounds of referral and arranging a hearing would be inappropriate and, if the prosecution had been initiated, probably incompetent. Also, technically, if grounds of referral were stated and the referral was for any reason discharged, for example if the grounds were denied and held by the sheriff not to be established after proof and the sheriff had discharged the referral under s 68(9) of the Children (Scotland) Act 1995, it would in theory be competent for the procurator fiscal to*

---

17. Criminal Procedure (Scotland) Act 1995, s 17(1).
18. Children (Scotland) Act 1995, s 53(3)
19. 'The terms of the caution, sometimes known as the common law caution, are that the suspect is not obliged to say anything but that anything he does say will be noted and may be used in evidence.' – Sir Gerald Gordon, *Renton and Brown's Criminal Procedure*, 6th edition, paragraph 24–40.

prosecute. It would however be contrary to practice for the Crown to do so – the writer is aware of no case where this has been attempted. In this case the reporter took the initiative by telephoning the procurator fiscal. As long ago as 1982 the good working relationship was recognised by researchers[20]. If anything this valuable feature has become consolidated since then and reporters and procurators fiscal confer on a regular basis[21]. (In a case where a young person over the age of 16 and under 18, it will be prudent for a procurator fiscal to check whether such a person may be a 'statutory child', that is a child within that age group who is under the supervision of a children's hearing – see Children (Scotland) Act 1995 s 93(2)(b)(ii), definition of 'child'; cf Children's Hearings (Scotland) Rules 1996 r 3. In practice a procurator fiscal might ask the local reporter.)

Note [5]   In Scots criminal law there must be evidence from more that one source (corroborated evidence) identifying the accused as the offender. The case of Moorov v HM Advocate 1930 JC 68 contains an important discussion of this principle in relation to cases where more than one offence is alleged. Its import has been summarised thus: 'Where an accused is charged with two or more crimes and only one witness implicates him in each they afford mutual corroboration if the crimes are so interrelated by character, circumstances and time as to justify an inference that they are parts of a course of criminal conduct systematically pursued by the accused[22].'

Tuesday, 13 December 2005, afternoon

The reporter asks the Social Work Department for a further Report. He requests that the report be submitted as soon as possible since he is anxious to get such a serious matter addressed before the New Year if possible. The department, in view of the recent report already obtained, say they will try to present a Report within a week or so. The reporter considers asking the head teacher for a report, and in view of the urgency attending the investigation of such a serious offence he obtains a verbal report from Mr Black (to be confirmed in writing) stating that William's conduct has deteriorated over the last few weeks, and citing his verbally abusive manner at the interview mentioned above.

---

20. See *Prosecution in the Public Interest* by Sue Moody and Jacqueline Toombs, Scottish Academic Press, Edinburgh, 1982 at page 79.
21. The same researchers reported one view that children's reporters at the time enjoyed a wider discretion in deciding whether or not to proceed than that exercised by procurators fiscal (*op cit* p 58). But this view seems not to have been supported by the Crown Agent of the day, the late William G Chalmers CB (*ibid*, Foreword).
22. Walker and Walker on Evidence, second edition, paragraph 5.10.1.

Friday, 16 December 2005, mid-morning[23]

The reporter receives the following report from Social Work:

Social Work Department
Kirklenton Office
8 Laverock Road
Kirklenton LE6 4DV
Tel: 012104 545 554
Fax: 012104 545 555

SOCIAL BACKGROUND REPORT

Subject: William Brown (dob 01/08/1991) in 3rd Year, Kirklenton High School.

Address: Flat 3/1, 27 Morrison Street, Kirklenton LE2 7EH.

Family

Hugh Brown, Father, at present unemployed; born 1951, married, in 1990, for the second time, to

Sylvia Watson or Brown, Mother, born 1969;

Isobel Brown, half-sister, (daughter of Hugh Brown by his first marriage) born 1972, now living outwith the home;

Merle Brown or White, half sister, (daughter of Hugh Brown by his first marriage) born 1973, now married and living outwith the home;

Angela Watson, known as Brown, half sister (the daughter of Mrs Sylvia Brown in consequence of a youthful liaison but accepted into the family), born 30th June 1988, unmarried and living in the home, at present attending Muirbrachlan College.

Basis of Report

The writer compiled a report on William Brown on 23rd November 2005 in relation to a referral to the reporter alleging that William Brown had assaulted a fellow pupil Stephen Green. That report was based on:

1. A meeting at Kirklenton High School on 18 November 2005 with William and Guidance Teacher Miss Reilly.

---

23. This is an exceptionally swift response (normally such a report would require several weeks to compile) – it has been made possible because Social Work were already working with the family.

2.   Two visits to the family home. On the first visit the writer interviewed William Brown's mother when William was at school and on the second occasion at a time when William was at home when he was seen by the writer at first alone and then in the presence of his mother when there was a general discussion. On neither occasion was William Brown's father available and the mother became evasive when asked where he was. There had been no previous Social Work involvement with this family.

For the purpose of the present report the writer had a further interview with the Guidance Teacher, Miss Reilly, a further interview with William at home and a further interview with the mother at home. Once again it was not found possible to interview the father.

The present report consolidates the information obtained for the first report with the latest information.

Analysis of Family Background

Morrison Street is in a housing scheme dating from the 1950s. The house is a three-bedroom, kitchen, and bathroom flat. While the area is not one of multiple deprivation it is not prosperous. The majority of the residents are, like William Brown's father, unemployed and the area is known to the writer's office as having a higher than average component of offending and alcohol and drug abuse. However the Brown family are not known to the department and the house was clean and tidy when the writer visited it – on the first and second occasions without advance warning – and there were no patent signs of alcohol or drug abuse.

William Brown's mother is a catering superintendent in Muirbrachlan General Hospital. His father is unemployed. His half-sister, Angela, is at Muirbrachlan College studying for a qualification in computer technology. Both his mother and Angela are out all day and his father also does not seem to be in the house at the time when William returns from school and accordingly he is a 'latchkey' child.

Mrs Sylvia Brown is substantially younger than Mr Hugh Brown. Although the writer did not meet Mr Brown the impression was conveyed that he would like to be a dominating personality who 'rules the roost' but in reality it is his younger wife who is the main influence in the family. She holds down a responsible and relatively well-paid job. Mr Brown slightly resents this since he, formerly a skilled 'banksman' at the local steel works, was made redundant some years ago and has been unable to find employment since. He spends a lot of time in the pub. He also feels somewhat inadequate because Angela, who was born to Mrs Sylvia Brown as a result of a youthful romance, is doing well in tertiary education – the only one connected with the family who has made anything of her education. The writer did not see Angela Brown but got the impression that she does not bother much about William Brown. There may be some sibling rivalry – see below. Mrs Sylvia Brown presents as a caring mother, and is in fact the dominating figure in the household.

The Child William Brown

William Brown had a normal birth. He has attended mainstream school where his performance is academically poor. The writer found William Brown to be un-communicative and verging on the surly. He is not interested in any particular academic subject but is top of the class for PT. He is fond of football but is not allowed to play in the school team because of alleged persistent 'foul' playing. He has recently had several unexplained absences from school and if these continue he may find himself referred to the reporter for truancy. Mrs Sylvia Brown says that her husband is disappointed that William, the only child of herself and Hugh Brown, has not done better and he 'casts this up' and seems to blame his wife for producing a comparatively clever child – Angela – as a result of her youthful affair. William Brown sometimes overhears these quarrels and this has created a tension between him and Angela.

Grounds for Referral

It was originally alleged that at about 6.30 pm. on Friday 4th November 2005 at Attlee Quadrant near Morrison Street, Kirklenton William Brown assaulted Stephen Green, aged 14, by punching him in the stomach and head, knocking him down and kicking him on the head, all to his injury. William accepts that he punched Stephen Green on the chest, having been taunted by Stephen Green about having been detained in school, he agrees that Stephen Green fell to the ground as a result of the punch but vehemently denies kicking him on the head. He admitted as much to the police and accepts that when interviewed by the police he admitted what he had done, adding words to the effect that Stephen Green was a 'grassing bastard'. William was aware that the police had seen the knocking down incident but is emphatic that no kicking took place. William said there were no marks on Stephen Green's head or face suggesting that any kicking had taken place and, if this were true, and the writer had no information of such marks, then the writer was at the time inclined, and still is inclined, to believe William Brown's account. The writer understands that the reporter decided to take 'no action' in connection with this matter.

At the writer's first interview William Brown volunteered to the writer that Stephen Green's allegation was another example of the type of thing represented by allegation that Stephen had made that he (William) had spray-painted a school door prior to 5th November 2005. This is one of the incidents which now forms the subject matter of the present referral. When questioned by the writer about this allegation he said he had an 'alibi witness' in relation to that incident but was very vague about who this was or, for that matter, how he could have an alibi for doing something which, if innocent, he would not know the time of.

In relation to the allegation about the burning of part of a school outhouse William Brown totally denies all knowledge of this. He suspects that Stephen Green may have 'planted' the empty petrol can and the spray-paint container, but does not think Stephen Green would have had the 'bottle' as he puts it, to set fire to the shed himself as part of a carefully thought out revenge scheme.

William Brown is contemptuous of all forms of authority. In particular he is resentful of most of the teaching staff in his school and thinks that they, led by Mr Black, have 'picked on' him for alleged fouling on the football field. He says he played 'hard ball' but no more than any of the others. He regards Mr Black, who is a lay preacher in an evangelical church, as a hypocrite. (The Brown family have no apparent religious affiliation.) There is no evidence that William Brown abuses alcohol or drugs, although the writer is aware that both are available, and sometimes consumed, by his peers in Kirklenton High School.

Mrs Sylvia Brown believes her son's account and is horrified at the allegations. She regards herself as a good parent but feels a little guilty that she requires to be away from the home all the working day and sometimes at week-ends. She says that her husband shares her horror at the allegations and that they both believe William in his denials. If the matter goes to a panel both William Brown and his parents will deny the grounds for referral.

Assessment and Recommendation

The family seems to be comparatively stable and are concerned about the allegations which have been made. William Brown's progress at school, while not at all distinguished, would not seem at present to give more cause for concern than that of many of his peers. The recent absences from school, while concerning, may, if continued, require action in the future but not, in the writer's opinion, at present. In relation to the original incident (the assault on Stephen Green) the writer was at the time, and still is, of the opinion that it was no more than part of a schoolboy brawl and would not, against the relatively stable family background, have warranted social work intervention. However the new allegations, particularly that of fire-raising, suggest a pattern of conduct. As stated above the parents will deny the grounds. The writer believes they are likely to remain in denial even if the grounds were to be held as established by the court. Consequently, in the event of the grounds being upheld, the writer would advise social work intervention in the form of cognitive therapy which would help William Brown to think about the consequences of his actions. Such therapy is available in the Kirklenton Social Work team from Lorraine Carter, Project Team Leader, and the writer himself. In order to progress this the writer recommends that William be made the subject of a supervision requirement.

Mark Fox
Social Worker
16th December 2005

Friday, 16 December 2005, afternoon

The reporter now considers the matter in the light of the considerations set out in paragraph *[3]* above. He is influenced by the following:

•   the alleged fire-raising is a serious offence;

•   it is now no longer a first reported offence but the second reported offence and indeed the third offence over-all if one counts assault on Stephen Green;

•   the circumstances, involving setting fire to property by a flammable substance, involve danger to the perpetrator and others;

•   William's conduct at school has deteriorated.

Putting all these considerations together the reporter decides that compulsory measures of supervision are necessary and that he will frame grounds of referral as soon as possible.

> *Note [6]   The decision by the reporter to rely on only the two incidents is understandable, competent, and in accordance with good practice. The formal letter to William and his parents stating that no action in relation to the alleged assault is to be taken by the reporter has the effect of preventing the reporter from bringing proceedings 'on the basis solely of the information obtained during the initial investigation...'[24] and this would technically not bar the reporter from founding on the original 'assault' incident now that other grounds have arisen, but it would be very unusual for a reporter to resurrect a ground in respect of which he had intimated 'no action'. The reporter has taken the view that the essential concerns surround the other two incidents. It has long been regarded as good practice to aver 'the real grounds of referral'[25]. (In the case of O v Rae[26] it was held that the hearing were entitled to have regard to matters which had been referred to in a Social Background Report and which could have been made the subject of a substantive ground of referral, but that case has been called in question in the important case of S v Miller[27].)*

---

24. Children (Scotland) Act 1995 s 56(5).
25. See *In the Child's Best Interests*, Russell Meek et al (Scottish Child and Family Alliance and HMSO 1991) page 28, quoted in *Kearney, op cit* at 16.07.
26. 1992 SCLR 318, 1993 SLT 570.
27. 2001 SLT 531 per Lord President Rodger at 542 H and I; see also *Kearney, op cit* at 16.08 and discussions by Professor Kenneth McK Norrie in his *Children's Hearings in Scotland*, second edition pp 116 and 117 and *In Defence of O v Rae*, 1995 SLT (News) 38.

Friday, 16 December 2005, later in the afternoon

The reporter states grounds of referral as follows:

Form SCRA F

SCOTTISH
CHILDREN'S REPORTER
ADMINISTRATION

The children's reporter has referred the case of William Brown (dob 1st August 1991), 3/1, 27 Morrison Street, Kirklenton LE2 7EH to a children's hearing for LENTONSHIRE on the following grounds:

That in terms of section 52(2)(i) of the Children (Scotland) Act 1995 [he]/[she] has committed an offence.

Statement of Facts

In support of the above it is stated:

1. That William Brown did on or about Wednesday 2nd November 2005 paint abusive words on the door of class-room number 7 of Kirklenton High School, Aberfeldy Road, Kirklenton, LE5 4DL – this being the offence of malicious mischief.

2. That William Brown did at or about 10 pm. on Saturday 5th November 2005, using a flammable substance, set fire to an outhouse situated in the north eastern corner of the playground of Kirklenton High School, Aberfeldy Road, Kirklenton, LE5 4DL whereby fire took hold and damaged the door and part of the front wall of said outhouse – this being the offence of wilful fire-raising, or, alternatively, the offence of culpable and reckless fire-raising.

Date: 16 December 2005

Hector Somerville, Authority Reporter
SCRA, 17 Laverock Road, Kirklenton LE6 7EK
Telephone: 012104 545 700. Fax: 012104 545 710

Notes

The children's hearing will ask the child and relevant persons if they accept the reasons for arranging the hearing. If the reasons are accepted the children's hearing will discuss with the child and relevant persons what is best for the child. If any of the reasons are not accepted, the hearing may either discharge them or tell the reporter to apply to the sheriff who will decide if any of the reasons are proved.

If the sheriff decides that any of the reasons are proved, the children's hearing will then discuss what is best for the child, as if these reasons had been accepted. If the sheriff decides that no reasons are proved the case will be discharged.

Rehabilitation of Offenders Act 1974

If the grounds are accepted or established are offences committed by the child, then they will form a record that may have to be disclosed at a later date to potential employers. The reporter can give you a leaflet explaining the Act in more detail.

> Note *[7]   This represents a fairly typical Statement of Grounds for Referral in an 'alleged offence by the child' case. The form is not contained in the current Children's Hearings (Scotland) Rules 1996. It has been created by Scottish Children's Reporter Administration which has adapted 'Form A' of the now superseded Children's Hearings (Scotland) Rules 1986. The grounds of referral in this case are very straightforward – this has assisted the reporter in stating the grounds quickly. In view of the imminence of Christmas and Hogmanay he is anxious to get the case moving with the minimum of delay.*

> Note *[8]   The substance of the Form is in two sections, viz the 'grounds' for the referral and the Statement of Facts supporting that reason. The 'grounds' must comprise at least one of the 'conditions' set out in section 52(2) of the Children (Scotland) Act 1995*[28]*. The Statement of Facts comprises those facts which the reporter intends to prove if, in the event of the reasons not being accepted by the child and his parents (the 'relevant persons') the case goes to the sheriff for proof. The substantial facts are the facts in relation to the allegation in the 'grounds' section justifying the alleged 'grounds', viz., that William has committed two offences. The distinction between the 'ground(s)' section and the Statement of Facts section is important because while the Statement of Facts may, with the permission of the sheriff at proof, be amended*[29]*,the 'ground(s)' section may not be amended.*

> Note *[9]   The law provides that where an offence by a child is alleged the Statement must 'specify the nature of the offence in question'*[30]*. That is why in paragraphs 1 and 2 of the Statement*

---

28.   Section 52 of the Children (Scotland) Act 1995, as amended, is reproduced as Appendix 1.
29.   Child Care and Maintenance Rules, 1997, rule 3.48; cf rule 3.50 which empowers the sheriff, where the alleged offence has not been proved, to hold that some other offence has been proved.
30.   Children's Hearings (Scotland) Rules 1996 rule 17(2).

particular crimes are identified by name. Where, as in the fire-raising offence there are two possible versions of the offence it is proper practice to specify both alternatives.

Friday, 16 December 2005, later in the afternoon

The reporter instructs sheriff officers to notify the grounds of referral giving Tuesday 27 December 2005 at 4.30 pm. within Room Number 2, St Lenton's House, 1 Laverock Place, Kirklenton LE5 1AA as the date and location of the children's hearing. The grounds are to be notified separately to (1) the child William Brown and (2) and (3) his parents Hugh Brown and Sylvia Brown and (3) the Chief Social Work Officer of Lentonshire Council.

Note [10]   The provisions governing notification of hearings are contained in rules 6, 7 and 8 of the Children's Hearings (Scotland) Rules 1996. Under rule 6(1) of these Rules the notification to the child, the relevant persons, and the Chief Social Work Officer of the local authority within whose area the hearing is to sit must be given notice 'not less than 7 days before the hearing'. This means 7 clear days, but it does not mean 7 working days, so that the interposition of a Saturday and Sunday and of Christmas Day and Boxing Day do not affect the position. In a case in 1980[31] the Court of Session had to consider the meaning of section 42(4) of the Social Work (Scotland) Act, 1968, which provided that an application to the sheriff for a proof had to be heard 'within twenty-eight days of the lodging of the application. Counsel argued that a Sunday and perhaps a holiday should each be regarded as a dies non. The court dealt with this rather tartly: 'He [counsel for the appellant] was unable to cite any Act or any authority for that proposition, which has perhaps the superficial glamour of latinity ... where s 42(4) of the [1968] Act states that the sheriff shall hear an application 'within twenty-eight days of the lodging of the application' it means exactly what it says. An initial hearing outwith twenty-eight days is incompetent.' It is now accepted that the same principle applies to the interpretation of rule 6. Accordingly the reporter here is just in time with his notifications. It should be said that a reporter would not normally cut matters so fine but our reporter's anxiety to expedite matters has, rightly or wrongly, impelled him to take this course.

Note [11]   The mode of notification chosen by the reporter was by sheriff officer. The rules in relation to notifications given under the Children's Hearings (Scotland) Rules, 1996 are contained in rule 30 of these Rules[32]. It would have been more normal for the reporter in an alleged offence by the child case to have employed postal citation under rule 30(2)(d). Under rule 30 the reporter

31.   *S v Galbraith* (8th July 1980) Court of Session, unreported.
32.   Rule 30 is reproduced as Appendix 3.

could have delivered the notification himself, or instructed one of his staff to do so, but, having regard to what he now regarded as the serious and indeed delicate (having regard to his earlier letter saying that there would be no action regarding the alleged assault) he decided, wisely it may be thought, to instruct 'the professionals' in relation to the service of documents, viz, the sheriff officers.

Friday, 16 December 2005 – still later in the afternoon.

As with the form setting out the Grounds for Referral there is no statutory provisions governing the wording of the notification and SCRA have created a style. Using this style, adapted for the purpose of the present case, the sheriff officer delivers to William the following letter, along with the Grounds for Referral and a copy of the Social Background Report:

TO *WILLIAM BROWN, (D.O.B. 01.08.1991),*
3/1, 27 Morrison Street,
Kirklenton LE2 7EH

Dear *William*

I have arranged a children's hearing to consider the Grounds of Referral attached to this letter.

The hearing will be held at 4.30 pm on Tuesday 27 December 2005 at Room 2, St Lenton's House, 1 Laverock Place, Kirklenton LE5 1AA.

You have the right to attend the hearing, and it is very important for you to be there. If you do not come the hearing may arrange for you to be brought. You may be kept in a place of safety until the next hearing can be arranged. If there is a good reason why you cannot come to the hearing, such as illness, please contact my office. My address and telephone number are printed at the bottom of this letter.

There is a leaflet with this letter which will tell you about the hearing.

You may want to tell the hearing what you think would be best for you. You have the right to do that. If you do want to, you can tell me before the hearing starts or you can say it at the hearing.

You can write to me if you want. Whatever you tell me or write to me will be passed on to the panel members and also to your parents or main carers and to the safeguarder if one is appointed by the hearing. **You can either write to me on the page which is attached, or on another piece of paper.**

If you want to, you can bring someone with you to the hearing, a representative, to help you talk to panel members. Travel expenses will be paid to you and your representative.

Date: 16 December 2005

Signed: Hector Somerville
Children's Reporter
Scottish Children's Reporter Administration,
17 Laverock Road, Kirklenton, LE6 7EK,
Tel: 02104 545 700
Fax: 012104 545 710

[The accompanying page:

To the Panel Members from *William Brown, aged 14.*

I would like you to know what I think before you make a decision at the children's Hearing.

(Write what you want to say here and remember that a copy will be given to your parents or main carers and any safeguarder. You can say as much as you like but you do not have to fill the page. If you want, you can ask someone to help you write down what you want to say.)

Please bring this to the children's hearing or send it to the reporter at *17 Laverock Road, Kirklenton LE6 7EK*]

Friday, 16 December 2005 – even later in the afternoon

The sheriff officer delivers to each of Hugh and Sylvia Brown, the parents, notification of the time and place of the hearing together with the Grounds for Referral, an explanatory leaflet and the Initial Enquiry Report. The sheriff officer delivers the same papers to William Brown[33]. The notification tells each of them that they are obliged to attend the hearing and to bring a representative if they wish.

The reporter arranges for delivery to the Social Work Department of Lentonshire Council notification of the time and place of the hearing, enclosing a copy of the Grounds for Referral.

Note [12]   In this case the parents of William, as 'relevant persons', have, under section 45(8) of the Children (Scotland) Act

---

33. There is nothing in the rules requiring service of reports on children, but considerations of fairness, inspired by the provisions of the European Convention on Human Rights, have led to the practice of notifying children who are judged to be sufficiently mature of the contents of Reports, where necessary editing out any material which would seriously harm the child.

*1995 both the right to attend 'all stages of the hearing (s 45(8)(a)
of the Act and (s 45(8)(b)) and an obligation to attend all stages
unless the hearing are satisfied that insisting on such attendance
would be unreasonable or unnecessary for the proper consideration of the case. In theory any person who fails to attend a hearing
having been lawfully cited can be reported to the procurator fiscal
and face prosecution under s 45(9). Such prosecutions are so rare
as to be almost, but not quite, unknown.*

Saturday, 17 December 2005

Mr and Mrs Brown discuss the matter with William and all agree that they
will deny the grounds for referral. They notice the statement in the
Grounds of Referral that if the grounds are not accepted the matter may
go to the sheriff. They have never had occasion to instruct solicitors but
take note of the right to do so mentioned in the leaflet which accompanied
the Grounds of Referral. In all the circumstances, and having a lot on their
minds in the run-up to Christmas, they decide to put off consulting a
solicitor until after the hearing fixed for Tuesday 27 December 2005. Mr
Brown hints that he may leave it to his wife to attend the hearing and is
unimpressed by her saying that he might get into trouble with the law if he
does not attend.

Tuesday, 27 December 2005 at 4.30 pm

William Brown and his mother attend the hearing[34]. The social worker is
not in attendance – he phoned the office to say that he had got stuck in the
snow. William and his mother do not accept the Grounds for Referral. The
hearing decide unanimously (they not being at all inclined to discharge the
referral in terms of the concluding words of section 65(7) of the Children
(Scotland) Act 1995) that the reporter should be directed to make
application to the sheriff for a finding as to whether the grounds are
established[35]. The hearing discuss whether a warrant should be granted.
Two members of the hearing express the view that the child's failure to
explain why he was arrested for the assault on the child G and his failure
to explain, in relation to the 'paint' incident, how he could have an 'alibi
witness' to an event which, had he been innocent, he could not have
known the time of all indicated that he was guilty. The reporter states that
it is the child's right to remain silent, but the two members are uncon-
vinced. The same two panel members express the view that the failure of
the child's father to be present when the social worker has gone to the
house, and the father's failure to come to the hearing suggest that the child
is not under proper control. The Chair of the hearing argues that this does
not accord with the social worker's view and invites William and Mrs
Brown to comment. William says that the social worker had said that he

---

34. For examples of how hearings are conducted, see Part One of this book at pages 54 et
      seq and 123 et seq.
35. Children (Scotland) Act 1995 s 65(7).

was going to tell the hearing that he (William) was not at a high risk of 're-offending'. One of the hearing members says, 'Why should we accept that? – it's not in the Report.' The reporter says that it is not unusual for a social worker to make a supplementary verbal report. William becomes abusive and his mother, unsuccessfully for quite a while, tries to calm him down. After matters have settled down the two panel members say they think this proves their point.

Ultimately the hearing, by a majority of two to one, grants warrant for William to be detained for a period of twenty two days in a place of safety on the ground that this is necessary in order to safeguard or promote his welfare[36]. The hearing were satisfied that the parents should have unsupervised contact with William and that the Social Work Department would arrange this[37]. The formal order is:

1.   To direct the Reporter to make an Application to the sheriff for a finding in relation to grounds not accepted – s 65(7).

2.   Not to appoint a Safeguarder – s 41.

3.   To issue a warrant under s 66(1).

The hearing stated its reasons thus:

1.   In respect that William Brown and his mother did not accept any of the Grounds for Referral the hearing unanimously decided not to discharge the referral and directed the reporter to make application to the sheriff for a finding as to whether said grounds were established.

2.   The hearing decided not to appoint a safeguarder or legal representative on the basis that at the proof before the sheriff the child would almost certainly be legally represented – this was confirmed by the child's mother.

3.   The hearing, by a majority, ordered the child to be detained in a place of safety[38] because the child refused to discuss the case and said nothing beyond denying the Grounds for Referral. The majority of the hearing thought that his failure to explain why he was arrested for the assault on the child G and his failure to explain, in relation to the 'paint' incident, how he could have an 'alibi witness' for an event which, had he been innocent, he could not have known the time of, all indicated that he was guilty. Moreover since fire-raising was such a serious matter and since the child's father had not attended the hearing and the majority thought his mother was not able to control him, the majority therefore concluded that he was a danger to

---

36.   Children (Scotland) Act 1995 s 66(2)(b).
37.   Cf Children (Scotland) Act 1995 s 66(4)(b).
38.   Form 12 of the Children's Hearings (Scotland) Rules 1996 indicates that the place of safety should be named. It is now the practice, approved by SCRA, to treat this part of the form as directive rather than mandatory and not to name the place.

himself and others and that it was therefore necessary for his safety and welfare to require his detention.

The reporter arranges for the decision and the written reasons for the decision to be given to the child and his mother immediately after the hearing.

Tuesday, 27 December 2005 at 5.30 pm

The reporter makes out a 'Form 12' (of the Children's Hearings (Scotland) Rules, 1996, SI 96/3261), headed 'Warrant under Section 66(1) of the Act for Keeping a Child in a Place of Safety'[39], and the chair of the hearing signs it. He conveys a copy of this to the Out of Hours Team of the Social Work Department[40] and to the manager of the local residential establishment, which is St Thenew's Residential School. The Out of Hours Team take William to St Thenew's.

Tuesday, 27 December 2005, Wednesday 28 December 2005

Mr and Mrs Brown are horrified that their son has been, as they see it, 'locked up'. They have had no contact with lawyers but have noticed the name of Messrs Campbell and MacDonald, Solicitors, Kirklenton. Mrs Brown phones them on Wednesday morning and finds that Jamie Wynford, who is their procurator (ie legal assistant) and has considerable experience in the hearings field, is in the office and able to see her at short notice on the following morning.

Wednesday, 28 December 2005

The reporter phones the social worker, Mr Mark Fox, and tells him what has happened. He faxes to Mr Fox a copy of the Form 12 and copies of the written decision of the hearing and the Statement of Reasons.

Thursday 29, December 2005 at 10 am

Mrs Brown meets Mr Wynford on Thursday 29 December 2005. She gives him her copy of the Grounds for Referral the SBR, Statement of Reasons and the written decision of the hearing, as well as Form 12. He advises that Mr and Mrs Brown and William have the right to appeal to the sheriff against the warrant, and that when the appeal is lodged it will require to be dealt with within three days. Mrs Brown says she wants action as soon as possible. Mr Wynford says that he might be able to lodge the appeal papers later in the same day and in that event the appeal hearing would be likely to be fixed for Sunday 1 January 2006. Mrs Brown says she would like this to be done.

---

39. For an example of 'Form 12', see Part One of this book at p 135.
40. Had the social worker Mr Fox been present a copy would have been given to him right away.

Mr Wynford, who is an experienced court practitioner, and trusted to take on new clients, explains the formalities which nowadays attend the instruction of a solicitor (see paragraph *[14]* below). He says that, as mentioned already, William himself and both Mr and Mrs Brown (as 'relevant persons') have the right to appeal and draws attention to the provisions of section 2(4A) of the Age of Legal Capacity (Scotland) Act 1991[41]. He mentions that in any event he would wish to see William before the hearing and suggests that, as William is an obviously mature 14½ year old, it might be appropriate for William to be the 'client'. Mrs Brown agrees.

Mr Wynford says he will argue that the decision of the hearing was most unusual in detaining a child for a first 'offence' of this nature where the information that William was a continuing danger to himself or others was conspicuously thin. He says he thinks the decision will be open to attack on the ground that the social worker was not present, and because there was no indication in the decision itself or in the Reasons provided that the hearing had considered whether making an order would be better for the child than making no order at all[42]. He says that he is fairly confident that the appeal will be successful, though, cautiously, warning Mrs Brown that he cannot guarantee this.

Mr Wynford says he will contact the residential establishment and try to arrange to see William later on the same day and, as well as interviewing him on the merits of the case, ask him to sign an application form for Legal Advice and Assistance, which will cover the pre-court work and an application for full Legal Aid in respect of the appeal hearing in the Sheriff Court[43]. He mentions that Legal Aid is not available for appearances before Children's Hearings themselves but indicates that his firm will appear with William without charge at any hearing at which any important decision is likely to be taken. Mrs Brown asks if he will ask the managers of St Thenew's about contact with their son and Mr Wynford agrees to do this.

Mr Wynford then telephones the managers of St Thenew's and they agree that Mr and Mrs Brown can visit William each day in the meantime. While on the phone to St Thenew's he asks if he can speak to William and this is arranged. He explains to William that William's mother has asked him to arrange an appeal against the decision of the hearing to grant the warrant. William enthusiastically agrees that Mr Wynford can act for him. Mr Wynford passes on all this to Mrs Brown. Before leaving Mrs Brown asks if there is any way she can get William out pending the appeal. She is told that this is not possible under the Children (Scotland) Act 1995[44].

---

41. 'A person under the age of sixteen years shall have the legal capacity to instruct a solicitor, in connection with any civil matter, where that person has a general understanding of what it means to do so; and without prejudice to the generality of this subsection a person twelve years of age or more shall be presumed to be of sufficient age and maturity to have such understanding'.
42. The 'No non-beneficial order' principle, enacted in section 16(3) of the Children (Scotland) Act 1995.
43. Legal Aid (Scotland) Act 1986 s 29(2)(b)(i) and s 29(3), as substituted by the Children (Scotland) Act 1995 s 92.
44. See discussion in Kearney, op cit, at 53.02.

Note [13]   Mr and Mrs Brown are fortunate to have secured (and at the festive season!) a solicitor who is familiar with the system and ready and willing to act promptly. Appeal is in the first instance by Note of Appeal[45]. The time-limit for appealing against any decision of a hearing is 'within a period of three weeks beginning with the date of any decision of a children's hearing'[46], but owing to the obvious importance of trying to get the boy home as soon as possible the solicitor aims to get his Note of Appeal in later on the same day, even although this will require a hearing of the appeal on or before New Year's Day. Once the Note of Appeal has been lodged it must be disposed of 'within three days of the lodging of the appeal' and if it is not disposed of within that period the warrant ceases to have effect at the end of that period[47]. In this case the day of lodging is 'day one' and the reference is to calendar days, not working days[48]. Accordingly a Note of Appeal lodged on Thursday 29 December 2005 would have to be disposed of by Sunday, 1 January 2006 or the warrant would fall. It is unlikely that the court would fix the hearing of the appeal on the day after lodgement, or even on the day after that (which would give parties almost no time to prepare) and accordingly the solicitor correctly anticipates that the appeal hearing will, most exceptionally, be held on New Year's Day.

Note [14]   The professional obligations of a solicitor on taking on a client are now governed by detailed rules including the Solicitors (Scotland) Practice Rules 1986 and the Solicitors (Scotland) (Client Communication) Practice Rules 2005[49]. Mr Wynford explains what he has to explain[50] and promises that the firm will send out its 'Terms of Business' to William and Mr and Mrs Brown in the evening's post.

Note [15]   In relation to possible conflict of interest the Law Society of Scotland has issued 'Law Society Guidelines on Conflict of Interest', as amended on May 1999[51]. It is beyond the scope of this work to discuss these rules in detail, but it should be noted that the 1986 Rules include, as Rule 2, the following: 'A solicitor shall not act for two or more parties whose interests conflict'. The 1999 Guidelines include: 'Neither the Rules nor the Code of Conduct contains a definition of conflict of interest. ... Conflict of interest is not a matter for the judgment of the client – it is a

---

45. Act of Sederunt (Child Care and Maintenance Rules) 1997, r 3.53(1), Form 62.
46. Children (Scotland) Act 1995 s 51(1)(a). This has been held to mean that the date of the hearing is 'day one' but this has been doubted and the suggestion made that the day after the hearing is 'day one'. See discussion in *Kearney, op cit* 50.09.
47. Children (Scotland) Act 1995, s 51(8).
48. *S v Galbraith* (8 July 1980, unreported) Court of Session, and *B v Kennedy* 1992 SLT 870; see discussion in *Kearney, op cit*, 50.10 and 50.11.)
49. Reproduced respectively in the Parliament House Book, section F, at pages 271 and 336/2.
50. See Part One of this book paragraph *[21]*.
51. Reproduced in the Parliament House Book, section F, at page 1204.

matter for the judgment of the solicitor.' In the present situation Mr Wynford judges (a) that there is no foreseeable conflict of interest between Mrs Brown and William and (b) that Mrs Brown has not in any real sense become his client. The decision to have William as 'the client' instead of the mother (or both) is based on the realities of the situation and a reasonable reading of section 2(4A) of the Age of Legal Capacity (Scotland) Act 1991[52].

Thursday, 29 December 2005 at 12 noon

Mr Wynford attends at the Residential School and meets William. He explains to William the formal position in relation to the appeal procedures and as to the concept of instructing a solicitor. In relation to Legal Aid he explains the position as already conveyed to Mrs Brown at their meeting that morning. He then takes detailed notes[53] of William's stance in relation to the allegations in the Grounds and the whole background. He advises William, as he has advised Mrs Brown, that he is reasonably confident of a favourable outcome, but again cautions that he cannot guarantee this. He later converts his notes into William's precognition as follows:

Children's Reporter (Kirklenton) v William Brown (d.o.b. 01.08.1991)

29 December 2005

PRECOGNITION

of

William Brown (14), school student,
residing at 3/1, 27 Morrison Street,
Kirklenton LE2 7EH.
Phone number: 012104 552 777

I attend Kirklenton High School and am at present in Secondary Three. I live with my parents at the above address. My friends at school are Douglas Leitch and Henry Galbraith. I know Stephen Green but for some reason, possibly connected with his allegation that I once injured him in a 'foul' when playing football, he regards himself as my enemy and is always trying to get me into trouble. We are all in the same class in school. None of us is particularly interested in school subjects except PT at which we are all pretty good. I also quite like Science.

On the morning of Thursday 3rd November 2005 Henry came up to me at break time and told me that the door to one of the science labs had been

---

52. The issue of conflict of interest arises in the case treated in Part One of this book – see Part One, paragraphs [21] and [22] and intervening passages.
53. It might not always be practicable for a solicitor to take such a full statement at such short notice but by chance a whole day meeting for Mr Wynford has been cancelled at the last moment.

spray-painted with the rude words about Mr Black. Henry had been told of this by the janitor, Mr Donaldson. Henry's uncle is the janitor of St Anastasia's School here in Kirklenton and socialises with Mr Donaldson and sometimes comes to Henry's house. As a result Mr Donaldson and Henry are kind of friendly and that would be why Mr Donaldson would give this information to Henry. Mr Donaldson had told Henry that he (Mr Donaldson) had noticed the paint on the Wednesday evening, 2nd November, when doing his evening round up about 7 pm. The science teacher, Mr McNeill, had reported that the door was in its normal condition when he left the school at 5.30 on the Wednesday. He left school at that time because he ran the school Stamp Club which met in his science lab between 4.15 and 5.15. Mr McNeill, according to what I was told by Henry, locked the door of his science lab, but left open the outer door of the Science building, leaving it to the janitor to lock the outer door when doing his evening round. As a result the science block was open to anyone between 5.30 and 7. (I believe this has now been changed and it is now locked when the last teacher leaves.) Stephen Green regularly goes to the Stamp Club. I have of course no direct knowledge but I suspect that Stephen himself may have done the painting and blamed it on me in order to get me into trouble.

I usually go the Kirklenton swimming baths after school on Wednesdays with Henry and Douglas. I went to the baths on Wednesday 2nd November and lingered there till quarter past seven and didn't get home till half past seven. My mum can confirm that I came home with wet swimming things at that time, but on this particular Wednesday Henry and Douglas weren't able to come with me so I went alone. I cannot give the name of anyone who saw me at the baths. I said I had an alibi witness because I thought that Henry would back me up, but it turned out that he had been to his mother's birthday party that afternoon and evening and was afraid that if he said he was at the baths he would be found out. I'm now sorry I told a lie about that but I was really afraid of being wrongly blamed for the paint incident, since I think Stephen is a bit of a teacher's pet and would be believed in preference to me – as in fact happened. Stephen is a member of the Stamp Club and would have had the opportunity of painting the door by hanging about after the club meeting after Mr McNeill had gone.

After the break on Thursday morning I was summoned to the Head's office and he, in the presence of the school secretary, Miss Webster, asked me if I knew anything about the spray painting. He didn't give me much chance to explain but I said I had an alibi. He asked who that was and I refused to give a name, since I had not yet checked with Henry if he would back me up. I think Mr Black took that as indicating that I was lying and also that I was guilty. He said he had an eye-witness to say that I had done it. He refused to tell me who the witness was. I am sure that it was Stephen because he had been called out of the class earlier on. I guess Stephen had hinted to Mr McNeill that he knew something about the painting incident and that Mr McNeill had told the Head. I said to the Head that I had the right under the Human Rights Act to know who my accuser was and the Head then got angry and told me not to try to be clever. I then got very angry and I am afraid I lost my temper and said words to the effect that he'd bloody well better be careful about making false allegations or I would sue him and the school. I didn't use any other bad language, because I, and all of the others, like and respect Miss Webster and would not dream of, for example, using the 'f' word in her presence. The Head then said he was satisfied that I was guilty and that I would be suspended. He told me to go back to the class meantime while he attended to the formalities. About an hour later I was summoned back to the Head's office. This time Mr McNeill, who is the Assistant Head Teacher, was also present. Mr Black then told me that, having discussed the matter with Mr McNeill, he had decided to limit my punishment to one and a half hours' detention on the Friday afternoon. I felt like saying 'Thanks for nothing' since I was still being punished for something I hadn't done, but, like most of us, I like and respect Mr McNeill and, since I believed and still believe that he had advised against suspension, I did not want to appear ungrateful. However I just said nothing and was told to go back to the class.

On Friday 4th November 2005 I was detained till half past five. I live about half a mile from the school. My route home takes me past Attlee Quadrant which is round the corner from Dalton Causeway, where Stephen Green stays. When in Attlee Quadrant I saw Stephen across the street and he shouted over to me in a taunting manner 'Have you had a nice afternoon?' I saw red and ran across the road – I am a very fast runner and I think Stephen was too surprised at the speed of my reaction to run away. I gave him one punch on the chest which winded him and he fell to the ground. That was the only blow. I wanted to hit him again but I was not prepared to do so when he was 'down'. I told him to get up and I'd give him a real doing. Then the police arrived and, seeing Stephen on the ground with me standing over him, took hold of me. I think they may have heard what I said to Stephen because my voice was raised. Stephen shouted to them that I had punched him in the guts. That was not correct – I had however hit him quite hard on the chest.

The police said something about detaining me under some Act and asked my name, age and address. They said I didn't need to say anything but that if I did say anything it would be noted and might be given as evidence. They spoke to Stephen Green and he said I had punched him in the stomach and kicked him on the head when he was on the ground. I strongly denied this and said words to the effect: 'That grassing bastard is lying. I only punched him on the chest. He had it coming to him.' The police then put me into the police car. They asked Stephen if he wanted a lift but he said he was near enough home. The police then drove me the short distance to my home. Only mum was in. They explained what had happened and said they were going to charge me with assaulting Stephen Green. The female police officer said that I did not need to say anything but that if I did say anything it might be used as evidence. She then charged me with assaulting Stephen Green by punching him in the stomach and kicking him on the head. I replied that I had only punched him on the chest, that it was a lie that I had kicked him and that the grassing bastard had it coming to him. She then asked me what I meant by that and said I was still under caution. I said 'Oh nothing' and that was the end of the interview. They said they would be reporting this to the procurator fiscal or the reporter to the children's panel and then left.

After the police had gone I told my mum about everything that had happened that day. She knew about the detention because the school had phoned. I'm not sure that she believed my denials about the painting since I have done daft things like writing on walls before and she has heard about them. I know she did believe me when I said I only punched Stephen Green because she knows that, though I get into trouble for graffiti and fighting, I never fight dirty.

The next thing to happen was that about a fortnight later a social worker called Mark Fox came to the school. He first saw my guidance teacher Miss Reilly and then me along with Miss Reilly. I told him more or less what I've told you and also a little about the set up at home. He said he would contact my mother and get further details directly from her. He told me that there would not be a prosecution in court but said the reporter might take me to the panel. That was for the reporter to decide. Much might depend on whether the reporter believed that I had kicked as well as punched. I think it was on the afternoon of the same day that the social worker came to see mum. A few days later he came in the evening to see mum and dad and me, but my father was not in.

You have asked me about the set-up at home and explained that you have to know about it in case the case is upheld and you have to talk to a hearing about what they should do then as to 'disposal'. Mum is the dominant force. Dad is all right but he was a steel worker and there is now no work in his line near here. He is very depressed about this and goes to the pub rather a lot. He was out at the pub when the social worker came to the house. Mum works as the head of catering in the big hospital in Muirbrachlan. Mum takes the car to her work and Dad feels a bit 'put down' by this. I get on well enough with Angela but she puts it on a bit about being in college. Actually I find some of the school subjects more interesting than I let on. It is not a good idea to appear to be a 'swot' and as I am strong physically I make the most of this by concentrating on football and PT. The only thing I allow myself to work on at school is Science, partly because Mr McNeill is such a good teacher. But actually I quite like English – particularly plays. If it was not seen as missy I think I would like to try acting.

On the evening of Saturday 5th November 2005 my mum had to go out to attend a staff meeting in the hospital in Muirbrachlan and she left the house about 8 pm, leaving me with Angela, who was not too pleased about this as she wanted to spend part of the evening in the Wine Bar with her boy-friend. Angela actually slipped out and did not come back till 10 pm, just before my mum came back from her meeting. Dad had been at the pub and did not return till late. Accordingly I was in the house alone from 8 till 10 and therefore have no alibi for a time which may have been the time when the school shed was set fire to. I know nothing at all about the petrol container and the spray-paint container. The fact that they were found together doesn't seem to me to mean very much. The anonymous information was given to Mr Black a few days after the reporter had written to my mum and dad on 29th November 2005 saying that he was taking no action against me. I have now been told that notification of this was sent to the Greens. I think this is suspicious. I think Stephen Green may have planted these things so as to frame me. I have no idea who set fire to the shed. I don't think it would be Stephen Green. I don't think he would have the bottle.

As to the hearing on 27th December I thought it was 'a shambles' [William's own words]. The social worker was not there. I knew he regarded me as at a low risk of offending again. He said to me that he had intended to put that in his report but had forgotten but re-assured me that he would say that to the hearing. I tried to explain this to the hearing but they would not listen. The chairman and the reporter tried to see things from my point of view but they were overruled and, I thought, bullied by the other two members who seemed to have a 'down' on me.

In case there should be any doubt I confirm that Mr Wynford's firm have my permission to tell my parents everything about the progress of this case.

Note [16]   A precognition does not reproduce the exact words of the witness. In this it is different from a 'statement', which should do that. A precognition, on the other hand is, in the words of Lord Justice Clerk Thomson in Kerr v HM Advocate[54], *' filtered through the mind of another, whose job it is to put what he thinks the witness means into a form suitable for use in judicial proceedings'. That is the reason why reference in evidence to precognitions, as opposed to statements, is, in Lord Justice-Clerk Thomson's words in Kerr, 'frowned upon'*[55]. *His Lordship, with cheerful cynicism, goes on to say of the 'filtering': 'This process tends to colour the result. Precognoscers as a rule appear to be gifted with a measure of optimism which no amount of disillusionment can damp.' One wonders if he was speaking from bitter experience at the bar of witnesses not coming 'up to precognition'. The precognition of William taken by Mr Wynford seems not to be of the type thus stigmatised. Although not using the witness's exact words (except where Mr Wynford has specifically indicated) – it is too tidy and grammatical to be the exact words of a fourteen year old child – it seems to follow his words reasonably closely. For example, he refers to the police saying something about detaining him 'under*

---

54. 1958 JC 14 at 19; see discussion in Part One of this book at paragraph *[3]*.
55. The extent to which statements can be used in evidence is a big subject. For further discussion see *Macphail on Evidence* (1987) at *19.29 to 19.30 and, in the criminal sphere, *Renton and Brown's Criminal Procedure*, 6th edn at paras 24–31 to 24–67.

some Act'. It differentiates between information which the witness knows directly and information which he knows by having been told. This is very important. It greatly weakens the impact of evidence when it emerges at the proof that what the witness is saying is hearsay. In criminal cases this can be disastrous since in such cases hearsay evidence is generally inadmissible to prove its contents and this case, being a referral under section 52(2)(i) counts under the law of evidence[56] as a criminal case[57]. The precognition covers the assault incident in some detail, even although it is not in the Grounds for Referral. This is not just because William was anxious to talk about it (never by itself a good reason for including something in a precognition) but because it bears upon the relationship between William and Stephen, which is highly relevant to the line that Mr Wynford will require to take in trying to counter the evidence of Stephen by establishing malice. Mr Wynford has not yet decided whether it will be (a) admissible and (b) desirable to use this evidence in the proof, but it is important to have a record of it, if only because it might emerge anyway.

The precognition is also satisfactory in that it gives some impression of the character of the witness. This is helpful because the person taking the precognition will not necessarily be the person taking the proof. Some precognoscers add a written note giving some guidance, eg, 'This seems a very nervous witness'. This may be appropriate in a particular case but the author did not often do this.

---

56. Civil Evidence (Scotland) Act 1988, s 9, as amended by the Children (Scotland) Act 1995, Sch 4 para 44: definition of 'civil proceedings'.
57. For further discussion of the admissibility of hearsay evidence see *Kearney*, op cit, at 43.10 to 43.22.

Thursday, 29 December 2005, 2.30 – 3.30 pm

Mr Wynford frames his Note of Appeal thus:

APPEAL TO SHERIFF AGAINST ISSUE OF WARRANT BY CHILDREN'S HEARING UNDER SECTION 51(1) AND (8) OF THE CHILDREN (SCOTLAND) ACT 1995

Act of Sederunt (Child Care and Maintenance Rules) 1997 Rule 3.53(1)

Sheriff Court of Lenton and Muirbrachlan at Kirklenton

APPEAL

under

Section 51(1) of the Children (Scotland) Act 1995 by

The child William Brown, d.o.b. 01.08.1991, at present accommodated in St Thenew's Residential School, Kirklenton

APPELLANT

against

A decision of the children's hearing for the Lentonshire Council at Kirklenton to issue a warrant for the detention of the said William Brown.

1.   On 27 December 2005 a children's hearing at Kirklenton granted warrant for the detention of the said child under section 66(2)(b) of the Children (Scotland) Act 1995 and the child was taken to and kept at St Thenew's Residential School. A copy of the decision and of the reasons stated therefor is attached. The hearing also had before them a Social Background Report dated 16 December 2005. A copy of this is also attached hereto.

2.   No safeguarder was appointed.

3.   The said warrant is unnecessary because the child is not a danger to himself or others. The Social Worker's report did not suggest that the child was a danger to himself or others and the Social Worker was not present to give his views on this matter.

4.   The said warrant is unnecessary because it does not tend to promote the welfare of the child throughout his childhood in respect that it removes him from his secure home environment for no good or sufficient reason.

5.   The action of the said hearing in granting said warrant was irregular because the hearing did not give the child an adequate opportunity to express his views.

6.   The action of the said hearing in granting said warrant was irregular because they did not consider, or, *separatim* did not consider adequately, whether it would be better for the child that the warrant should be granted as opposed to no warrant being granted. The hearing deliberated in the absence of the child's social worker which was unusual and to that extent irregular and prejudicial to the interests of the child in that it limited the ability of the hearing to assess whether it would be better for the child that the warrant should be granted as opposed to no warrant being granted.

7.   The action of the said hearing in granting the said warrant was irregular because it is clear from the third reason stated by the hearing that the hearing (a) exceeded their powers by purporting to conclude that the child was 'guilty' of the first offence in the Grounds for Referral and, (b) took into account an alleged offence not founded on in the Grounds for Referral and purported to conclude that the child was guilty of that also and (c) having so concluded, they appeared, without any foundation, to extend this conclusion to the more serious second offence in the Grounds for Referral.

8.   The action of the said hearing in granting the said warrant was irregular in respect that a hearing which is contemplating granting warrant for the detention of a child should, it is submitted, appoint a safeguarder.

9.   In any event the action of the said hearing was irregular in that the hearing as a public authority, had a duty to respect the child's right under Article 6(3)(c) of the European Convention on Human Rights to allow the child legal assistance to defend himself before having his liberty abridged, and failed in said duty.

10.   The said William Brown appeals to the sheriff against said decision.

Signed: Jamie Wynford
Solicitor,
Messrs Campbell and MacDonald,
17 Wallace Square,
Kirklenton LE6 9ZE
Telephone: 012104 878 200
Fax: 012104 878 201.

Note *[17]   There is no formal provision, in the context of an appeal to the sheriff from a decision of a hearing, permitting or prohibiting the putting forward of a new ground of appeal at the appeal hearing itself[58]; however, rather than taking the chance that the sheriff might consider that bringing in a new ground at the last minute would be unfair to any other party, Mr Wynford has decided, in the limited time at his disposal, to err on the side of comprehensiveness rather than brevity[59]. The arguments will be summarised and ruled upon by the sheriff in the Note to her judgement.*

Thursday, 29 December 2005 at 4.30 pm

Jamie Wynford attends at the sheriff clerk's office and obtains a court order in these terms[60]:

Kirklenton 29th December 2005.

The court assigns 1st January 2006 at 2.30 pm. in chambers within the Sheriff Court of Lenton and Muirbrachlan at Kirklenton, 1 Wallace Place, Kirklenton, LE6 4DD, for the hearing of the application[61].

APPOINTS the Sheriff Clerk forthwith

(a)   To intimate a copy of the application and this warrant on

    i.   The Principal Reporter; and

    ii.   The relevant persons, viz Mr Hugh Brown and Mrs Sylvia Brown, 3/1, 27 Morrison Street, Kiklenton, LE 6 1AA.

    iii.   The Chief Social Work Officer, Lentonshire Council, The Council Buildings, Bruce Gardens, Kirklenton, LE6 1AA.

AUTHORISES the Sheriff Clerk to effect said intimation orally in terms of Act of Sederunt (Child Care and Maintenance Rules) 1997 r 3.15(3).

Eo die

The court finds it unnecessary to appoint a safeguarder under section 41(1) of the Children (Scotland) Act 1995.

Fiona Grey
Sheriff

---

58.   In contrast to the situation in an appeal from the sheriff to the Sheriff Principal where, under Act of Sederunt (Child Care and Maintenance Rules) 1997 r 3.59(9) which allows new points to be raised 'on cause shown'.
59.   For discussion of amplification of grounds of appeal at the appeal hearing, see *Kearney, op cit*, at 52.03.
60.   Following the wording of Form 62 relevant to r 3.53(1) of the Act of Sederunt (Child Care and Maintenance Rules) 1997.
61.   Here, as elsewhere in this style, the word 'application' is used whereas this is not an application but an appeal. Mr Wynford, however, follows the style!

The sheriff clerk effects the required notifications. The sheriff clerk confirms to the sheriff that arrangements have been made for the court building to be open on New Year's Day 2006 for the hearing of the appeal at 2.30 pm.

> *Note [18]   While considering the Note of Appeal Sheriff Grey also considered, as she was bound to under section 41(1) of the Children (Scotland) Act 1995, 'if it is necessary to appoint a person to safeguard the interests of the child in the proceedings'. (In practice some sheriffs consider appointing a curator ad litem[62].) It is thought that sheriffs, in considering this matter, are entitled to take such advice as they think fit, eg by asking the sheriff clerk to speak to the solicitor, the reporter or any social worker known to be involved. A safeguarder is concerned with 'the interests' of the child and not simply with his instructions and therefore the consideration that William is represented by a competent solicitor (while a relevant point) is not conclusive against the appointment of a safeguarder. However, having regard to the terms of the SBR, which suggests no serious significant worries as to William's general welfare, and the fact that William is in effect legally represented, Sheriff Grey decided not to appoint a safeguarder or a curator ad litem.*

Thursday, 29 December 2005 at 7.30 pm

Mr Wynford attends, by arrangement, at Mr and Mrs Brown's house, reports on progress so far and also takes Mrs Brown's precognition, including her account of what happened at the hearing of 27 December 2005.

Sunday, 1 January 2006 at 2 pm – In Sheriff Grey's chambers

The sheriff has before her: The Note of Appeal, which has been lodged in the court; and its attachments, viz the Hearing's decision, with Statement of Reasons, and the Social Background Report dated 16 December 2005. (In an Appeal against the granting of a Warrant, as opposed to appeals against substantive decisions of hearings[63], there is no provision for the other side to lodge answers.) Having re-examined these papers the sheriff tells the sheriff clerk that she is ready and the sheriff clerk confirms all parties are ready. The hearing is to take place in the small court which will be the sheriff's 'chambers' for this occasion. As in all court procedures in relation to children's hearings, the general public is excluded.

> *Note [19]   Since the proceedings are 'in chambers' the sheriff has a discretion as to who, apart from those principally involved, may*

---

62. For discussion of the appointment and functions of safeguarders and curators *ad litem*, see Part One of this book, paragraph *[28]*.
63. Act of Sederunt (Child Care and Maintenance Rules) 1997 r 3.55.

be present in her chambers[64]. In practice it is extremely unusual for any person other than those principally involved (the child, the relevant persons, the reporter on behalf of the hearing, and any author of any report or statement whom the sheriff may wish to examine[65]) to be present. A police officer is generally present but for today's proceedings the sheriff, judging that there is no foreseeable risk of disorder, has dispensed with police presence. It is competent for the sheriff to admit a bona fide representative of the media if she thinks it appropriate. It is generally an offence for anyone to publish any matter which could identify any child concerned in the proceedings or his or her address or the address of any school[66], but publication may be permitted by the sheriff, the Court of Session or the Scottish Ministers. Such permission would be highly exceptional.

Sunday, 1 January 2006 at 2.30 pm – In Sheriff Grey's chambers

The persons appearing before the sheriff are: Mr Wynford, solicitor, with his client, William, the child's mother, as relevant person, and the reporter, on behalf of the hearing. Also in court (but not in the sheriff's chambers) is one of the managers of St Thenew's. In practice the minimum number of persons appearing before the sheriff would be the solicitor for the appellant and the reporter, but in an appeal against a warrant it is normal for the appellant(s) to be present also.

The appeal hearing takes place. Mr Wynford addresses the sheriff in support of his Note of Appeal. The reporter responds and advances such arguments as he thinks proper in support of the decision of the hearing. The sheriff asks William if he wishes to express a view[67]. He says he does. The sheriff asks if he wishes her to hear these views in private but William says he would like everyone to hear his views. The sheriff invites William to state his views and he says he would like to return home. The sheriff makes a written record of these views. The sheriff asks the solicitor and the reporter if they have any comment on this and they say they have not. The sheriff then states orally that the appeal is allowed and that the warrant is recalled[68]. She adds that she will issue a written opinion summarising the arguments and giving the reasons for her decision within 7 days[69]. The manager of St Thenew's is invited into the sheriff's chambers and the sheriff tells him of her decision. William is formally re-united with his mother and they go home. Mr Wynford arranges for Mrs Brown and William Brown to come to his office on Monday 9 January 2006 for a full discussion of the case.

---

64. For a fuller discussion of this see *Kearney, op cit,* at 28.03 – 28.08 and *Norrie, op cit,* Chapter Five.
65. Children (Scotland) Act 1995 s 51(3) (b) and (c).
66. Children (Scotland) Act 1995 s 44(1)
67. Children (Scotland) Act 1995 s 16(2); Act of Sederunt (Child Care and Maintenance Rules) 1997 r 3.5(1),(2) and (3) – particularly (3).
68. Act of Sederunt (Child Care and Maintenance Rules) 1997, r 3.58(1).
69. Act of Sederunt (Child Care and Maintenance Rules) 1997, r 3.58(2) & (3).

Sunday, 1 January 2006 at 4 pm

The sheriff signs an interlocutor in these terms:

Kirklenton 1st January 2006

For the Principal Reporter: Somerville

For the appellant (the child), personally present: Wynford

Mrs Sylvia Brown, mother of child and relevant person, personally present

The sheriff, having considered the appeal and having heard the views of the child, ALLOWS the appeal and DISCHARGES the warrant granted on 27 December 2005.

(Sgd) Fiona Grey

Friday, 6 January 2006.

The sheriff issues the following:

Note:

The background

[1] This is an appeal against a warrant for the detention of a child whom I will refer to as WB in a residential establishment. The appeal runs in the name of the child WB. Mr Wynford explained to me that he had originally been instructed by the mother but that the child had indicated that he was in favour of the appeal and that he, Mr Wynford, should argue it on his behalf. I of course accepted this from Mr Wynford, and it was in any event obvious from the stance of the child throughout the appeal that this was the child's wish. The consideration that Mr Wynford had been instructed, the apparent maturity of the child, and the whole background confirmed me in my view, formulated in my interlocutor of 29th December 2005, that it was not necessary to appoint a safeguarder.

[2] The said child, with his mother, MB, appeared before a hearing here in Kirklenton on 27th December 2005 in respect of grounds stated in terms of section 52(2)(i) of the Children (Scotland) Act 1995, namely that the child had committed offences. The Statement of Facts averred that the offences were these:

    1.   That William Brown did on or about Wednesday 2nd November 2005 paint abusive words on the door of class-room number 7 of

Kirklenton High School, Aberfeldy Road, Kirklenton, LE5 4DL – this being the offence of malicious mischief.

2.   That William Brown did at or about 10 pm. on Saturday 5th November 2005, using a flammable substance, set fire to an outhouse situated in the north eastern corner of the playground of Kirklenton High School, Aberfeldy Road, Kirklenton, LE5 4DL whereby fire took hold and damaged the door and part of the front wall of said outhouse – this being the offence of wilful fire-raising, or, alternatively, the offence of culpable and reckless fire-raising.

[3] The hearing had before it a Report prepared by the Social Work Department of the local authority dated 16th December 2005 which the appellant's agent had annexed to his Note of Appeal. In general this report gave a reasonably favourable account of the child and his background. I shall say more about the terms of this report presently.

[4] Mr Wynford outlined the heads of appeal set out in paragraphs 3 to 9 of the Note of Appeal. Mr Wynford had not been present at the hearing on 27th December 2005. He told me that he had had the opportunity of discussing the matter with the reporter Mr Somerville in relation to his instructions from the mother and the child and that if I were to use my powers to 'examine' the reporter under s 51(3)(a) of the Children (Scotland) Act 1995 then the reporter's information would be substantially agreed. I expressed satisfaction that this agreement had been reached and invited the reporter to tell me what had happened at the hearing.

[5] The reporter told me that there were present at the hearing: the child, his mother and the reporter himself, Mr Somerville. There was a message from the social worker Mr Fox that he had become stuck in the snow and did not expect to be able to attend any time on the day.

[6] The chairman of the hearing, after introducing the parties, explained the grounds for referral, as required by s 65(4) of the Children (Scotland) Act 1995. In view of the fact that the child and relevant person ultimately did not accept the grounds of referral nothing hung upon the adequacy or otherwise of this explanation, but the reporter assured me that he regarded it as satisfactory both in relation to the definition of malicious mischief and in relation to fire-raising, wilful and culpable and reckless.

[7] After explaining the definition of the offences in the grounds for referral the chairman asked the child if he accepted that he had carried out the actions amounting to the offences in the grounds of referral. The mother replied that the child did not accept this. The chairman said the hearing would like to hear from the child and the child said his mother was correct: he did not accept the grounds. The chairman asked if there was any question, in relation to the charge of fire-raising, of the child accepting that he had been involved in some way such as lighting a fire for fun and then it turning out by accident that the outhouse had caught fire. The boy said he knew nothing of either the spray-painting incident or the fire. The

boy and his mother emphatically denied that he had been anywhere near the incident. The chairman then said words to the effect that it looked as if the hearing, unless it was inclined to discharge the referral, would have to direct the reporter to make application to the sheriff for a proof. He said he thought it was unlikely that the hearing would wish to discharge a referral containing such a serious allegation as fire-raising and therefore he proposed, if there was nothing more to be said, that the reporter be directed to apply to the sheriff for a proof.

[8] At this point one of the other hearing members, whom I will refer to as 'the second hearing member' said that there was something more to be said: how did the child account for the fact that he had been charged with an offence such as fire-raising. The chairman interrupted and said he thought this was not a line they should go down. This matter was not 'before' the hearing and could not, in the light of the child's non-acceptance of the grounds, be inquired into by the hearing. The third hearing member then said that the Social Work Report was 'before' the hearing and it contained the statement that the child had said he had had an 'alibi witness' to the spray-painting incident – How did this square with the child's statement a few minutes ago that he knew nothing of either incident? The chairman said they could not cross-examine the child as to his non-acceptance of the grounds and the other two hearing members did not pursue these points but said they thought they were significant.

[9] The chair repeated her suggestion that the hearing should direct the reporter to apply to the sheriff for proof. The second hearing member agreed but suggested that, having regard to the seriousness of the fire-raising charge, the hearing should grant a warrant for the detention of the child. The third hearing member reverted to the point about the 'alibi witness' and supported this suggestion. The chair said that the latter point should not form part of the hearing's deliberations but the third member said he maintained his reservations. The reporter, although thinking that the chair's view is preferable, does not intervene to say this because he regarded the proposed action as competent. The reporter also suggested that the hearing might wish to appoint a legal representative and/or a safeguarder since the liberty of the child was involved. The chair agreed with this suggestion but was out-voted by the other two members on this matter also. The mother interjected to say that she strongly objected to the proposal that a warrant be granted. She said that they would appeal and that the appeal would be conducted by a solicitor.

[10] After some further discussion amongst the hearing members the hearing decided unanimously to direct the reporter to apply to the sheriff for proof and, by a majority, with the Chair dissenting, to grant a warrant under section 66(1) of the Children (Scotland) Act 1995 on the ground that it was necessary to do so in order to safeguard or promote his welfare under s 66(2)(b) of the Act. The chair formally advised of the right of appeal. Thereafter arrangements were made to take the child to the residential establishment and there he remained until the conclusion of the appeal, which I granted.

[11] The hearing stated reasons for their decision thus:

[*The sheriff reproduces the Statement of Reasons as above at page 187*].

The submissions for the appellant

[12] Mr Wynford, for the appellants, opened by examining the powers of the sheriff in an appeal from the decision of a hearing. He referred to the discussion of this matter by Sheriff (as he then was) Mowat in *D v Sinclair*, 1973 SLT (Sh Ct) 47. In that case the learned sheriff stated: 'Accordingly, I considered that a sheriff should not allow an appeal unless there was some flaw in the procedure adopted by the hearing or he was satisfied that the hearing had not given consideration to some factor in the case'. Mr Wynford acknowledged that this approach had been given indirect approval by Lord President Hope in *O v Rae* 1992 SCLR 318 at 325. He said that, even accepting that Sheriff Mowat's analysis was correct, his appeal would succeed since he would submit that there had been serious flaws in the procedure and important matters which the hearing had not applied its mind to but should have done. There were also significant matters which the hearing had taken into account which it should not have. He did, however, submit that the restrictive approach adopted by Sheriff Mowat might no longer be regarded as appropriate having regard (a) to the consideration that the sheriff under section 51(5)(c)(iii) now had the power (not included in the appeal provisions of the Social Work (Scotland) Act, 1968) to substitute his own decision for that of the hearing; and (b) the Human Rights Act, 1998, which, by defining a tribunal such as a children's hearing as a public authority, imposed on the hearing the obligation under article 6(1) European Convention on Human Rights to accord to the child a 'fair' hearing. The consequence of this was that even if a hearing had not acted as identified by Sheriff Mowat, it could nonetheless have acted unfairly, in contravention of article 6(1); and it was unthinkable that a contravention of this article could not be corrected on by an unrestricted right of appeal.

[13] Mr Wynford submitted that the decision to grant a warrant was one which had to be made on the basis of the three principles set out in section 16 of the Children (Scotland) Act 1995. These are: the paramountcy of the welfare of the child during his childhood (s 16(1)); the principle of giving the child the chance to state his views if he wishes and taking account of any such expressed views in the light of the age and maturity of the child (s 16(2), read with s 16(4)(b)(ii); and the principle that no order should be pronounced which left the child no better off than he would have been had no order been pronounced (s 16(3)). Mr Wynford described these principles for short as, respectively, 'the paramountcy principle', the 'consulting the child principle' and 'the no non-beneficial order principle'.

[14] In relation to the paramountcy principle, Mr Wynford argued, under reference to paragraphs 3 and 4 of his Note of Appeal, that although the hearing had used the words of section 16(1) in their third reason ('the

majority thought his mother was not able to control him it was necessary for his safety and welfare to require his detention') it was clear, in Mr Wynford's submission, that this represented little more than lip-service to the principle. This was a child with no known record of or propensity to violent or dangerous conduct who had, taking the reporter's averments *pro veritate*, committed one fairly minor and one admittedly potentially very dangerous act of damage to property. The hearing had leapt from this to the unreasonable conclusion that the child was a danger to himself and others, and that this, linked with his mother's perceived inability to control him, rendered detention necessary.

[15] Moreover, said Mr Wynford, the reference to the mother's supposed inability to control the child was eloquent of the confusion which underlay the approach of the majority of the hearing. Was it being suggested that if the father had attended the hearing that this would have indicated that the child was more under control? This seemed to be the logic of the majority's position. But how, asked Mr Wynford, did the father's non-appearance at the hearing, which was not a matter which was explored by the hearing, lead to the inference that the child was beyond the control of his mother? It was very common for mothers to play the leading role in bringing up the family and if this were evidence of 'beyond control' then there would be many more children brought to hearings than the system could easily cope with. In any event the reporter had not brought a case of 'beyond the control of any relevant person' under section 52(2)(a) of the Act.

[16] Turning to the seventh paragraph of his Note of Appeal Mr Wynford referred to the second sentence in the hearing's Reasons: 'The majority of the hearing thought that his failure to explain why he was arrested for the assault on the child G and his failure to explain, in relation to the 'paint' incident, how he could have an 'alibi witness' for to an event which, had he been innocent, he could not have known the time of, all indicated that he was guilty of these offences.' This represented, said Mr Wynford, the hearing stepping out of its role as a body charged with deciding on the best interests of children and assuming the jurisdiction of a tribunal of fact. Moreover they had acted ineptly as a tribunal of fact. They had, perhaps taking a lead from an observation on the second page of the Social Work Report, erroneously inferred that, because the child had said he had an alibi in relation to the spray painting incident, he therefore must have participated in that incident. It did not require much imagination to think of other ways whereby the boy could have acquired this knowledge – most obviously, the information as to when the incident was thought to have taken place could have been acquired by hearsay. This was particularly likely in a close society such as a school – the incident would have been 'the talk of the steamie', as Mr Wynford put it.

[17] Also under reference to paragraph 7 of his Note, Mr Wynford mentioned the hearing's having founded upon the boy's 'failure to explain' (a) why he was arrested for the assault on the child G and (b) how he knew of the time of the paint incident. This was totally improper both in law and fact. It was wrong in law because there was no obligation on an accused person to explain anything and it was wrong, unsafe and unfair as a factual

inference since there was information in the Social Work Report and generally that the child was uncommunicative and suspicious of authority figures such as social workers and (from the child's perspective) hearing members. The reliance on the incident involving the child G was particularly inappropriate since that incident did not form part of the Grounds for Referral and had indeed been the subject of a 'no further action' decision of the reporter under section 56(4) of the Children (Scotland) Act 1995.

[18] Under reference to paragraph 6 of his Note of Appeal Mr Wynford accepted that it was competent for a hearing to deliberate in the absence of a social worker but said that this was unusual – see Sheriff Kearney's *Children's Hearings and the Sheriff Court*, second edition, paragraph 22.17. He accepted that the absence of the social worker who prepared the report, Mr Fox, was unavoidable because of the weather conditions but commented that it was unfortunate that the hearing had not considered an adjournment till later in the day under Children's Hearings (Scotland) Rules 1996 rule 10(4) for the purpose of inviting a social worker from the Out of Hours team to attend. Mr Wynford further focused this criticism by saying, as anticipated in said paragraph 6, that the advice from such a worker would have enabled the hearing to address the question of whether granting a warrant would be an order which was more beneficial to the child than making no order at all. For example it was Mr Wynford's information from his client the child that some of the residents in St Thenew's were long-term 'high tariff' offenders who might potentially exert undesirable influence on a young boy who had never been exposed to such company before. Mr Wynford did not ask me to hold that this was the case, but simply argued that a social worker could have advised the hearing on this matter and thus enable them the better to apply the 'no non-beneficial order' principle. As it was, there was no indication that the hearing had applied this principle at all.

[19] It would have assisted the hearing's position, Mr Wynford maintained, if they had had the advice of a safeguarder as to what might constitute the best course in the child's interests. It was of course incumbent on the hearing under section 41(1) of the Children (Scotland) Act 1995 to consider whether or not to appoint a safeguarder and it was evident from their Reasons that the hearing had applied their minds to this, but in deciding not to appoint one they had come to a decision which was not only wrong but, Mr Wynford argued, one which no hearing which was contemplating granting a warrant could reasonably have arrived at.

[20] Turning to his point about the need for legal representation under the European Convention on Human Rights Mr Wynford submitted that a hearing was clearly a public authority under section 6(3)(a) of the Human Rights Act 1998 and the child was a 'victim' as defined in section 7(1) of that Act. Article 6(3)(c) of the European Convention on Human Rights required that a person 'charged with a criminal offence' had the right to legal assistance if he chose to have it. Of course the case of *S v Miller* had decided that a child being dealt with by a hearing was not 'charged with a criminal offence' but it had been held in the same case that where

deprivation of liberty was in issue then a legal representative would gener-ally be necessary. It was, he submitted, to provide for this contingency that *The Children's Hearings (Legal Representation) (Scotland) Rules 2002*, and in particular rule 3(2) of these Rules, had been enacted.

[21] In concluding Mr Wynford referred to his fifth ground of appeal (hearing had not given the child an opportunity to express his view) and said that, while it would have been more regular for the child to have been asked specifically what his view was, the strong expression of opposition by the mother had effectively conveyed this view. He therefore said that this ground of appeal was not insisted upon except for the consideration that it represented yet another informality in what Mr Wynford finally described as a thoroughly bad and unfair hearing. However, he concluded there were ample reasons in his other heads of appeal to convince the court that the hearing's decision was, in the words of Lord Macmillan in *Thomas v Thomas* 1947 SC (HL) 45 at 59, 'plainly wrong.'

The submissions of the respondent reporter

[22] Mr Somerville, for the Principal Reporter, began by outlining briefly the role of the reporter in an appeal. This role, in relation to appeals to the sheriff, is not specifically defined in the Children (Scotland) Act 1995, but Mr Somerville drew my attention to section 51(12) of the Act which, in relation to appeals from the sheriff or sheriff principal, refers to the Principal Reporter as acting 'on behalf of the children's hearing'. He also referred to *Miller v Council of the Law Society of Scotland* 2000 SLT 513 at 516L where the reporter's duty to advise hearings on legal matters is recognised. Putting these considerations together Mr Somerville said he regarded his task before me as being to represent the stance of the hearing as best he could but be free to comment on their decisions in the light of his view of the law. He did not, however regard himself as entitled, as the Lord Advocate's representative would be in a criminal appeal, to 'not support' the stance taken by the court of first instance. I have no doubt that he was correct in this.

[23] In defending the stance of the hearing Mr Somerville argued at the outset that I should adopt the 'restrictive' view of the sheriff's powers at appeal, as originally set out by Sheriff Mowat in *D v Sinclair*, followed by Sheriff Principal G A Nicholson QC in *W v Schaffer* 2001 SLT (Sh Ct) 86 and, as Mr Wynford had conceded, substantially supported by Lord President Hope in *O v Rae*. Professor Norrie had summed the matter up stating that the words of section 51(5) of the Act, 'do not permit the sheriff to allow the appeal merely because he has a difference of opinion with the hearing as to the correct disposal of the case or as to whether a warrant ought to have been granted.[70]' Mr Somerville rejected the conten-tion that the enactment of section 51(5)(c)(iii) of the Children (Scotland)

---

70. *Children's Hearings in Scotland*, second edition, page 213.

Act 1995 had made any difference to the statutory position. In this regard he maintained that the sheriff's approach to an appeal must be in two stages. In the first place the sheriff must decide whether the appeal has failed (s 51(4)) or succeeded (the first two lines of s 51(5)). Only if the sheriff decides that the appeal is to succeed may he turn his mind to how that success is to be put into practice. This two stage procedure was in all material respects the same as the procedure enacted under s 49(4) and s 49(5) of the Social Work (Scotland) Act, 1968 and the introduction of the power to substitute the court's own decision could not influence the interpretation of the first stage in the court's deliberations.

[24] On the merits of the decision of the hearing Mr Somerville submitted that although the hearing may not have fully observed certain formalities their decision had been substantially the right one. Mr Wynford's most sustained attack had been on the length to which the hearing had gone in exploring the likely evidence against the child. There was a dearth of authority on the matter. He did however seek to derive some support from Lord Clyde's *Report of the Inquiry into the Removal of Children from Orkney* in February 1991 (Edinburgh, HMSO, 1992). At one stage the issue of the continued detention of the children had arisen. The results of certain medical examinations might have had a bearing on the merits of the Grounds for Referral and the reporter opposed the contents of these examinations being referred to at a hearing. At paragraph 13,72 of his Report Lord Clyde concluded: '... it would appear to be competent and relevant when considering the question of whether the continued detention of a child under a Place of Safety Order is in the child's best interests to have regard to evidence bearing on the strength of the grounds of referral.' Applying this approach to the instant case Mr Somerville submitted that the hearing were well entitled to try to assess 'the strength of the grounds of referral'.

[25] As to the argument that the hearing had not given due weight to the 'paramountcy' principle Mr Somerville submitted that there was no ground for this conclusion. They had relied principally on two factors, viz., the seriousness of the charge of fire-raising and their perception that the child's mother, apparently unsupported by the child's father who had not troubled to come to the hearing, would not be able to control him. This was a reasonable stance to adopt. This may not have been the stance which all hearings would have adopted, but it could not be said that no reasonable hearing could have adopted it.

[26] The argument that the hearing were invoking facts which could have been, but were not, the grounds of a ground of referral stated under section 52(2)(a) of the Children (Scotland) Act 1995 was, submitted the reporter, a red herring. *O v Rae* was binding on me until and unless overruled by the Inner House of the Court of Session but, perhaps more importantly in realistic terms, the extent to which the hearing in this instance had relied upon a ground of referral not stated fell far short of the facts in *O v Rae*, which was a case wherein an allegation in a report by a social worker which the hearing had had before it repeated an allegation that the child's father had been guilty of sexual abuse of the child – an

allegation which had been made by the reporter in the original grounds for referral but withdrawn before the father had accepted the reduced grounds for referral based only on lack of parental care. The situation here was quite different. There was no question of an allegation of 'beyond control' having been formulated and withdrawn. The hearing were bound to have regard to the controlling abilities of the only parent who seemed to be willing to accept responsibility, viz., the mother.

[27] In relation to the ground of appeal based on the absence of the social worker Mr Somerville pointed out, as conceded by the appellant, that there was no statutory requirement for the social worker to be in attendance. He submitted, however, that this absence was caused by matters beyond anyone's control and that there would have been scant purpose in seeking to secure, during the deliberative part of the hearing, the attendance of a social worker from the Out of Hours team who would know little or nothing about the background of a child whose family, as revealed in Mr Fox's report, was not known to the Department.

[28] Mr Wynford had linked the absence of the social worker to an argument to the effect that the hearing had not given attention to the 'no non-beneficial order principle' embodied in section 16(3) of the Children (Scotland) Act 1995. Mr Somerville accepted that this principle was one which governed the granting of a warrant and that the hearing had not made specific reference to it in their statement of reasons. He maintained, however, that statement of reasons should address the matters of substance rather than of form. What is required, in the words of Lord President Hope in *H v Kennedy*, 1999 SCLR 961 at 964F '... is a clear statement of the material considerations to which the children's hearing had regard in their decision. The statement must be intelligible to the persons to whom it is addressed and it must deal with all the substantial questions which were the subject of the decision'. Judged by this standard the statement of reasons was adequate and would not have been improved on by the hearing's having in addition repeated the wording of section 16(3). Mr Wynford had said that the child might be exposed to the company of 'high tariff' offenders in St Thenew's and this could not be to his benefit. There was not evidence of this and the court should not indulge in such a speculation.

[29] As to the appellant's point in relation to representation under reference to the European Convention on Human Rights, Mr Somerville referred to the case of *K and F, Applicants*, 2002 SLT (Sh. Ct.) 38, 2002 Fam 44. In this case Sheriff Principal Nicholson, upholding Sheriff A M Bell, had refused to allow a caveat to be taken in where a Child Protection Order was in prospect and had observed that the ready access to review of the CPO made it unlikely that a breach of article 6 had taken place. The same principle, said Mr Somerville, applied here and the appellant's arguments failed on this issue also.

[30] In relation to the absence of any reference in the reasons to the appointment of a safeguarder Mr Somerville said that obligation under section 41(1) of the Children (Scotland) Act 1995 was <u>to consider</u> the

appointment of a safeguarder. He accepted that the issue of the appointment of a safeguarder should have been more clearly focused, particularly when it became apparent that the granting of a warrant was in issue, but said frankly that the move to grant a warrant had taken him by surprise and that when the wording of the Statement of Reasons was being settled his main concern had been that the justification advanced by the majority should be clearly stated. He accepted, standing the mandatory provisions of s 41(1) of the Act, that the failure to consider the appointment of a safeguarder constituted an irregularity but argued that it was not a fatal irregularity in view of the fact that there was ready access to an early appeal. He also referred to the distinction drawn by Lord President Hope in *Sloan v B* 1991 SLT 530 at 546 F-G between a defect in procedure which was fundamental and 'a defect in the procedure which could be put right'. In the instant case the early access to an appeal constituted the 'putting right' and therefore while the failure to consider the appointment of a safeguarder was unfortunate it was not a fundamental defect and that I should consider the issue of whether a warrant should have been granted on its merits. The position had some affinity with that in *K and F Applicants*. In any event, the reporter concluded, the appointment of a safeguarder could have made no real difference to the outcome, since such an appointment would not have prevented the granting of the warrant.

DISCUSSION AND DECISION

The powers of the sheriff on appeal from a decision of a hearing

[31] As will be seen my decision on this appeal does not turn on whether or not I adopt a 'restrictive' or 'non-restrictive' approach to this appeal, but I think, out of deference to the arguments addressed to me, I should deal with this, albeit briefly.

[32] I have always had a reservation about the universal applicability of the restrictive approach as a matter of legal theory although it has been adopted in practice (partly at least owing to the high respect accorded to any decision of the late Sheriff Mowat) by most of the sheriffs in Scotland (but not by all – it seems not to have been followed by Sheriff William Fulton in *Humphries v S*, 8 September 1980, Inverness Sheriff Court, unreported, but mentioned in *Kearney*, op cit, at para 47.03). Section 51(3)(c) of the Children (Scotland) Act 1995, like its predecessor, section 49(3) of the Social Work (Scotland) Act, 1968, confers on the sheriff power 'to call for any further report which he thinks may assist him in deciding the appeal'. It seems to me that such a power sits ill with the concept of the appellate court having the merely re-active role of ascertaining if the tribunal has taken into account some matter which it should not have done or had not taken into account some matter which it should have taken account of. As to whether or not the additional power to 'substitute ones own view' affects the initial decision of whether or not to allow the appeal I am inclined to think that this power fortifies the

argument that the sheriff's appellate role should not be re-active, but since, as I have mentioned, my decision does not turn on this issue, I do not think I need express a concluded view on this controversial issue.

Non-appointment of safeguarder (Ground of Appeal 8)

[33] The hearing had an obligation under section 41(1) of the Children (Scotland) Act 1995 to <u>consider</u> appointing a safeguarder and if appropriate to appoint one. Where such an obligation is placed on a tribunal I think that tribunal should, where obliged to issue a statutory statement of reasons, include a reference to how it has complied with such an obligation. It was accepted that the hearing here had not focused its attention on the issue of the appointment of a safeguarder and had, as a consequence, not dealt with the matter in their Statement of Reasons.

[34] It seems to me that the failure adequately to consider the appointment of a safeguarder must be regarded as an *ex facie* irregularity in the conduct of the proceedings. I also think, however, that the consideration that when a warrant is granted the child has a right to an early appeal at which full legal aid is readily available is a highly relevant consideration, in that it tends to place the irregularity into the category of 'a defect in the procedure which could be put right'. In any event I think the reporter's comment that even if the issue of the appointment of a safeguarder had been more precisely focused this would not be likely to have influenced the hearing's decision to grant a warrant has much merit. Further I do not think that by failing to consider a safeguarder the hearing was in fact acting counter to the 'paramountcy principle' or indeed either of the other section 16 principles. The majority of the hearing believed that what they did was in the child's interests and of course it has been recognised that it may be in the interests of a child to be kept in detention in order to prevent him from committing further offences – see *Humphries v S.* 1986 SLT 683. In all the circumstances, but principally because there was a right to early appeal, thus making the irregularity one which could readily be 'put right', I am of opinion that this irregularity is not one which impels me to sustain the appeal.

Failure explicitly to give child opportunity to express his views (Ground of Appeal 5).

[35] This ground was departed from by Mr Wynford, correctly in my view. While it was clear from the narration of the proceedings in front of the hearing given to me by the reporter that the hearing did not explicitly ask the child for his views, thus on the face of things contravening the relative section 16 principle, I think the hearing's having been unequivocally informed of the child's views by his mother cures this defect. In addition the considerations mentioned in the foregoing paragraph in relation to an early appeal at which the child was effectively represented would also have persuaded me that this technical irregularity was immaterial. However I should not like my approach here to be treated as encouraging the practice of not paying explicit attention to the section 16

principles: while not wishing to commend a 'tokenistic' formalism I hope that hearings, when giving reasons, will convey that they have observed the section 16 principles.

Purporting to find the child 'guilty' (Ground of Appeal 7)

[36] In relation to this the hearing stated: 'The majority of the hearing thought that his failure to explain why he was arrested for the assault on the child G and his failure to explain, in relation to the 'paint' incident, how he could have an 'alibi witness' for to an event which, had he been innocent, he could not have known the time of all indicated that he was guilty of these offences.' I agree that this wording is on its face suggestive of 'pre-judging.' The hearing had of course no authority to 'judge' the case in the sense of making provisional findings in fact, but I agree with Mr Somerville in drawing an analogy between what the hearing did here with the matter which Lord Clyde was discussing at paragraph 13.72 of his Report. Accordingly I do not think the hearing went wrong in trying to assess the weight of the case against the child. Whether or not the hearing came to the correct conclusion, on the basis of the information before it, as to the likelihood of the ground of referral being proved, is a separate matter which I will deal with in relation to Grounds of Appeal 3 and 4.

Alleged failure to apply 'No Non-beneficial Order' principle (Ground of Appeal 6)

[37] I refer to what I have said about the hearing's not having explicitly applied the principle of consulting the child. I think the concept of paying explicit attention to the 'No Non-beneficial Order' principle is particularly important. It is a natural human tendency to think, as King Edward VIII is reputed to have said about the plight of the unemployed in Wales in 1936, 'Something must be done', and then to presume that action is preferable to inaction. I suspect it was to correct this tendency that the section 16(3) of the Children (Scotland) Act 1995 was enacted.

[38] It must be recognised that the Reasons stated by the hearing, although not mentioning explicitly the No Non-beneficial Order Principle clearly indicated that they had thought about it, in that they stated: 'Moreover since fire-raising was such a serious matter and since the child's father had not attended the hearing and the majority thought his mother was not able to control him, the majority therefore concluded that he was a danger to himself and others and that it was therefore necessary for his safety and welfare to require his detention.' I therefore think that it could not be said, in the words of the first arm of Ground of Appeal 6, that 'granting said warrant was irregular because they did not consider' the No Non-beneficial Order Principle and that the argument must really be under the second arm of this Ground which is that the hearing 'did not consider adequately, whether it would be better for the child that the warrant should be granted as opposed to no warrant being granted.' The resolution of this question turns largely on the degree of risk which the child

presented to himself and others and therefore merges with the issues raise in Grounds of Appeal 3 and 4 and to these I will now turn.

Warrant unnecessary because child not a danger – and because it did not promote child's welfare (Grounds of Appeal 3 and 4)

[39] As already mentioned, I think it is appropriate for a hearing to make an assessment of the weight of the case 'against' the child on the basis of the information before it. I think it is also open to me, as the appellate judge, to examine the reasoning of the hearing on the basis of the information available to them.

[40] The core of the decision of the hearing was the view that the case 'against' WB was strong and that he was consequently in need of the control which would be provided by detention. This is represented by the words: 'The majority of the hearing thought that his failure to explain why he was arrested for the assault on the child G and his failure to explain, in relation to the "paint" incident, how he could have an "alibi witness" for an event which, had he been innocent, he could not have known the time of all indicated that he was guilty of these offences. Moreover since fire-raising was such a serious matter and since the child's father had not attended the hearing and the majority thought his mother was not able to control him, that he was a danger to himself and others and that it was therefore necessary for his safety and welfare to require his detention.'

[41] I think that the most concrete of these considerations is the reference to the 'alibi witness' point. This, as submitted by Mr Wynford, seems to be drawn from the passage in the Social Work Report, 'for that matter, how he could have an alibi for doing something which, if innocent, he would not know the time of?' I agree with Mr Wynford's criticism of this comment. The supposed time of such an incident would, in my view, very likely to have been common talk in the school and it seems to me that to treat this statement of the child WB as indicative of likely guilt is to ascribe to it almost the status of a circumstantial confession (cf *McAvoy v HM Advocate* 1983 SLT 16 per Lord Justice Clerk Wheatley at 18) – a status which in my view it comes nowhere near to attaining. I further think that the hearing attached far too much importance to the alleged failure by the child to explain why he was arrested for the alleged attack on the child G. This attack was the factual basis of a potential ground of referral no longer insisted upon by the reporter. If it had been made a ground of referral, and if the matter had gone to proof, the child might have been found not to have committed the offence, and this could well account for his refusal to comment. To have pre-judged this *against* the child was, in my view, clearly unfair. In any event WB was said to be uncommunicative.

[42] I also thought the hearing's assumption that the absence of the child's father from the hearing indicated in some way that the mother's 'control' of the child was inadequate was without foundation.

[43] The fourth ground of appeal invokes the paramountcy principle. I refer again to what I have said about the importance of conveying explicitly in the Statement of Reasons that regard has been accorded to the section 16 principles. Once again I direct my attention to the substance as well as to the form. In this instance I hold that by coming to unfounded conclusions as to the weight of the evidence 'against' WB the hearing's conclusion that he was a danger to himself and others was unjustified as was their conclusion that the mother's control was inadequate. I accept that, although there was no mention of the paramountcy principle in the Statement of Reasons, the hearing were acting in what they thought was WB's best interests, but having regard to the flawed inferences to which I have referred, I think that their decision must be regarded as not adequately promoting these interests and 'plainly wrong'. I conclude that the appeal must succeed on the bases of Grounds 3 and 4 of the Note of Appeal.

No legal representation for the child at the hearing (Ground of Appeal 9)

[44] Having decided that the appeal has succeeded on other grounds I do not propose to say much in relation to this ground. I think that the general principle must be that where the limitation of the liberty of the subject is at stake there must be effective access to legal representation. This is in accordance with Article 6(1) of the European Convention on Human Rights and the relative jurisprudence of the European Court of Human Rights. This approach was re-enforced in relation to the Hearings System in the case of *S v Miller* which in turn led to the enactment of *The Children's Hearings (Legal Representation) (Scotland) Rules 2001* and the provision of the present government scheme to fund representation when it is provided under these Rules, although it must be remembered that the 2001 Rules only refer to legal representation in the context of the child requiring this effectively to participate in the hearing or where a requirement that 'secure accommodation' criteria are present[71]. I reserve my opinion as to whether the early access to this court as an 'unrestricted' appellate court may 'cure' the lack of legal representation at the meeting of the hearing. I suspect it would have been impracticable, in the absence of a 'duty solicitor' scheme similar to that which operates in the sheriff's criminal custody court, for a solicitor to have been instructed in mid-hearing.

Conclusion

[45] It follows from all the foregoing that the appeal succeeded and I accordingly sustained it and recalled the warrant granted on 27 December 2005. I should add that I considered, as I was bound to under section 41(1) of the Act, appointing a safeguarder but decided against this since I

---

71. The Children's Hearings (Legal Representation) (Scotland) Rules 2001, SI 2001/478, r 3(2).

understood that Mr Wynford was going to continue to act for the child and I did not perceive any conflict between the interests of the child and the likely instructions of the child[72] which would render it necessary or desirable to appoint a safeguarder to represent the interests as distinct from the instructions of WB.

(Initialed) *F.G.*

> *Note [20]   The sheriff's Note is very full and self-explanatory. It calls for no comment except perhaps that a Note of this length (or indeed of any length!) would not normally be issued in an appeal against a warrant. The sheriff clearly regarded the appeal as raising important matters of principle and her anonymising the name of the child may indicate that she thought there was a possibility of her decision attracting the attention of the law reporters.*

> *Note [21]   It will be recalled that it was on Tuesday, 27 December 2005 that the hearing directed the reporter to make application to the sheriff for a finding as to whether the not-accepted grounds of referral were established, pursuant to the provisions of section 65(7) of the Children (Scotland) Act 1995. It then became the duty of the reporter under rule 3.45(1) of the Act of Sederunt (Child Care and Maintenance Rules) 1997 to make application to the sheriff within 'a period of seven days beginning with the date on which the Principal Reporter was directed' to make the application. On the face of it this would be Monday, 2 January 2006, which along with Tuesday 3 January was a day on which the court was closed for ordinary business. The reporter plans to lodge the application on Wednesday 4 January, 2006, relying on the principle that where a time-limit on lodging papers expires on a day when the court is closed for ordinary business the papers will be accepted on the first court day thereafter[73]. (The reporter might have been more prudent and lodged the Application on or before Friday, 30 December 2005. One should never 'test' the law unnecessarily: but Mr Somerville no doubt knows the practices of his local court!)*

Wednesday, 4 January 2006

The reporter lodges with the sheriff clerk at Kirklenton the following Application and the sheriff clerk fixes Monday 30 January 2006 as the date for the proof in relation to the Application.

---

72. Cf at [28] (c) of Part One of this book: '*The rôle of the safeguarder and curator ad litem is to be distinguished from the rôle of a solicitor acting for the child: the solicitor takes the instructions of the child, whereas the safeguarder or curator ad litem represents what he or she judges to be the interests of the child*'.
73. *B v Kennedy*, 1992 SLT 870 at 872K; cf *Lanark County Council v Docherty*, 1959 SLT (Sh Ct) 12.

Here is the document, as lodged by the reporter (the shaded words are here reproduced so as to reflect the statutory style, but would not in practice be included in this case):–

SW 1/06

FORM 60

SCOTTISH
CHILDREN'S REPORTER
ADMINISTRATION

Form of Application to Sheriff Under Section 65 of the Act

Rule 3.45(1)

Sheriff Court of Lenton and Muirbrachlan at Kirklenton

APPLICANT

Hector Somerville, Authority Reporter, 17 Laverock Road, Kirklenton LE6 7EK. Telephone 012104 545 700; Fax: 012104 545 710.

in the case of

William Brown, d.o.b. 01.08.1991, residing at 3/1, 27 Morrison Street, Kirklenton LE2 7EH.

1. On 27 December 2005 a children's hearing for Lentonshire Council gave a direction to the Principal Reporter under section 65(7) or 65(9) of the Children (Scotland) Act 1995 in respect of the child William Brown. The hearing appointed [insert name of safeguarder] as a safeguarder / No safeguarder was appointed.*

2. A copy of the Statement by the Principal Reporter of the grounds for the referral of the case of the said William Brown to the children's hearing is attached together with any report of the safeguarder appointed for the purpose of safeguarding the interests of the child in the proceedings.

3. *The said William Brown and Mrs Sylvia Brown, 3/1, 27 Morrison Street, Kirklenton LE2 7EH, the mother and as such a relevant person, did not accept the grounds of referral so far as relating to the sole condition (under section 52(2)(i) of the Children (Scotland) Act 1995) of the Statement of the Principal Reporter.

OR

3. *The children's hearing were satisfied that the said William Brown will not be capable of understanding or has not understood the explanation of the grounds of referral given under section 65(4) of the Act.

4. The Principal Reporter therefore makes application to the sheriff to find whether the grounds of referral not accepted by the said William Brown or the said Mrs Sylvia Brown or not understood by the child are established.

5. The Principal Reporter requests the sheriff to remove the obligation on the child to attend the hearing in view of [insert reasons]. And to dispense with service on [insert name and give reasons].*

Date: *29th December 2005*

> Signed: *Hector Somerville*
> Children's Reporter
> Scottish Children's Reporter Administration,
> 17 Laverock Road, Kirklenton, LE6 7EK,
> Tel: 02104 545 700
> Fax: 012104 545 710

Here is the warrant which the sheriff clerk grants. This will be attached to the above:

Kirklenton, 4 January 2006.

The court assigns 30 January 2006 at 10 a.m. within the Sheriff Court of Lenton and Muirbrachlan at Kirklenton for the hearing of the application; APPOINTS the Principal Reporter forthwith*

a. to serve a copy of the application and relative statement of grounds of referral and this warrant on:

    i. the child, together with a notice in form 31 or orders service of the following documents only [insert details of documents to be served on the child, e.g. notice in form 31 only].

    ii. Mr Hugh Brown and Mrs Sylvia Brown, being relevant persons as father and mother of the said child, together with a Notice in form 39;

    iii. The safeguarder [insert name and designation] appointed by the sheriff,*

*b. Orders that the address of [insert name] should not be disclosed in the application.

*c. Dispense with service on the child or any other person for the following reasons [insert details].

*d. Dispenses with the obligation on the child to attend the hearing in view of [insert details].

And grants warrant to cite the witnesses and havers[74].

Anne McGibbon
Sheriff Clerk Depute

*delete as appropriate

Attached to this Application is a copy of the Form SCRA F, reproduced *supra* at pages 181, 182. It is an exact copy of that which is printed at pages 181, 182 except that there are handwritten notes in the left-hand margin. Beside the Condition of Referral ('That in terms of section 52(2)(i) of the Children (Scotland) Act 1995 [he]/[~~she~~] has committed an offence') is written: 'Not admitted by child and relevant person' Beside each of the Statements of Fact, there is written as follows: beside Statement of Fact 1: *Not admitted by child and relevant person*; beside Statement of Fact 2: *Not admitted by child and relevant person.*

Wednesday, 4 January 2006, later

The sheriff clerk, in accordance with good practice, brings the Application to the sheriff. Kirklenton is a 'two sheriff' court and any sheriff could have dealt with the matter, but as Sheriff Grey is in court the sheriff clerk takes it to her as the sheriff having knowledge of the case. The only statutory function the sheriff has to attend to is the obligation to consider the appointing of a safeguarder in terms of section 41(1) of the Children (Scotland) Act 1995. This is a decision to which only the 'paramountcy' principle of the three Section 16 principles applies. Sheriff Grey, as before, takes the view that since the main interest of the child is to have his case presented properly the consideration that a solicitor has been instructed makes it unnecessary to appoint a safeguarder. She is aware that it is the duty of the safeguarder to ascertain and pass on the views of the child[75] but thinks that William and his solicitor between them will be quite able to do this without the intervention of another. [Sometimes the sheriff will require to make, or have made, inquiries before deciding on the appointment of a safeguarder.] The sheriff clerk has already, again in accordance with good practice, asked the reporter if the proof in the case is likely to last long and been told that the likely duration is about half a day.

Monday, 9 January 2006, afternoon

William Brown and his mother attend at Mr Wynford's office as arranged. For the first half-hour or so all three are present and the case is discussed in general terms. William Brown and his mother make it clear that they want to 'defend the case all the way', as they put it. Mr Wynford explains the general position, viz, that the case against the child will have to be

---

74. A 'haver' is someone who is alleged to possess (have) a relevant document.
75. Act of Sederunt (Child Care and Maintenance Rules) 1997, r 3.8(c).

proved to the criminal standard and that it will be up to the reporter to establish guilt in respect of each alleged offence. He explains that under the criminal law it is not for the person accused, even when that person is a child, to prove his innocence, but advises that in cases of this type it is generally necessary and desirable, unless there is 'no case to answer' for the person accused of the offence to give evidence on his own behalf. William says he will certainly wish to give evidence. Mr Wynford then explains the somewhat complex provisions Part 2 of the Vulnerable Witnesses (Scotland) Act 2004 and mentions the 'special measures' which a child witness such as William may be entitled to in the prescribed circumstances (see below paragraph *[21]*). William says he is not in the least interested in any special measures. Mr Wynford mentions that he will require to apply to the court for certification that the court is satisfied that the child does not want any special measure.

> Note *[22]*   *The detailed provisions of Part 2 of the Vulnerable Witnesses (Scotland) Act 2004 are summarised at paragraph 38 (ii) to (v) of Part One of this book. William Brown says he does not wish any special measure but, as noted at paragraph 38(iii) of Part One, it is nevertheless obligatory for the party citing the witness to lodge a Child Witness Notice in order to obtain an order of court that the child is to give evidence without any special measure.*

Mr Wynford explains that the reporter will supply him with a list of the witnesses on whose evidence the reporter intends to rely and says he will interview these witnesses. He gets William to sign an Application Form for full Legal Aid for the 'proof' before the sheriff. He says he is confident that Legal Aid will be granted and fairly confident that he will have been able to prepare the case in time for the proof on 30 January 2006, but explains that if the case has not been fully prepared by the date of the proof it is possible to ask the court to postpone the proof and that the court is likely to grant such a motion provided a good reason can be put forward.

Monday, 9 January 2006 – later in the afternoon

Mr Wynford phones the reporter to confirm that there is no likelihood of this case 'settling' by the child accepting the grounds of referral. He also asks the reporter for a list of the reporter's witnesses when it becomes available. The reporter says he has not yet decided on the final list of witnesses as he still has some investigations to carry out, but obviously his witnesses will include Stephen Green, the Head Teacher Mr Black, the janitor Mr Donaldson, someone from the Fire Service and possibly also Mr McNeill. He adds that for his part he has no intention of abandoning the referral. He asks Mr Wynford if there is any prospect of the child accepting only one of the disputed statements of fact and gives Mr Wynford the impression that he (the reporter) is more confident of proving the alleged spray painting offence and might, if the child were ready to admit to that, give up the more serious fire-raising ground. Also mentioned is the possibility of any formal evidence being agreed by Joint Minute[76]. Mr Wynford says he doesn't know Mr Donaldson's first name and would like to know it because he will be writing to him. The reporter says he will be phoning the school later that day and will phone back. The reporter later phones Mr Wynford's office with the name. Both sides refer to the Vulnerable Witnesses (Scotland) Act 2004 and state that their respective child witnesses, William Brown and Stephen Green will not require any 'special measures' and that they will be lodging with the court applications for orders under section 12(1)(b) of the Vulnerable Witnesses (Scotland) Act 2004 declaring that these children are to give evidence without the benefit of any special measure. They agree to advise the sheriff clerk that neither has any opposition to the other's application in this regard and that consequently the sheriff will almost certainly not require a formal hearing.

> *Note [23]   It is one of the satisfactory features of the legal side of referrals proceedings that, when working well, there may be early and frequently informal contact between the reporter and the other party or parties' lawyer. This saves time and tends to avoid unnecessary delay and misunderstanding. It does not however derogate from the duty of the lawyer for the child to defend his client by all lawful and ethical means. The sheriff clerk will be grateful to be informed as to parties' agreement about the Vulnerable Witness Applications – see paragraph [22] above.*

Tuesday, 10 January 2006, morning

Both sides prepare Applications to the court – the reporter in relation to Stephen Green and Mr Wynford in relation to William Brown – under section 12(1)(b) of the Vulnerable Witnesses (Scotland) Act 2004. Mr Wynford's Application is as follows:

---

76. A 'Joint Minute' is a document lodged in court, signed, in referrals procedure, by the reporter and the lawyer for the child, agreeing any non-controversial evidence, such as the ownership of a car, or the contents of a medical or other technical report.

Rule 3.67

FORM 75

Vulnerable Witnesses (Scotland) Act 2004
Section 12

Received the *12th* day of *January 2006*.
(Date of receipt of this notice)

(Sgd) *Elaine MacFadzean*
Sheriff Clerk

CHILD WITNESS NOTICE

Sheriff Court: *Lenton and Muirbrachlan at Kirklenton*   *10 January 2006*

Court Ref. No: SW 1/06

1. The applicant, Jamie Wynford, solicitor, Kirklenton, is a party[77] to an application under section 65(7) of the Children (Scotland) Act 1995.

2. The applicant has cited William Brown (dob 01.08.1991) 3/1, 27 Morrison Street, Kirklenton LE2 7EH as a witness.

3. William Brown is a child witness under section 11 of the Vulnerable Witnesses (Scotland) Act 2004 and was under the age of sixteen on the date of the commencement of proceedings.

4. The applicant considers that no special measures are required for the said William Brown in giving evidence.

5. The reasons for this opinion are: the Applicant has seen William Brown on several occasions and is satisfied that he is mature and not likely to be unduly intimidated by giving evidence without any special measure. The nature of the allegations, malicious mischief and fire-raising, while serious, do not raise any issues of delicacy which would cause embarrassment.

6. William Brown has expressed the firm view that he would prefer to give evidence without any special measures and his mother, Mrs Sylvia Brown, agrees that special measures are unnecessary.

7. Other information considered relevant to this application is as follows:-
The children's reporter has intimated that he has no objection to this application.

---

77. It is odd to categorise a party's agent as himself a 'party' – but this is the wording of the style.

8. The applicant asks the court to:

(a)   consider this child witness notice;

(b)   make an order authorising the giving of evidence by William Brown without the benefit of any special measure.

Signed: *Jamie Wynford*
      Solicitor,
      Messrs Campbell and MacDonald,
      17 Wallace Square,
      Kirklenton LE6 9ZE
      Telephone: 012104 878 200
      Fax: 012104 878 201.

NOTE: This form should be suitably adapted where section 16 of the Act of 2004 applies.

Tuesday, 10 January 2006 – in the Sheriff Clerk's office at 2.30 pm

Mr Wynford lodges this with the sheriff clerk who books it and takes it to one of the sheriffs for signature. The following interlocutor is granted:

Ref: 1/06

Child: William Brown

Witness: William Brown

Kirklenton 10 January 2006.

Before: Sheriff Ralph Thomson

The sheriff, having considered the foregoing application under section 12 of the Vulnerable Witnesses (Scotland) Act 2004, Finds it unnecessary to fix a hearing and GRANTS same; and in terms thereof ORDERS that William Brown is authorised to give evidence without the benefit of any special measure at the proof on 30 January 2006 in the Application at the instance of the Principal Reporter in relation to William Brown and at any adjournment thereof.

Ralph Thomson
Sheriff

Wednesday, 11 January 2006

Mr Wynford now writes to Mr Black, Mr McNeill and Mr Donaldson at the school telling them that he acts for William Brown and requesting them to allow him an appointment at which he can take a statement about the allegations against his client. He offers to come to the school or to fix an appointment in his office at a mutually convenient time but adds that an early meeting would be helpful in view of the nearness of the proof on 30 January.

Mr Wynford also writes to Stephen Green's mother and father (whose names and addresses Mrs Brown was able to supply) in these terms:

---

11 January 2006

Dear Mr and Mrs Green

Children's Reporter (Kirklenton) v William Brown

I have been instructed by William Brown to represent him in the pending proceedings under the Children's Panel system. As you will know your son Stephen is likely to be called as a witness by the children's reporter to the hearing before the sheriff which has been fixed for Monday 30 January 2006 in Kirklenton Sheriff Court.

It is my duty as William Brown's solicitor to investigate the grounds of referral stated by the children's reporter and as part of my investigations I should like to take a statement from all the reporter's witnesses, including Stephen. I would therefore be glad if Stephen and you would consent to Stephen's being interviewed by me and, if so, could let me know what arrangement for an interview would be suitable to you. I could meet you in my office at any mutually convenient time, including evenings and the week-end. Alternatively I could call at your home. I would not expect the interview to last more than an hour or so. If coming to my office I would expect that one of you would accompany Stephen. Wherever the interview may take place I should like to interview Stephen without anyone else present except my secretary, but if you prefer that a parent should be present at the interview then that is how it will be.

I look forward to hearing from you. As the hearing before the sheriff is only some three weeks away I should be grateful if you would contact me as soon as possible. If phoning please ask for me in the first instance and, if I am not in or cannot take the call, for my secretary Miss Quinn. As you can see we are also accessible by fax and e-mail, but a phone call might be the easiest way of fixing an appointment.

Yours sincerely,
Jamie Wynford

Friday, 13 January 2006

While Mr Wynford is out at court his secretary takes a somewhat irate phone call from Mrs Green saying that she does not see why her son should help a bully like William Brown. Also Stephen has already given a statement to the reporter and is it legal for him to talk to 'the other side'? She leaves her phone number and asks Mr Wynford to phone back. Mr Wynford writes to Mrs Green as follows:

---

13 January 2006

Dear Mrs Green

Children's Reporter (Kirklenton) v William Brown

Thank you of phoning so promptly. I have noted from my secretary that you have reservations about Stephen giving a statement to me. I think you have two difficulties. In the first place you do not see why Stephen should 'help' someone whom he regards as a bully and obviously does not like. In the second place you are worried that, having given a statement to the reporter it may be against the law to give a statement to 'the other side'.

On the second point, I can give you my assurance that it is not illegal to give a statement to a solicitor acting for one party when one has already given a statement. I should mention that you are not alone in thinking that it may be illegal but I can assure you that it is not.

As to your other point, there is of course no obligation on Stephen to give a statement to me. That is why my letter of 11 January asked for your consent. However it has long been recognised in our law, to borrow the words stated many years ago by a very senior judge of the High Court 'that every good citizen should give his aid, either to the Crown or the defence' where the facts relating to a criminal charge require to be ascertained.

I repeat that there is no question of Stephen being forced to give a statement if he or you do not want that, but I hope that, in the light of what I have said, you and Stephen may come round to agreeing to an interview.

You asked me to phone you but I thought, because of the importance of the matters you had raised, that it was preferable for me to set out the position in writing. I hope to hear from you again early next week if possible.

Yours sincerely
Jamie Wynford.

Note [24]   Mr Wynford, as one would expect in a solicitor expert in children's law, is a master of the riposte tactful. He is also careful. It would have been dangerous to get into an unstructured telephonic discussion with the irate mother of a child whom his client has admitted to having knocked down. Also he knows that he may have to challenge the credibility of Stephen quite strongly, so it is necessary to keep relations with Stephen and his family at a formal level. It is generally preferable, and in the case of adults it is normal and proper practice, to interview witnesses without any third party, particularly a potential witness, present, but in the case of a child the parent can insist on being present. It is also prudent, at least in the view of the author, to have another person from the office, such as a female secretary, present when inter- viewing a child because: (a) it will assist the interviewer to concen- trate on questioning the child without the barrier of a note-book or dictating machine; and (b) it provides a witness to speak to any allegation which may be made at a later stage of impropriety on the part of the interviewer.

The old case in the High Court to which Mr Wynford refers is HM Advocate v Monson[78] and the words are those of Lord Justice-Clerk Macdonald[79].

Monday, 16 January 2006

Mrs Green phones Mr Wynford and says that Stephen and she now agree to be precognosced and Mr Wynford fixes a meeting at which a precog- nition from Stephen is taken.

Monday, 16 January 2006 – Friday, 27 January 2006

Both the reporter and Mr Wynford prepare their cases and have some phone conversations. The reporter tells Mr Wynford of the witnesses he proposes to call and Mr Wynford reciprocates. The reporter intends to call: Stephen Green, PCs Margaret Myles and Wilfred MacTaggart, the Head Teacher, Mr Black, the Assistant Head and science teacher, Mr McNeill, the janitor Mr Donaldson and, as an expert, the Assistant Chief Fire Officer, Mr Leonard Kivlichan, who has prepared a report saying that fire to the outhouse was caused by a comparatively small amount, about a gallon at most, of flammable material being applied to the wooden door of the outhouse and ignited, causing the external, painted, surface of the door to be damaged, but not spreading owing to the wood of which the shed was constructed having been damp, apparently because of disuse. Mr Wynford says his witnesses will probably be William Brown, his mother, and his sister Angela. He asks the reporter to supply a copy of Mr Kivlichan's Report, with a view to agreeing its contents. The reporter sends a copy and they prepare a Joint Minute[80].

Mr Wynford instructs his precognition clerk to precognosce Mr Black, Mr McNeill and Mr Donaldson. The latter states that he passed the outhouse

---

78.   (1893) 21 R(J) 5
79.   Discussed in *Kearney*, op cit, at 30.30.
80.   The legal term for a note of agreed matters.

at 8 pm. on Saturday 5 November 2005 when it was intact and that he
was called out to inspect it at about 10 pm. when it was damaged by fire
but the fire had gone out. He had not examined the shed very carefully. It
was old and disused. There had been a bonfire and fireworks display in a
neighbouring field and he assumed that the comparatively minimal
damage had been caused by a misdirected firework and, beyond noting the
damage in the school log-book, he took no further action.

Mr Wynford himself takes brief precognitions from William's mother and
from Angela Brown. The latter states that she left William in the house on
the evening of Saturday 5 November 2005 at about 8 pm. in order to have
a quick drink with her boy-friend. When she left the house William was
watching the television. When she returned at about 10 pm. she found
William was still watching the television. He did not look as if he had been
out. She had not noticed anything special about him, although she agrees
that she had not (and would not normally) pay much attention to him. She
had not detected any smell of petrol from his clothes, but could not say if
he was wearing the same clothes at 10 as he had been at 8. She was not in
the habit of memorising what her kid half-brother wore, except that he
always (in her opinion) looked awful.

About a week before the proof fixed for 30 January 2006 Mr Wynford
phones the reporter to advise that he will be leading an affirmative defence
of alibi in respect of the fire-raising charge to the effect that William
was at home during the hours of 8 pm. and 10 pm. on 5 November
2005, being the hours between which it was believed that the incident
happened.

> *Note [25]   The communings between the reporter and the child's
> solicitor, although informal, comply with good practice[81]. If an
> affirmative defence such as 'alibi' were 'sprung' on the reporter
> without notice he would be entitled to ask for an adjournment in
> order to prepare his response[82]. Mr Wynford's use of a precog-
> nition clerk to interview the teachers and the janitor are reason-
> able. The precognition of the mother and Angela could have been
> delegated to a competent precognition taker, but Mr Wynford's
> decision to interview them himself is sensible and normal. The
> precognition of the child himself was undertaken by Mr Wynford
> in person and this is in accordance with good practice[83]. Had the
> reporter considered that further inquiry was necessary he would
> have taken the precognitions himself, or instructed one of his staff
> to take them, but in a relatively straightforward case such as the
> present one he is content to rely on the statements supplied by the
> police.*

81. For fuller discussion of this see *Kearney*, op cit 30.29 (exchange of information re
witnesses etc) and 41.08 (advance notification of affirmative line of defence).
82. He might not get the adjournment – that is always a matter for the discretion of the
court – cf *G v Scanlon* 2000 SCLR 1; 1999 SLT 707.
83. See the discussion in *Kearney*, op cit, 30.32 and the authorities therein cited.

Friday 20, January 2006

The reporter and Mr Wynford cite their witnesses. The reporter cites: Stephen Green; the Head Teacher, Mr Black; the Assistant Head and science teacher, Mr McNeill; Mr Donaldson, the janitor; PC Margaret Myles; PC Wilfred MacTaggart and, as an expert, the Assistant Chief Fire Officer, Mr Leonard Kivlichan. Mr Wynford cites William Brown, Mrs Sylvia Brown and Miss Angela Watson. Both the reporter and Mr Wynford employ first class recorded delivery post[84] as the mode of citation of the witnesses.

Both the reporter and Mr Wynford write letters to accompany the citations. The letters are along these lines:–

---

20 January 2006

Dear Mr Donaldson

The Children's Reporter (Kirklenton) v William Brown (d.o.b. 01.08.1991)

I enclose citation requiring you to attend at the Sheriff Court House, 27 Nelson Street, Kirklenton, LE5 9DG at 10 a.m. on Monday 30 January 2006 in order to give evidence in the case which I have initiated involving the referral of William Brown to a children's hearing.

SCRA will re-imburse travelling expenses and, up to certain maximum amounts, subsistence expenses and loss of earnings. I enclose a Claim Form in this connection. Please complete this in due course and hand it to the reporter at the court or return it to me at the above address within a month of the day in court.

If you wish to discuss with me any matter concerning this citation. Please telephone me here and ask for me or, if I am not available, for my colleague, Miss Ruthven. I can also be contacted by letter, fax, or e-mail.

Yours sincerely
Hector Somerville

In relation to the citation of the 14 year old Stephen Green a slightly different letter is appropriate:

---

84.   Act of Sederunt (Child Care and Maintenance Rules) 1997 r 3.15(2)(e).

FIRST CLASS DELIVERY POST

20 January 2006

Dear Stephen

The Children's Reporter (Kirklenton) v William Brown (d.o.b. 01.08.1991)

As I mentioned when I met you to take you statement I need to have you in court as a witness to tell the court what you know about the incidents in which William Brown is said to have spray-painted a door on 2 November and set fire to a shed on 5 November 2005.

In order to do this I enclose a formal document known as a citation which imposes a legal duty on you to come to the Sheriff Court, 27 Nelson Street, Kirklenton, LE5 9DG at 10 a.m. on Monday 30 January 2006 for the proof hearing before the sheriff. This will take place in a private room and not in open court.

You may wish to come to court with one of your parents or a suitable relative or friend and such a person will be entitled, with the approval of the sheriff, to sit in the room when you are giving evidence. I think you told me that your mother would be likely to come and I am writing to her separately.

I also enclose a Claim Form for Expenses by Witness. If you incur any travelling or subsistence expenses please complete this form and hand it to the reporter at the court or send it to me here within a month of the day in court.

If you wish to discuss anything about the case with me, please phone me here. If I am not in my colleague Miss Ruthven will see to it that I get your message.

Yours sincerely
Hector Somerville

The letter to Mrs Green is as follows:

---

20 January 2006

Dear Mrs Green

The Children's Reporter (Kirklenton) v William Brown (d.o.b. 01.08.1991)

As I mentioned to you when I was at your house to take Stephen's statement I have to call Stephen as a witness. The proof hearing will take place in a private room in the Sheriff Court, 27 Nelson Street, Kirklenton, LE5 9DG at 10 a.m. on Monday 30 January 2006.

In order to make sure that Stephen attends the court I have written to Stephen by First Class Recorded Delivery post enclosing a citation which requires Stephen to come to the Sheriff Court, 27 Nelson Street, Kirklenton, LE5 9DG at 10 a.m. on Monday 30 January 2006 for the proof hearing before the sheriff. I have enclosed with the citation a form for Stephen to fill up in order to claim any expenses incurred in attending court.

As you know Stephen has indicated that he is quite happy to give evidence without you being present in the court room to 'support' him, but I think you indicated that you would be bringing him to court. I assume that you will take Stephen home after he has given his evidence. SCRA will re-imburse your travelling expenses and, up to certain maximum amounts, subsistence, and baby-sitting/childminding expenses. I enclose two Claim Forms in this connection. Please have one or both completed and either convey them to the reporter at the court or return them to me at the above address within a month of the day in court.

If you wish to discuss anything about the case with me, please phone me here. If I am not able to take the call my colleague Miss Ruthven will see to it that I get your message.

Yours sincerely
Hector Somerville

Both the reporter and Mr Wynford prepare executions of citation in relation to the witnesses they have cited[85].

> *Note [26]   Unless otherwise provided by a specific rule, the period of notice for the service of documents is 48 hours where the service is 'personal', i.e. handed over directly by a sheriff officer to the person being notified, and 72 hours where the service is by first class recorded delivery post. Accordingly the last time for effecting personal service for a proof hearing at 10 a.m. on Monday 30 January 2006 would be 9.59 a.m. on Saturday 28 January 2006 and the last time for effecting postal service by first class recorded delivery would be 9.59 a.m. on Friday 27 January. In practice no reporter or solicitor would willingly run up against such limits and, as here, would allow a reasonable margin. The ultimate sanction for compelling a witness to attend court is the granting of a warrant for the witness's apprehension[86]. A sheriff would, unless the circumstances were exceptional, generally be reluctant to grant a warrant for the apprehension of a witness*

---

85. Act of Sederunt (Child Care and Maintenance Rules) 1997 r 3.17.
86. Rule 3.24 of the Act of Sederunt (Child Care and Maintenance Rules) 1997 in effect preserves for the Hearings System procedures Rule 29.10 of the Ordinary Cause Rules 1993, which provides inter alia that the sheriff may, on production of a certificate of citation, grant warrant for the apprehension of such witness and for the bringing of him to court. For discussion of modes of citation in relation to these proceedings in the Sheriff Court see paragraph [29] of Part One of this book.

who had been cited at the last minute. Also a warrant would not generally be granted unless the sheriff was satisfied that there was no obvious impediment to the witness's attending, such as possible lack of the bus fare – hence the emphasis on re-imbursement of expenses. (In Kirklenton the hearings venue is within walking distance of Stephen Green's house – in more scattered jurisdictions it might be thought prudent to send an advance to cover travelling expenses[87].)

Monday, 23 January 2006

The reporter and Mr Wynford adjust a Joint Minute in these terms:

Sheriff Court of Lenton and Muirbrachlan at Kirklenton

Joint Minute of Admission

in the case of

Hector Somerville, Authority
Children's Reporter (Kirklenton)

concerning

William Brown (d.o.b. 01.08.1991),
school student, residing at 3/1,
27 Morrison Street, Kirklenton
LE2 7EH, the Referred Child,

Somerville, for the Principal Reporter, and Wynford, for the Referred Child, concur in stating to the Court that it has been agreed as follows:

The contents of the report by Assistant Chief Fire Officer Leonard Kivlichan, dated 18 November 2005, headed 'Report on fire at outhouse of Kirklenton High School', are in all respects true and accurate.

> *Hector Somerville*
> Authority Reporter (Kirklenton),
> for the Principal Reporter
>
> *Jamie Wynford*
> Solicitor,
> for the Referred Child

Monday, 30 January 2006

The reporter and Mr Wynford arrive at the court building at about a quarter to ten in the morning. They find that their witnesses have arrived

---

87. Cf *Gerrard, Petitioner* 1984 SLT 108 and discussion at *Kearney*, op cit, paras 30.34 to 30.40.

and been put in separate witness rooms. They have brought with them the executions of citation for possible lodgement[88], but as their witnesses have all turned up it would seem that this will not be necessary. The reporter has brought the Joint Minute, duly signed. The reporter and Mr Wynford meet briefly and confirm with each other that the proof will be going ahead – i.e. there is no chance of the child admitting the grounds or the reporter abandoning the application[89] at the last minute. The reporter tells Mr Wynford that there is another proof to call but the sheriff will be asked to adjourn it to a later date.

> *Note [27]   It sometimes happens that proofs are not able to proceed at the first calling, frequently because, in contrast with the case of William Brown, children and parents sometimes leave obtaining legal advice to the last minute. While adjourning or not is always a matter for the discretion of the court[90], the court frequently feels that it is in the interests of justice to grant an adjournment in such circumstances. There is no formal provision in referrals procedure for any form of preliminary or 'inter-mediate' diet, as in criminal procedure, but sometimes a (non-statutory)'pre-proof hearing' may be fixed at which the time-tabling of the case and possible agreement of non-controversial evidence can be discussed.*

THE PROOF BEFORE THE SHERIFF

PROCEDURAL PRELIMINARIES

Kirklenton, uses, as noticed already in relation to the Appeal on 1 January 2006, a small court room as the sheriff's 'chambers' in which these cases are heard. Glasgow Sheriff Court enjoys the luxury of a special room within what is referred to as the 'Children's Referral Suite' which is reserved for the hearing of Children's Hearings cases. This facility includes a crèche and small kitchen which is staffed by professional child carers.

(Following a 'pre-proof hearing'[91] for an earlier case the sheriff has withdrawn to the retiring room behind the main room in order to attend to some paper work including looking at some new applications which have been lodged and considering such matters as the granting of legal aid and whether or not a safeguarder or curator *ad litem* should be appointed.)

---

88. Act of Sederunt (Child Care and Maintenance Rules) 1997 r 3.17.
89. Act of Sederunt (Child Care and Maintenance Rules) 1997 r 3.46.
90. *G v Scanlon* 1999 SLT 707, 2000 SCLR 1.
91. A 'Pre-proof Hearing' is a non-statutory but permissible procedure adopted by some sheriffs in order to ascertain from parties, particularly in complex cases, their state of preparation, whether some evidence can be agreed and the like.

Accordingly in the main room there is at first only the sheriff clerk, Miss McGibbon, PC Marjory Dale (the court police officer), and the sheriff's bar officer, Miss O'Hara. The main feature of the room is an oblong table. The sheriff's chair is at the head of the table. The sheriff clerk is sitting on the left of the sheriff's place. The police officer is sitting on a chair against the wall opposite the sheriff's place. The reporter enters and sits to the right of the sheriff's place. Mr Wynford enters with William Brown and his mother and they sit at the end of the table opposite the sheriff's place. On seeing that everyone is present the sheriff clerk indicates to Miss O'Hara that she should bring the sheriff on and she, using the door behind the sheriff's place, goes into the retiring room.

After a short pause the sheriff comes in preceded by Miss O'Hara who says, quietly but firmly, 'Court – all stand'. The sheriff comes in and bows to all present, and this bow is reciprocated by the members of the 'bar', i.e. the reporter and Mr Wynford. All sit down. The sheriff is not wearing the wig and gown which she would wear in all criminal and most civil business, but a black jacket and skirt and a white blouse. Mr Wynford, who, as a solicitor, would require to wear a black gown if appearing in any criminal and most civil courts, is not gowned, and wears a dark suit. The reporter, Mr Somerville, is not a solicitor, and therefore would never wear a bar gown. He is however a reporter having at least one year's experience and is therefore, by statutory instrument[92], entitled to appear before the sheriff. He wears a dark suit. All present sit down and the sheriff clerk calls the case by saying: 'The case of the child William Brown'.

> *Note [28]   I apologise to those well acquainted with the ways of courts for going on and on about such details, but they are interesting to those not so acquainted. They are also significant. Although 'in chambers' the proceedings are in 'a court of law'; it has been said – 'The genius of this reform [the introduction of the hearings system], which has earned it so much praise which the misfortunes of this case should not be allowed in any way to diminish, was that the responsibility for the consideration of the measures to be applied was to lie with what was essentially a lay body while disputed questions of fact as to the allegations made were to be resolved by the sheriff sitting in chambers as a court of law'[93]. Accordingly while a degree of informality is secured by the practice of the sheriff not wearing the full shrieval garb, by the lawyers and the clerk not wearing black gowns, a degree of formality is maintained by the requirement that those present should stand and that the old-fashioned practice of exchanging bows with the bar is retained. The practitioners will address the sheriff as 'My Lady'. Sheriffs sitting in hearings cases have to make decisions which have potentially devastating effects on families. A degree of formality is essential.*

---

92. Reporters (Conduct of Proceedings before the Sheriff)(Scotland) Regulations 1997, SI 1997/714; cf Reporters (Conduct of Proceedings before the Sheriff (Scotland) (Amendment) Regulations 1997, SI 1997/1084.
93. *Sloan v B* 1991 SLT 530 per Lord President Hope at 548E.

Reporter: My Lady, I represent the Principal Reporter. I am ready to proceed.

Mr Wynford: I represent the child William Brown, my Lady. The child's mother, Mrs Sylvia Brown is in the building but, as I think Your Ladyship is aware, William has indicated that when he comes to give evidence he does not require any 'support' and he is happy to sit beside me without his mother being present.

Sheriff Grey: You are representing the child?[94]

Mr Wynford: Yes, my Lady. And I can confirm that the grounds are still not accepted by the child?[95]

Sheriff: Thank you. Mr Somerville, would you like to begin?

Reporter: I tender to your Ladyship my list of witnesses. Also, there is one preliminary matter: my friend Mr Wynford and I have been able to adjust a Joint Minute agreeing the Report of the Assistant Chief Fire Officer dated 16 November 2005. I lodge this now with the Report itself, which I have marked as Reporter's Production No 1.

Sheriff: Good, it is always satisfactory when such matters can be agreed. Would you like to call your first witness?

THE EVIDENCE OF THE REPORTER

Examination in chief of Stephen Green

Reporter: My first witness is Stephen Green. He is a mature 14 year old and, as your Ladyship is aware, is to give evidence without any special measures under the vulnerable witnesses procedures and though my friend would had no objection to his mother, who is in the waiting room, being present during his evidence Stephen himself has indicated that this will not be necessary.

Sheriff: Good, then let's get started.

The sheriff's bar officer goes out of the room and then returns with Stephen Green and leads him towards the chair near the sheriff which is used as the witnesses' chair.

Bar officer: Stephen Green, my Lady.

Sheriff: Stephen – is it 'Stephen' I should call you, is that all right?

---

94. The sheriff expects no difficulty in this case, but it is as well to check routinely. In *Kennedy v S* 1986 SLT 679 there was confusion as to whether the solicitor was acting for the parent or the child – see per Lord Hunter at 681.
95. This informs the sheriff that there is no prospect of evidence being dispensed with under s 68(8) of the Children (Scotland) Act 1995.

Stephen: Yes.

Sheriff: Stephen, I have been told you are 14, is that correct?[96]

Stephen: Yes, my date of birth is 7th July 1991.

Sheriff: The law is that a person of your age is old enough to be placed on oath or make a solemn affirmation. I have been told that you would prefer to affirm?[97]

Stephen: Yes.

Sheriff: Then please, while still standing, repeat the words of the affirmation as follows: 'I do solemnly, sincerely and truly,'

Stephen: I do solemnly, sincerely and truly,

Sheriff: 'declare and affirm,'

Stephen: declare and affirm,

Sheriff: 'that I will tell the truth,'

Stephen: that I will tell the truth,

Sheriff: 'the whole truth,'

Stephen: the whole truth,

Sheriff: 'and nothing but the truth.'

Stephen: and nothing but the truth.

Sheriff: Thank you. Please sit down. Mr Somerville, whenever you are ready.

Reporter: I am obliged to your Ladyship. Stephen, could you tell us your full name?

---

96. The age of a child witness is important. A child of 14 or over is generally sworn or asked to take the affirmation. In the case of a child between 12 and 14 the matter is one for the sheriff's discretion – the sheriff can either 'admonish' (i.e. direct) the child to tell the truth or, if the child appears to understand the significance of the oath, administer the oath. In the case of a child under 12 the sheriff should admonish her or him to tell the truth and judge the child's credibility and reliability as would be done for any other witness. Thanks to s 24 of the Vulnerable Witnesses (Scotland) Act 2004 the requirement to 'examine' a child witness as to whether she or he understands the difference between truth and the importance of telling the truth in court has been abolished. See further discussion of this matter In Part 1 of this book at page 151.
97. It is good practice, although it does not always happen, for court officials to find out in advance if there is any speciality in relation to the form of oath/affirmation which a witness wishes to take; e.g. a particular religious oath may be required.

Stephen: Stephen McKillop Green.

Reporter: I think you live with your mother at 17 Dalton Causeway here in Kirklenton and that you are in third year at Kirklenton High School in the same class as William Brown?

Stephen: Yes.

Reporter: Do you see William in this room today, and if so would you point to him?[98]

Stephen: Yes. Over there. [Pointing.][99]

Reporter: I would like you to think back to Thursday 3rd November of last year, the year 2005, do you remember that day, the Thursday before Guy Fawkes' Day?

Stephen: Yes.

Reporter: Did something emerge that day which caused a lot of talk in the school?

Stephen: Yes.

Reporter: My Lady, my friend and I have agreed that I may lead the witness as to the background facts of this aspect of the case.

Mr Wynford: I confirm that. I shall let my friend know if I think he is straying from the background into the foreground.

Sheriff: Very good. Carry on, Mr Reporter.

Reporter. I'm obliged. Stephen, I believe that at about morning break-time, between 10 past and half past eleven, the news came that the words 'F*** Boozer Black' were found to have been painted by red spray paint on the outside of the door of the Science Lab, which is room 27 in what is known as the New Block of the school?

Stephen: Yes

Reporter: How did you hear about this?

---

98. Although hearings procedures are 'civil proceedings *sui generis*', section 68(3)(b) of the Children (Scotland) Act 1995 provides that the standard of proof required in criminal proceedings shall apply in cases where one of the grounds (as here) is under s 52(2)(i) of the Act. This entails all the rigorous application of the criminal law of evidence, including the rule that the unambiguous identification of the person accused is an essential fact.

99. Although the proceedings are 'civil proceedings *sui generis*', this is a criminal charge and the rules of evidence and safeguards for the accused person applicable to the criminal law apply: cf *Constanda v M* 1997 SCLR 510 per Lord President Rodger at 512D. One of these rules is that the witness in court who identifies the person accused must do so unequivocally, almost always by pointing.

Stephen: Charlie Galbraith, Henry Galbraith's wee brother who is in first year, came running up to us and told us – he had just come from a science lesson. He thought it was all very funny.

Reporter: Who all were there when Charlie came with this news?

Stephen: There was Henry, Douglas Leitch, William Brown, Jason McHugh and some others. And of course me.

Reporter: How did they all react?

Stephen: They all seemed surprised. Except that William didn't seem in the least surprised. I think that was because ...

Mr Wynford: I think my friend's witness is straying into speculation. He cannot read minds. I would object if this is to be pursued.

Reporter: My Lady, I don't intend to pursue this. Stephen, I don't want you to theorise about William's thoughts. We have to stick to the facts. Leaving aside what you thought that William thought, how did your various pals react?

Stephen: We all thought it was very funny. We were surprised, but William did not seem surprised. I was suspicious of this because I had seen William going into the New Block after school on the previous Wednesday when I was coming away from the Stamp Club.

Reporter: What time was this and what exactly did you see?

Stephen: The Stamp Club finished at about quarter past five and I stayed a bit later to show Mr McNeill one of the stamps in my collection which had what looked like a flaw on it. I must have left about half past five. I left by the main gate of the school into Aberfeldy Road.

Reporter: What happened then?

Stephen: I saw Bill in Muthill Lane.

Reporter: Which is where?

Stephen: It runs into Aberfeldy Road and runs along the side of the school. There is a side entrance to the school in it. Bill was heading in the direction of the side gate. I don't think he saw me.

Reporter: Did you notice anything about William? Did he have ...

Mr Wynford: I really must object, my friend is starting to lead beyond the common ground.

Sheriff: Mr Somerville?

Reporter: Sorry, my Lady. Stephen, could you see what he was wearing?

Stephen: He had a dark bomber jacket with the hood up.

Reporter: Did anything special strike you about his appearance?

Stephen: He seemed to have something in his jacket, inside it, up against his chest.

Reporter: What kind of 'something' – can you tell us?

Stephen: Not exactly. It seemed to drag down the front of the jacket though. So it must have been a bit heavy.

Reporter: What happened then?

Stephen: He looked round and then slipped in at the side gate.

Reporter: What distance is there between the side gate and the science lab?

Stephen: I don't know exactly. It's quite near.

Reporter: Using this room as an example, how far away, more or less than the length of this room?

Stephen: About double the length of this room.

Reporter. So if this room is about ten yards, that would mean twenty yards?

Stephen: Yards? What do you mean?

Sheriff: This room measures nine point five metres in length.

Reporter: I'm most obliged to your Ladyship. Stephen, so, as this room is nine point five metres and the distance we are talking about is about double that, the distance between the side gate and the New Block would be about nineteen metres?

Stephen: I suppose so.

Reporter: Did you see anything else of importance on that Wednesday evening?

Stephen: No.

Reporter: Reverting to Thursday the third of November, what did you do after you heard about the spray-painting incident?

Stephen: At first I didn't know what to do. I didn't want to 'tell' on another boy, but I thought that I might be blamed because I had stayed on after the Stamp Club so at the end of the break I went to see Mr McNeill and told him what I had seen. I went back to my class but soon after the Head sent for me and I told him what I had seen. Later I noticed William leaving the class and I suppose that was when he got dealt with. That was all that happened during the day at school.

Reporter: Did anything of note happen on the following day?

AN OBJECTION IS RAISED

Mr Wynford: I think my friend is going to lead evidence about an incident between the boys in the evening of the 4 November. We have briefly discussed this matter and my friend and I agree that there is a legal issue here which would be best discussed in the absence of the witness.

Sheriff: What is the general line of the difficulty?

Mr Wynford: Without saying too much the issue is whether the incident might fall foul of the rule which was discussed in *Nelson v HM Advocate*.

Sheriff: Yes I see what you are getting at. Stephen, would you please go with Miss O'Hara to the witness room and wait till you are asked to come back. And of course please promise me not to discuss your evidence with any other witness. Will you promise that?

Stephen: Yes.

Reporter: I think it might be appropriate if William, who will obviously be giving evidence, were also to withdraw. I will require to discuss possible evidence and there is an obvious risk of contamination. This is a matter of agreement between my friend and myself.

Sheriff: I know I have power under rule 3.47(5) of the Rules to exclude children while evidence is being given; I do not think that rule covers the exclusion of the referred child while evidence is being discussed but I can see that this is desirable on the basis of possible contamination and I think I would have power at common law so to order. In any event the motion is made by agreement and I will grant it. [Turning to William] William, I think it would be preferable if you went out while this legal matter is being discussed. I think your lawyer will have explained this to you?

William: Yes, he has, and that's all right.

Sheriff: Very well. Will you promise me not to discuss your evidence with anyone?

William: Yes.

The bar officer accompanies William, Mrs Brown and Stephen out of the room and returns.

Note [29]   Sheriff Grey is quite right in saying that rule 3.47(5) is of no assistance here, since it deals with excluding a child where the nature of the case or the evidence to be given is such that it would not be in the interests of the child to be present. In assuming power to exclude the referred child other that under that rule the sheriff may be regarded by some as taking a bold step, but she would defend it as being in the interests of doing justice for the child, if necessary invoking the words of Lord Sutherland in WW v Kennedy 1988 SCLR 236 at 239:- ' ... the proceedings in front of the sheriff on referral are self-contained civil proceedings sui generis in which it must be borne in mind at all times that the principal purpose is to ascertain what is necessary to be done in the interests of the child. In our opinion it would be quite wrong for this objective to be thwarted by the application of rigid rules of evidence or procedure just because such rigidity may be appropriate in other kinds of proceedings.'

Sheriff: Now, Mr Wynford, would you like to elaborate your point?

Mr Wynford: Very briefly. It is known to me that the boys met each other at about 6 pm. on that day and that William assaulted Stephen, apparently in response to some taunting by Stephen. William admits to punching Stephen once and causing him to fall but Stephen says he only delivered one punch. The police arrived and William was cautioned and charged. He replied something like: 'That grassing bastard is lying. I only punched him on the chest. He had it coming to him.' If my friend is allowed to go down this line then that potentially damaging admission will be in the evidence.

The incident was reported to my friend the children's reporter who on Tuesday 29 November 2005 wrote to William and his parents saying that he was taking no action in terms of section 56(4) of the Children (Scotland) Act 1995. In my submission my friend cannot now lead evidence of this now because he has not included this in his Statement of Facts. As your Ladyship is aware the issue of whether or not the prosecutor is entitled to lead evidence of a crime not charged was authoritatively ruled upon in *Nelson v HM Advocate* 1984 SLT 389. In that case Lord Justice General Hope, delivering the opinion of a Court of Five Judges, set out the law on this matter at pages 395L to 396B of the report. In particular his Lordship stated (if I may paraphrase for brevity) that evidence of a crime not charged may be led unless fair notice requires that the other crime be specifically libelled or referred to and that fair notice will so demand where the other crime tends to show that the accused was of bad character and that the other crime 'is so different in time, place and character from the crime charged that the libel does not give fair notice to the accused that evidence relating to that other crime may be led.'

Now in this case fair notice has not been given, although it could have been. Section 56(5) of the Children (Scotland) Act 1995 provides that a reporter who has decided to take no action under s 56(4) shall not at any other time arrange a hearing 'on the basis solely of the information obtained during the initial investigation' However the Statement of

Grounds for Referral which has been raised in this case is not based solely on the 'information obtained during the initial investigation', but on the other information about the spray-painting and indeed about the fire-raising. So it would have been open to my friend to have included the assault in his Statement and he has not done so. Now while the detailed criminal law code is not applicable to hearings procedures I submit that in a section 52(2)(i) case where of course 'the standard of proof required in criminal proceedings' must be applied, the safeguards of the criminal code must be observed. This was the approach of Lord President Rodger in *Constanda v M* 1997 SCLR 510 wherein his Lordship stated at 511F – I have a copy here for your Ladyship – 'In that overall context it is plain that Parliament was not prepared to apply a lower standard to the proof that a child had committed a criminal offence for the purposes of condition (g).' His lordship was of course dealing with a case under s 32(2)(g) of the Social Work (Scotland) Act, 1968. His Lordship continued: 'For these purposes the child is entitled to receive exactly the same protection as an adult or child would receive if he were prosecuted for the offence in the criminal courts'. In my submission the alleged, and partially admitted, attack on the boy Stephen Green is not within the category of cases mentioned by Lord President Hope in *Nelson* as admissible without fair notice having been given in respect that it 'tends to show that the accused was of bad character' and is 'so different in time, place and character from the crime charged that the libel does not give fair notice to the accused that evidence relating to that other crime may be led". There has been no such fair notice, and therefore the evidence about what William Brown did on the evening of 4 November 2005 is inadmissible.

Sheriff: Thank you. Mr Somerville, how do you respond to that?

Reporter: First of all on a technical point, I do not agree with my friend's interpretation of section 56(5). The reference to 'the initial investigation' must surely be to the initial investigation of a particular ground, in this case the ground under s 52(2)(i) in relation to the alleged offence of assault on the other boy. The natural meaning of the section is that only where further investigation has disclosed additional evidence as to the original ground of referral the matter could be included as a Ground for Referral. Suppose the child who had received the 'no action' letter one day were to be violently and unacceptably 'chastised' by his parent on the evening of receiving the letter, the parent perhaps saying, in an old-fashioned way, 'Well if you are not being dealt with by the panel you are going to be dealt with by my belt'. Surely it cannot have been the intention of the legislature, in the event of a referral being made in respect of a Schedule 1 offence against the child, that the alleged offence by the child should be capable of being re-activated as a Ground for Referral of the child? Apart from anything else, if this came to be known it would deter children from reporting.

Sheriff: An interesting argument. Do the books help us at all? And wasn't there a case in the 1980s about the facts of a former referral being resurrected?

Reporter: I think your Ladyship may be thinking of *Kennedy v S* 1986 SLT 679. I have a copy and pass it to your Ladyship. It is, with respect, on a slightly different point. As your Ladyship will see from the rubric this was a 'care and protection' case wherein a previous case of lack of parental care had been found not to be established and the reporter wished to use the previous evidence in conjunction with new evidence which, in the words of Lord Hunter at page 681 K, L indicated that the previous conduct was repeated, thus rendering the earlier conduct not an isolated incident. The only references to section 56(5) in Sheriff Kearney's book are at paragraphs 2.29 and 16.25 wherein the matter appears to be treated mainly in the context of 'care and protection' cases and under reference to *Kennedy v S*. Professor Norrie does deal with the matter explicitly at page 51 of the second edition of his *Children's Hearings in Scotland* where he states, 'These new circumstances may indicate quite different grounds of referral or they may concern the same ...' but it is perhaps significant that, in giving an example, Professor Norrie goes on to say, ' – for example, when the decision not to arrange a children's hearing was made on the basis of lack of evidence which has now come to light.' Although Professor Norrie states that the new circumstances 'may indicate quite different grounds of referral' I doubt if this can be taken to mean circumstances in relation to a totally different event. I suggest that Professor Norrie is referring to the type of situation wherein, for example, it emerged in relation to a child in respect of whom a case based on 'beyond control' had been not proceeded in which it subsequently emerged that the child, while apparently 'beyond control', was also 'falling into bad associations'. Professor Norrie concludes that once the section 56(4)(a) notification has been given then the decision not to arrange a hearing becomes 'irrevocable'. In the present situation there is no question of new evidence about the alleged assault and I am therefore bound by my decision not to state it as a Ground for Referral and that therefore my decision not to do so should not be used by my friend as a prop to his argument that this evidence is irrelevant to the matters in hand.

In any event, and more importantly, I would submit that facts surrounding the assault charge are capable of proving that William Brown is guilty of the paint-daubing charge. I am able to lead evidence from the police to the effect that when cautioned and charged with the offence of assault on Stephen William said 'The grassing little bastard had it coming to him'. In my submission that reply is admissible in relation to the paint matter since by saying in effect that Stephen had 'grassed' on him, i.e. reported that he, William, was guilty of an offence, William was by reasonable implication accepting that he had committed an offence and it was a reasonable inference in all the circumstances that the offence concerned was the painting offence. I do not need to prove the assault charge and will not of course be asking your Ladyship to make a finding of guilt in relation to that charge, but I do require to lead evidence about the assault in order to put that answer into context. The case has some affinity with *HM Advocate v Cairns* 1967 JC 37, 1967 SLT 165 which held that it was competent to lead evidence in relation to a matter on which the accused had been acquitted in order to support a different charge. As to the issue of fair notice, if my friend feels he has been taken by surprise it is open to him to ask your Ladyship for an adjournment. Hearings procedure is flexible enough to allow this, as reflected in the oft-quoted words of Lord Sutherland in *WW v Kennedy* 1988 SCLR 236 at 239 wherein his Lordship deprecated 'rigidity' in relation to this type of procedure. I would certainly not object to such a motion.

Sheriff: What about the point that evidence as to the previous alleged assault tends, in the words of Lord Hope 'to show that the accused was of bad character'?

Reporter: Yes it does, but that is not an absolute bar to its admissibility. All that Lord Hope is saying is that for such a line to be adopted fair notice must be given.

Sheriff: Mr Wynford, would you like to respond?

> *Note [30]   In dealing with a relatively simple objection the sheriff will normally hear the objector and the questioner briefly and then give her decision. In the present situation, however, the reporter has developed substantial legal issues on which the other side is entitled to be heard in reply.*

Mr Wynford. Yes indeed. I am obliged. As to the technical matter about whether my friend could have averred the assault as a ground of referral, I would argue that in a system aimed at promoting the welfare of children it can never have been the intention of the legislature to exclude on technical grounds a ground of referral which might be relevant to the disposal of the case.

Sheriff: What about the point that the possibility of an 'old' alleged crime by the child being 'revived' would deter a child from reporting that someone had abused him?

Mr Wynford: I think it is fanciful to suggest that a child would think along these lines. Having received my friend's letter the child would assume that the offence was buried for ever. On the more substantial point I submit that the principle enunciated in *Nelson* is directed at the commission of the offence. It might have been admissible for my friend to lead evidence about the assault if the commission of the offence of assault probabilised the commission of one of the other offences. For example, if it were a similar offence it might re-enforce the attempt which I suspect my friend may make to invoke the *Moorov* principle[100].

Sheriff: If I were to allow the evidence, would you wish an adjournment in order to make further inquiries?

---

100. That is the 'doctrine', based on the case of *Moorov v HM Advocate* 1930 JC 68, that where more than one similar and interconnected offences are alleged that the evidence supporting one may in certain circumstances constitute the corroboration for the other. See *infra* at page 256.

Mr Wynford: No, my Lady. As it happens I think I have enough information to deal with this.

Sheriff: Do you want to come back Mr Somerville?

Reporter: No, I am happy to leave the matter in your Ladyship's hands.

Sheriff: I think I would like to give this matter some thought, but I am inclined to reserve the matter at this stage and allow the evidence to come out under reservation. I think Lord President Hope advised this course in the Orkney case[101]. Would you both agree to such a course?

Reporter and Mr Wynford: Yes, my Lady.

Sheriff: [To the sheriff clerk (for minuting).] 'Line of evidence relating to the alleged assault by William on Stephen on 4 November 2005 objected to by Mr Wynford on the ground that it tended to prove an offence not founded upon. Line allowed under reservation of all matters of competency and relevancy.'

Examination in chief of Stephen Green resumes

Sheriff: I think we might have Stephen and William back in now. Miss O'Hara, would you go and ask Stephen and William to come in again?

The bar officer goes out and returns with William, William's mother, and Stephen.

Sheriff: I have now attended to the legal matter which arose. Stephen, I will now ask the reporter to continue his questions. Mr Somerville, I think your question was, 'Did anything of note happen on the following day?' and by 'the following day' meaning Friday 4 November 2005. What do you say in answer to that Stephen?

The examination in chief of Stephen Green continues. In relation to the events of that Friday evening he says he saw William Brown in Attlee Quadrant at about 6.30 pm and may have shouted over at him. He thought he said simply 'Hi, pal', perhaps in a sarcastic way, but he did not agree that he asked him if he had had a nice afternoon. He says that William ran across the street towards him and punched him in the stomach, causing him to fall over. He said that when he was down William kicked him on the head twice and that then the police arrived. He told the police that he did not require medical attention. The lady police officer took him home and took a statement from him. In evidence he agreed that he said to the lady police officer that he would get his own back on William, but denied that his evidence against William was his way of getting back. He agrees that he and his parents received a letter dated

---

101. Yes, Lord President Hope did so recommend; see *Sloan v B* 1991 SLT 530 at 546L.

29 November 2005 (a copy of which is produced as a reporter's pro-duction) from the reporter stating that no action would be taken against William Brown in connection with the assault on him. He says he was initially annoyed about this but very soon put it out of his mind and was really quite glad that William was not being formally dealt with since, although he admitted not liking William, he did not want him to get into serious trouble. As to the fire in the shed, he, like the rest of the school, had heard about it at the time and went along with the theory that it had been caused by a mis-directed firework. Nobody had said much about it. He knew nothing at all about the finding of the can of spray paint or about any anonymous letter sent to the Head.

Examination in chief of Stephen Green concludes

The examination in chief of Stephen concludes about half past eleven and Sheriff Grey says she thinks the witness should have a break and says she will rise for about 15 minutes. Thereafter all assemble again.

Sheriff: Mr Wynford, do you wish to cross-examine?

Cross-examination of Stephen Green

Mr Wynford: If your Ladyship pleases. [Turning towards Stephen.] Stephen, I want to ask you first about the evening of Wednesday 2nd November 2005. You said you left the Stamp Club at about half past five after staying back to show Mr McNeill a stamp with a flaw in it?

Stephen: Yes.

Mr Wynford: By the way, what stamp was it, and what was the flaw?

Stephen: It was a 1949 Pitcairn Islands Two Pence, with a circular blob of white.

Mr Wynford: So Mr McNeill will be able to tell us about that?

Stephen: Yes.

Mr Wynford: You said that Muthill Lane runs into Aberfeldy Street and that you saw William in Muthill Lane?

Stephen: Yes.

Mr Wynford: How near were you when you saw him? How could you see it was him when he was presumably walking away from you?

Reporter: My Lady ...

Sheriff: That is two questions, one of which contains an assumption.

Mr Wynford: Sorry, my Lady.

> Note [31]   *It is appropriate for the lawyer adducing a witness to protect the witness from unfair questioning. It is also the duty of the court to intervene at its own hand to avoid the unfairness and/or confusion which can result from multiple or 'loaded' questions, particularly where the witness is a child or other vulnerable person. Mr Wynford is a competent court practitioner, but even good pleaders get carried away sometimes. He at once realises his infelicity and proceeds to put it right.*

Mr Wynford: Where were you when you saw William?

Stephen: I was crossing Muthill Lane where it comes into Aberfeldy Street.

Mr Wynford: How far away was he when you first saw him? – Again use the court as an example if you want.

Stephen: A bit more than the length of this room.

Mr Wynford: More than 9½ metres then? Much more?

Stephen: Maybe about half as much more.

Mr Wynford: How near was he to the side gate of the school?

Stephen: I don't know.

Mr Wynford: Please try.

Stephen: It was quite a bit.

Mr Wynford: Was it the same distance again, 9½ metres or more?

Stephen: Perhaps.

Mr Wynford: In what position was he when you saw him?

Stephen: What do you mean 'what position'?

Mr Wynford: What part of him could you see?

Stephen: He was walking away from me. I could see his back.

Mr Wynford: Did you see any other part of him?

Stephen: Not really.

Mr Wynford: You said to my friend the reporter, if I have noted you correctly, that he seemed to have something in his jacket, inside it, up against his chest. And that whatever it was must have been heavy because it dragged down the front of his jacket. How could you see that if you only saw his back?

Reporter: I think my friend should put to the witness that he looked round at one point and slipped into the school.

Mr Wynford: My Lady, I think my friend should let me cross-examine and not prompt the witness.

Sheriff: Mr Reporter, I think that is fair comment.

Reporter: Sorry, my Lady.

Mr Wynford [to Stephen]: Well, how could you see that?

Stephen: I saw it when he turned into the school.

Mr Wynford: And that was after he had walked another 9½ metres or more?

Stephen: I suppose so.

Mr Wynford: And had you walked another 9½ metres or more from the time you had first seen him?

Stephen: I don't know what you're getting at.

Mr Wynford: Never mind what I am getting at, just answer the question please.

Stephen: Oh yes. I might have stopped. I stopped because I wondered what William was up to and that was when he turned into the gate and I could see him from the side.

Mr Wynford: You did not say that earlier when the reporter was asking you questions. Why not?

Stephen: Because he didn't ask me.

Mr Wynford: Isn't the real reason you didn't say it because it didn't happen and you made it up when you worked out what I was 'getting at'?

Stephen: No.

> Note [32] 'A hit, a very palpable hit'. The apple, to change the metaphor, does not often fall so neatly into the cross-examiner's lap, but it sometimes does and is most satisfying. Stephen now seems to lack credibility. Of course the odd thing is he may be telling the truth. At this moment the reporter will be regretting that he did not cover this point in precognition.

Mr Wynford: You don't like William Brown very much, do you?

Stephen: Oh I don't know.

Mr Wynford: I could bring other boys to say this, do I have to do that?

Stephen: Well maybe we don't get on all that well.

Mr Wynford: You seem reluctant to admit it – isn't that because you'd prefer us not to know that since it is because you 'don't get on all that well' that you are prepared to make up these tales against him?

Stephen: No.

Mr Wynford: Like the liar you are?

Sheriff: Mr Wynford!

Mr Wynford: I'm very sorry, my Lady. I withdraw that.

> Note [33]   *It is the duty of the court to protect witnesses from badgering. What constitutes badgering as opposed to robust but fair cross-examination depends on circumstances and is a matter of fine judgement for the individual sheriff. Sheriff Grey, correctly it may be thought, as this is a child witness, is quick to step in. In any event such a bombastic question achieves little and tends to antagonise the court and, in a jury trial, to alienate the jury.*

Mr Wynford. I now move on to the events of the morning of Thursday 3rd November 2005.

The cross-examiner now presses Stephen on his evidence that 'William didn't seem in the least surprised' when the news about the spray-painting broke. He suggests to him that this is a fabrication, based on his dislike of William and Stephen denies this. Mr Wynford then moves on to the assault by William on him on the Friday evening. First of all he presses him on the issue of 'taunting', and suggests that he did indeed shout over to William in a taunting manner 'Have you had a nice afternoon?' and suggests that it is unlikely that anybody would have reacted in the way which William did had an innocuous remark been made. Stephen sticks to his evidence in chief.

> Note [34]   *The purpose of 'putting to'[102] a witness in cross-examination an alternative account of events is two-fold. In the first place the cross-examiner aims to damage the credibility of the witness and may even hope to get the witness to retract (which*

---

102.   I put this in quotation marks because while it is in order to use this as a descriptive term, I do not favour the use of this phrase when asking a witness questions. It is lawyers' language which may not be understood. I prefer 'I suggest that ...' or, 'Isn't it the case that ...'. However, 'I put it to you that ...' is very common.

rarely happens) or perhaps press him or her into adopting an
extreme stance which will make him seem unreasonable and
prejudiced. (Older readers may remember the court martial scene
in 'The Caine Mutiny' wherein José Ferrar achieves this by
'breaking down' Captain Queeg (Humphrey Bogart) and causing
him to rant and rave and claim that all are against him. I have
never seen this happen in real life, but keep hoping.) The other
purpose in 'putting' an alternative account to the witness is to lay
a foundation for evidence one is going to lead oneself. Failure to
give a witness the chance to comment on a matter within that
witness's knowledge does not make the subsequent evidence
inadmissible, but may materially weaken the force of that
evidence.

Mr Wynford then cross-examines on the events of the assault. He suggests
to Stephen that his description of the assault is grossly exaggerated and
presses him as to why the police, who saw the knocking down, didn't see
the rest. Stephen tends to stick to his account, saying that the police could
not have seen everything since they drove past the scene in the first
instance and therefore did not have an unimpeded view. Mr Wynford
suggests to Stephen directly that he is lying about this but Stephen
maintains his stance.

Mr Wynford asks briefly on the anonymous letter which put the Head in
contact with the tin of petrol and the spray paint container and the
circumstances surrounding the presence of these items in the locker room.
He suggests to Stephen that he knows more about them than he is
prepared to admit, drawing attention to the fact that the letter was
received not long after the reporter had notified parties that he was taking
no action against William on the assault, implying that he might have had
something to do with this himself. Stephen firmly denies knowing anything
about these matters and Mr Wynford, not having any positive evidence to
bring forward on this point, considers that he cannot properly go as far as
formally to 'put to' Stephen that he 'planted' the articles or wrote the
letter.

Mr Wynford concludes by reverting to the spray-painting episode and
suggests to Stephen that he had the same opportunity to carry it out as he
alleges William had. Indeed he (Stephen) had said that he had been afraid
that he himself might be accused. Wasn't his fear of being accused amply
justified because it was rooted in the knowledge that he had himself done
the deed? At this point the sheriff intervenes to 'warn' the witness that he
need not answer the question if he thinks the answer might incriminate
him in any offence. Stephen says he is happy to answer and vigorously
denies having had anything to do with the spray-painting incident.

Note [35]   Good practice in cross-examining embraces ethical
and good advocacy considerations, and they should co-incide. It is
improper to allege that a witness has committed an offence unless
one is in a position to lead evidence tending to prove this. It is bad
advocacy to raise the expectation of the court by pressing a

witness elaborately on a point and then be unable to lead evidence tending to prove that point.

Note [36] "'Warning' a witness". Where a witness is asked a question which seems to be aimed at eliciting evidence which might help a prosecutor make out a criminal charge against the witness the "sacred and inviolable" principle against self-incrimination, as it has been called[103], comes into play and court must "warn" the witness along the lines adopted by Sheriff Grey here[104]. This is the approximate Scottish equivalent of "pleading the Fifth Amendment" in the Unites States. In a prosecution a Crown witness generally has, by virtue of being called by the Crown, a degree of immunity from prosecution and a "warning" by the court may not be necessary, but a reporter's witness enjoys no such immunity and consequently the "warning" should be given, because the technical possibility exists that the witness may be prosecuted or referred to a hearing on a section 52(2)(i) ground and any admission made during his evidence could be founded upon'.

Cross-examination of Stephen Green concluded

Sheriff: Mr Somerville, any re-examination?

Re-examination of Stephen Green

Reporter: Briefly, my Lady. Stephen, you said you stopped at the end of Muthill Lane. Can you tell us what made you stop?

Stephen: I was puzzled because William was going in the direction of the school at that time and wondered what he was up to.

Reporter: You said you didn't say that in examination in chief – that is when I was asking the questions earlier – because you hadn't been asked. Was that then the first time you had been asked about this?

Stephen: Yes.

Reporter: Had you not been asked by me about this when I interviewed you in my office?

Stephen: No.

Reporter: Nor perhaps had you been asked about this by my friend Mr Wynford when he interviewed you?

Stephen: No.

---

103. See *Livingston v Murrays* (1830) 9 S 161 at 162 per Lord Gillies.
104. *W v Kennedy* 1988 SLT 583 at 584 I, reported sub nom *WW v Kennedy* 1988 SCLR at 236 at 237. For further discussion, see *Kearney*, op cit, at 37.12.

Reporter: Finally, you ultimately agreed that you did not like William very much?

Stephen: Yes.

Reporter: Is your dislike for William so intense as to make you want to get him into serious trouble and come here today and tell lies about him?

Stephen: No.

Reporter: So what you have told us is the truth?

Stephen: Yes.

Reporter: I have no further questions, my Lady.

Sheriff: On that Wednesday evening, the 2nd November, that was a winter evening, so it must have been dark?

Stephen: Yes.

Sheriff: How easy was it for you to see down into Muthill Lane?

Stephen: There is good street lighting.

Sheriff: Even in the lane?

Stephen: Yes. The local council last year decided that streets around schools should be especially well lit and extra lamp standards were put up. I could see down the lane fine.

Sheriff. Thank you. Mr Somerville, Mr Wynford, anything arising out of my questions? Or anything at all you want to ask while we have Stephen here? As you know I take the view that in this procedure the strict rules should not be applied.

Reporter: Thank you my Lady, but no.

Mr Wynford. Likewise I am obliged to your Ladyship but have no further questions.

Sheriff: Very well. Stephen, that is all. You can go now. Thank you for coming. Miss O'Hara will take you to the witness room where I think your mother still is.

> *Note [37]   The essential purpose of re-examination is to allow
> the person who has examined in chief to ask about any answer in
> cross-examination which he thinks requires clarification. The
> reporter takes the bold step of trying to retrieve the situation
> arising from the point about how Stephen was able to get a front
> view of William by bringing out that he had not covered that*

matter in precognition. In ordinary civil pleading it is not generally permissible for the pleaders to raise 'new matter' at this stage, but, as can be seen from the final comments of Sheriff Grey, a more relaxed approach may be adopted in these proceedings because the interests of the child may incline the sheriff to allow last minute points to be raised. This is very much a matter for the discretion of the sheriff and should not be relied on by pleaders as a substitute for careful and well thought out questioning.

Note [38]   As to the questioning by the sheriff, it is submitted that in these proceedings the sheriff may take a more active and interventional role than would be normal in ordinary civil procedure, but when the sheriff does intervene to raise new matter it is proper for her to ask parties if they have any questions arising out of the evidence she has elicited.

THE REST OF THE EVIDENCE FOR THE REPORTER

Sheriff: It is now just after twenty to one. The evidence of Stephen has taken longer than was perhaps anticipated. Mr Reporter, would you like to call your next witness? I think we might at least make a start with your next witness?

Mr Wynford: Milady, before my friend proceeds with his evidence could I respectfully ask your Ladyship to consider, perhaps at the end of my friend's evidence, ruling on the objection I took to my friend's evidence about the assault charge, which your Ladyship allowed under reservation, since obviously your Ladyship's view on that may affect how I present the case for the child.

Sheriff: Yes, I can see that. Any observation Mr Somerville?

Reporter: No, my Lady, except I think that would be entirely appropriate.

Sheriff: Very well I shall rise now to consider the matter and issue a short opinion at the conclusion of the reporter's case. We will resume at five past two.

THE AFTERNOON SESSION – THE REPORTER'S PROOF CONTINUED AND CONCLUDED

PCs MacTaggart and Myles state that they were on uniformed mobile patrol at 6.30 pm. on Friday 4 November 2005, with Mr MacTaggart driving. They saw William, whom they identified, run across the road, almost in front of the police car and decided to turn the car and investigate. PC Myles, being the non-driver, kept the boys in view most of the time and spoke to William punching Stephen on the chest and knocking him down. She did not see any kicking but could not be absolutely sure that she had witnessed every second of the incident. Both officers said that Stephen was still on the ground when they arrived. Both said that when they approached the boys on foot William was standing over Stephen shouting words to the effect 'Stand up and I'll give you a proper doing'. They also speak to the reply to caution and charge, 'The grassing little bastard had it coming to him'. Mr Wynford does not cross-examine.

> *Note [39]   The decision by Mr Wynford not to cross-examine the police witnesses was carefully considered. It might have been tempting to press the arresting officers about whether they were sure about their evidence. But Mr Wynford has precognosced them and is aware that they could not say any more. If he had decided to have another bite at the cherry in court there would be a chance of stirring up a latent memory of some detail which would tell against William.*

The head teacher, Mr Black, states that the spray-painting was reported to him by telephone by the janitor at about 8 pm. on Wednesday 2 November 2005. He had told the janitor to leave it in position so that he could see it on the Thursday. He had looked at it on the Thursday morning and decided not to report it to the police, partly because he did not want to give the perpetrator the satisfaction of publicity and partly, he admitted, because the words were a bit embarrassing. After the morning break on Thursday Mr McNeill had come to him and said that Stephen had told him of seeing William going into the school on the Wednesday evening with something heavy concealed in his bomber jacket. He had interviewed Stephen who had confirmed this. He then summoned William who denied having done the painting and said he had an alibi witness. The Head thought this was suspicious because he had taken care not to specify the time when Stephen had said he had seen him. He just said that 'from information received' it seemed clear that the offender was William. He concluded by saying that his initial inclination to suspend had been over-hasty and indeed not lawful in that the formalities for such a disposal had not been observed. After talking the matter over with his Assistant Head, Mr McNeill, he had decided on detention. He gave evidence that the anonymous note had arrived on his in-tray in an unexplained way. It was in a plain envelope and stated, in block letters, 'SHED FIRE GO TO LAST LOCKER ON RIGHT'. He had gone to the place and found the petrol can and the spray paint container. The reporter took from him, with consent of Mr Wynford, that the police had examined the letter and the articles and found them to contain no fingerprint or other evidence of their origin. When cross-examined Mr Black denied that he had a particular 'down' on William but agreed that he regarded him as a difficult pupil, although he could not cite any specific incident to justify this view. He was not aware of any alleged foul play on the football field. He did not consider he had set a trap for William by not telling him of the time of the alleged incident. He just regarded this as good investigative technique. No, he hadn't asked William how he could know of the time since that would warn him of the point and enable him to 'improve his story'. The reporter does not re-examine.

Note [40]   The reporter had not personally interviewed Mr Black before the proof and was a little surprised at what he thought the court would regard as a somewhat persecuting stance against a pupil. The reporter considered that any re-examination aimed at moderating this stance might have the opposite effect. Accordingly he decided that the safest course was to 'get him out of the witness box' as soon as possible.

The rest of the reporter's evidence is fairly routine evidence from Mr McNeill and the janitor, Mr Donaldson. Their evidence tends to establish that the spray painting incident happened before 8 pm. on Wednesday 2 November and the setting fire to the shed took place about 8 pm. on Saturday 5 November 2005.

Reporter: That is the case for the reporter my Lady.

Sheriff: Thank you. Now as requested by Mr Wynford I will rule on the objection. [*Reads*]:–

The question was whether or not certain evidence relevant to the assault on the child Stephen Green was admissible since the assault on Stephen was not included in the grounds of referral. It is of course on the face of it paradoxical that it was William's lawyer who was arguing that the reporter would have been entitled to state the assault as a Ground for Referral, but of course he was bound to argue this in the context of his legal submission on admissibility. Mr Wynford maintained that the fact that the events of the assault were not included as one of the Statements of Fact forming these Grounds of Referral made it illegitimate for the reporter to lead evidence as to what William had said in reply to caution and charge.

Mr Somerville replied by saying he was not entitled to include this matter as a ground of referral because he had intimated 'no action' under s. 56(4). Section 56(5) enacts that when a 'no action' notification has been sent out the reporter 'shall not at any other time, on the basis solely of the information obtained during the investigation referred to in that subsection [ie subsection 4] arrange a hearing ...'. In my view the reporter's answer to this was valid. As I read it the natural meaning of section 56(5) of the Act is that it only allows a ground in respect of which a 'no action' notification in terms of s 56(4) has been sent to be made the subject of a Ground for Referral if further information in relation to the earlier Ground has been discovered. I agree that if that information suggests a new condition of referral <u>in relation to the facts of the original ground of referral</u>, then the reporter would be able to state such a fresh condition of referral, but that is not the situation here. Of course, as mentioned by Mr Wynford, the courts, in a system designed to secure the interests of children, must be careful not unreasonably to abridge this purpose, but the courts must also be astute to attend to the rights of the child and I think that where the child has received notification that no action is to be taken then she or he is entitled, in the absence of fresh information as to the original allegation, to regard the matter as closed. I therefore conclude that the reporter was barred by law from stating the alleged assault on Stephen Green as a Ground for Referral.

This however, is not the end of the matter. Since, as argued by Mr Somerville, it is not the <u>commission</u> of the crime of assault which the reporter desires to found on, but something which was said while that crime was being investigated. All the reporter requires to prove is that the words were said and not that the crime of assault was committed. In *Nelson* Lord Justice General Hope stated that it was the lack of fair notice which rendered inadmissible evidence of a crime which had not been libelled, (being a matter which tended to show that the accused was of bad character). In the instant situation, as I have said, the proof of the crime is not essential to the reporter's case and the issue of fair notice does not arise since the procedure in cases of this type – unlike, for example, solemn procedure – is flexible enough to cope with evidence of which no notice has been given by allowing the sheriff the discretion in an appropriate case to allow an adjournment for any further investigation which might be required. Mr Wynford has indicated that he does not require such an adjournment. I therefore repel the objection and hold that the evidence in relation to the assault on Stephen and what William said when charged with it was admissible and therefore properly before the court.

Mr Wynford: I am obliged to your Ladyship.

Sheriff: Do you wish a few minutes to consider the implications of my decision?[105]

Mr Wynford: No, my Lady, I am happy to proceed and my motion to your Ladyship is that, even with the evidence about what was said in the course of the investigation of the assault charge admitted, my friend has not made out a case to answer in terms of rule 3.47(2) of the Act of Sederunt (Child Care and Maintenance Rules) 1997 and I ask your Ladyship to make a finding to that effect under r 3.47(3) and consequently to dismiss the application and discharge the referral by virtue of section 68(9) of the Children (Scotland) Act 1995.

Sheriff: Did not the Rules made under the 1995 Act do away with 'no case to answer'?

Mr Wynford: Yes, but for all grounds except cases wherein an offence by the child is averred.

Sheriff: Of course. Sorry. Carry on.[106]

Mr Wynford: In my submission my friend has not made out a *prima facie* case in respect of either of the two alleged offences.

---

105. Sheriff Grey is a most considerate judge. Pleaders should not count on being allowed time in the middle of a proof to work out the implications of a ruling whose contents they should have been able to anticipate as a real possibility.
106. Not all sheriffs know all the law or have it at the top of their minds all the time!

In respect on the 'paint' case, if I may call it that, he has of course the evidence of Stephen Green which, I concede, if believed, would be enough to provide one source of evidence. For corroboration, however, my friend has to rely on the evidence which your Ladyship has just ruled to be admissible, namely the reply, 'The grassing little bastard had it coming to him.' Of course your Ladyship has to take the reporter's evidence at its highest at this stage but, in my submission, even taken at its highest, that cannot be regarded as an admission by William that he had committed the 'paint' offence. My friend's argument must be that by calling Stephen a 'grass' William is implying not only that Stephen had grassed on him, but also that he, William had committed something which could be grassed on and, not only that, but that that something was painting rude words on the door. This in my submission goes beyond the bounds of reasonable inference and enters the realm of speculation.

In relation to the fire-raising charge there is virtually no evidence. All we have is the finding by a single witness, the Head Teacher, of a can of red spray paint beside a container which had, and I concede this in accordance with the evidence, once contained petrol. I have discussed this with my friend the reporter and understand that he will argue that your Ladyship may infer that the can of spray paint was the can used by William to write the rude words and that the contiguity on this can with the petrol container indicates that they belonged to the same person and that therefore that person must be William. Once again I submit that this is not reasonable inference but that it goes even beyond speculation and enters into the realms of fantasy. In any event the finding of the paint container beside the petrol can was only spoken to by one witness and therefore there is no corroboration.

I believe my friend will attempt to invoke the principle of *Moorov v HM Advocate* 1930 JC 68. This principle is conveniently defined in the article by Lord Macphail (as he now is) and Sheriff Ruxton in volume 10 of *The Stair Memorial Encyclopaedia* at paragraph 769 thus: 'Where an accused is tried on two or more charges alleging similar acts which are so connected in time, character and circumstances as to justify an inference that they are instances of a course of similar conduct systematically pursued by him, the evidence of a single witness in relation to one charge may be corroborated by the evidence of another single witness in relation to another'.

While I would concede that there is a colourable argument in favour of this principle coming into play here I would submit that in cases wherein the *Moorov* doctrine has been applied there has always been clear identification of the accused – see *M'Rae v HM Advocate* 1975 JC 34 wherein Lord Justice Clerk Wheatley said at 38: 'In our view where there is no identification of an accused in a particular instance such an instance cannot be used under the Moorov doctrine ...'. In the instant case the identification of William in relation to the fire-raising charge is, as I have argued, based on speculation rather than reason and therefore my friend's reliance on *Moorov* should not succeed.

Sheriff: Thank you. Mr Somerville?

Reporter: In my submission there is ample evidence supporting the paint charge. The only point my friend makes is lack of clarity as to what was meant by the reply to caution and charge. I submit that the ordinary person hearing this said would deduce that William was saying not merely that Stephen was a 'grass' in general terms but that he had 'grassed' on him (William), and probably recently. The only matter which could be the subject of this 'grassing' was the paint offence, and therefore the statement was, or at least could be – and your Ladyship has to take my case at its highest for the present purpose – reasonably interpreted as being an admission that William had carried out the offence, the paint offence, in respect of which Stephen had 'grassed' on William.

As to the fire-raising offence, my friend is correct, I do rely on *Moorov*. Of course I do not have the eye-witness identification which I have for the paint offence, but the evidence of the one witness, Mr Black, puts a spray-paint can beside an empty can of petrol. The only container of spray-paint can we have heard of – and they do not lie about in profusion like discarded drinks cans – is that possessed by William when he was seen going into the school. Its having been found beside a petrol can which it may be reasonably inferred was used to set fire to the shed, may reasonably be taken to implicate the possessor of the paint-sprayer, namely William. Had the Head Teacher had the prescience to take someone with him to witness the discovery (as would have been done had this been a police investigation) we should not have been in this artificial situation of having to rely on *Moorov*, but, as my friend has virtually conceded – inevitably in the light of the facts – the necessary elements of the *Moorov* test are present. All I require to do at this stage is to lay before the court evidence which, taken at its highest, tends to incriminate the accused child. I submit that I have done this and respectfully move my Lady to repel my friend's motion in respect of both alleged offences. If my Lady is against me in relation to the *Moorov* argument, I would urge my Lady to leave standing the case based on the paint offence.

Sheriff: Mr Wynford, do you want to come back?

Mr Wynford: I'm obliged to your Ladyship, but no.

Sheriff: In my view there is sufficient evidence which, if believed, would entitle me to make a finding of guilt in respect of the alleged 'paint' offence. In relation to the alleged fire-raising offence I think that the reporter was entitled to invoke *Moorov*. The second offence was of a sufficiently similar type to make it a reasonable inference that the person who had committed the first may well have committed the second. I thought there was just sufficient evidence from which the identification of the child William could be inferred . I accordingly repel in its entirety the plea of 'no case to answer'.

Mr Wynford: I am obliged. In that event I call my client, William Brown.

Note [41]   The submission of 'no case to answer', is, as shown by the interchange between Mr Wynford and the sheriff, now, thanks to the Act of Sederunt (Child Care and Maintenance Rules) 1997, SI 1997/291 rule 3.47(2), confined to cases where the condition of referral is an alleged offence by the child, i.e. under section 52(2)(i) of the Children (Scotland) Act 1995. The pleaders here do not cite authority for the legal concepts to be applied because they are so well known. The test is the same as that which must be applied in respect of a submission of 'no case' under section 97 (solemn procedure) and section 160 (summary procedure) of the Criminal Procedure (Scotland) Act 1995, viz, that the evidence of the witnesses must be taken as true (pro veritate)[107], and the case for the prosecutor must be taken 'at its highest', i.e. on the basis that the court should proceed on the basis that the most favourable inference in favour of the prosecution side may be drawn.

THE AFTERNOON SESSION CONTINUED – THE REFERRED CHILD'S PROOF

Examination in Chief of William Brown

William goes over to the witness's chair and the sheriff, after checking his age (14), administers the oath, with both the sheriff and William standing with right hand raised: 'I swear by almighty God – that I will tell the truth – the whole truth – and nothing but the truth'.

Mr Wynford: Please tell us your name and age?

William Brown: My name is William Brown and I am fourteen and a half.

Mr Wynford: I think your address is 3/1, 27 Morrison Street, Kirklenton and that you go to Kirklenton High School. What class are you in at present?

William Brown: Third year, secondary three.

Mr Wynford: What subjects do you like at school?

William Brown: I'm interested in PT, and quite good at it. Not at much else I'm afraid.

Mr Wynford: I want to ask you first of all about the evening of Wednesday 2nd November of last year. Will you please tell the sheriff exactly what you did that evening from leaving school at 4 pm?

Mr Wynford 'takes' from William evidence along the lines of his precognition, reproduced in pages 191–195 above. When the exam-ination in chief of William has finished the sheriff turns to the reporter.

Sheriff: Mr reporter, I take it you will wish to cross-examine. [Turning to William.] William, you've been answering questions for some time. Would you like a short interval?

---

107. *Williamson v Wither* 1981 SCCR 214 at 217.

William Brown: No, thank you, I'd rather get it over with.

Sheriff: Very well. When you are ready, Mr Somerville.

Cross-examination of William Brown

Reporter: About the alleged events of 2nd November and the paint incident. If I have noted you correctly you told the headmaster that you had what you described as 'an alibi witness'.

William Brown: Yes and I knew the time of the painting because ...

Reporter: Never mind that, I'll come to that presently if necessary. Just answer the question. You told the head that you had an alibi witness, is that correct?

William Brown: Yes.

> *Note [42]   By interrupting a witness a pleader will often meet with the caution from the bench, 'Let the witness finish'. Witnesses should answer questions, not launch into a narrative which anticipates later questions. Of course some answers have to be detailed, and that is when the witness must be allowed to give the appropriate detail, but here the sheriff does not intervene, having rightly assessed that William is going to go into the quasi-exculpatory explanation of how he knew about the time of the incident and that that is not necessary for the answering of this particular question*

Reporter: And that was a lie?

William Brown: I suppose so.

Reporter: What do you mean, you suppose so, it was a lie – you have admitted as much when you were answering Mr Wynford's questions?

William Brown: Yes.

Reporter: So you were prepared to lie to the Head in order to get out of trouble?

William Brown: I suppose so.

Reporter: Of course you now say that you were not involved in the paint incident?

William Brown: Yes.

Reporter: But if you were involved and if the Head had believed your lie then someone else might have got the blame?

Sheriff: I think that is a rather convoluted question for a fourteen year old.

Reporter: Very well, I'm obliged. William, you lied to the Head so as to get out of trouble?

William Brown: Yes.

Reporter: So aren't you again lying in order to get out of more serious trouble?

William Brown: No. I am on oath today. And there was no danger of anyone getting wrongly blamed because of my lie, because although I lied about an alibi I knew I hadn't done it.

> Note [43] *The sheriff underestimated William's ability to understand a 'convoluted' question. Having learned from the experience of the earlier question William gets this out quickly before the reporter can interrupt and stop him!*

Reporter: You said you were at the swimming pool on Wednesday 2nd November and stayed there till a quarter past seven?

William Brown: Yes.

Reporter: When did you arrive at the pool?

William Brown: About five or quarter past five.

Reporter: So you stayed there for over two hours. Isn't that a long time to be at the pool, especially when you are by yourself?

William Brown: No, there is plenty to do. There is the swimming and the flume – and the hot sprays. Also I had a coke and crisps in the café area.

Reporter: All by yourself?

William Brown: Yes.

Reporter: You usually go with your friends Henry and Douglas, but you say they were not there that evening. Why were they not there?

William: It was Henry's mother's birthday that evening and he couldn't come. I don't know what Douglas was doing. I expect he knew about that and didn't want to go alone.

Reporter: 'Go alone', you said. But Douglas could have gone with you?

William: Sorry, I meant 'go without Henry'.

Reporter: No, didn't you mean just what you said, 'go alone' and isn't that because Douglas knew that you were not going?

William: I don't know why Douglas didn't come, I was just guessing.

Reporter: And how much of the rest of your evidence is guess work? I suggest to you that you didn't go to the pool with Douglas as usual because you didn't go to the pool at all and that, as Stephen told us, you were at the school at the time?

William: No. My mum saw me come in with my swimming things at about half past seven.

Reporter: I suggest that you might have intended to go to the pool, but changed your mind and went to the school and spray painted the door in the science block?

William: No, I didn't.

Reporter: And did you give your mum your wet swimming things when you got back?

William: No, I always put them directly into the washing machine.

Reporter: How convenient. William, isn't that just another lie, like the lie you told to the headmaster about the 'alibi witness' and hasn't your evidence about that Wednesday evening been a pack of lies?

William: No, I'm telling the truth.

Reporter: And like the guess-work about Douglas, isn't it the case that you will say anything that will get you out of trouble, because you know full well that you painted the door?

William: No.

> Note [44]   This is fairly vigorous cross-examination but neither the sheriff nor William's solicitor has thought fit to intervene. The cross-examiner must be allowed to test the witness's credibility in any fair way. A younger or more vulnerable witness might have to be handled more gently, but William has demonstrated that he is able to look after himself. Questioning aimed at merely annoying or badgering a witness, whether a child or an adult, is never acceptable[108], but the reporter's line of questioning here is far short of this.

The reporter now turns to the events of the morning of Thursday 3rd November, suggesting inter alia that William was not surprised by the news of the painting because he had done it. The reporter then moves on to the assault on Stephen on the evening of the Friday, skating lightly over

---

108.   *Falconer v Brown* (1893) 21 R(J) 1; (1893) 1 SLT 277; (1893) 1 Adam 96; cf *Reid v Guild* 1991 SCCR 71, *McAllister v Normand* 1996 SLT 622.

the assault itself but concentrating on the remark, 'The grassing little bastard had it coming to him'.

Reporter: You agree you made that remark?

William: Yes.

Reporter: And you agree that a 'grass' is someone who reports an offender to the authorities?

Mr Wynford: I think I must object. William has not qualified himself as one who can give expert evidence on the *argot* of the underworld.

Sheriff: I think that's putting it rather high, Mr Wynford.

Mr Wynford: Sorry, perhaps so; but your Ladyship will appreciate there is an important innuendo in my friend's question.

Reporter: I will re-phrase the question in order to re-assure my friend. William, what did you mean by those words?

William Brown: I meant that he had got me into trouble by telling tales about me to the head. Obviously I didn't mean that I had done it. Grasses can tell lies you know. He knew the head didn't like me and would be delighted to find that I was the guilty party.

The reporter concludes his cross-examination inter alia by putting before William that he carried out the burning of the shed as an act of revenge against the school, which William vehemently denies.

Sheriff: Mr Wynford, have you any re-examination?

Re-examination of William Brown

Mr Wynford: Briefly, my Lady. William, you were asked about the phrase, 'The grassing little bastard had it coming to him'. You accept you said that?

William: Yes.

Mr Wynford: Did you in any way intend to imply that you had carried out the spray-painting and that *that* was what Stephen had 'grassed' about?

William: No, definitely not.

Mr Wynford: You were asked about why you did not seem all that surprised when the news about the spray-painting came through. Have you any further comment on that?

Reporter: Perhaps I should put in a tentative objection. It sounds as if my friend may be introducing new matter.

Sheriff: Well, we shall see. But if there is anything new our procedure is flexible enough to allow me to let you re-cross-examine. How would you answer Mr Wynford's question, William?

William: No, not really. The whole thing didn't seem all that important. There was a bit of a laugh about it, but I didn't see any point in going ape about it.

Mr Wynford: I don't think my friend will require to re-cross. [*The reporter nods agreement.*] That's all William, just go over and sit beside your mum.

Mr Wynford now leads his remaining witnesses. William's mother states that William came home on Wednesday 2nd November 2005 at about 7.30 pm. and seemed to have been at the swimming pool since he had a towel with costume presumably wrapped in it. She could not speak to their condition since William had, as he generally did, slipped them directly into the washing machine. As to the evening of 5 November she says she came back from her hospital meeting at about 10.15 pm. William was in and seemed to have been in all the time. Cross-examined briefly she concedes that obviously she could not say for sure whether William had gone out for a short while.

Angela says William was in when she slipped out at 8 pm. on 5 November. He was in the house when she came back at about five past ten. He was watching a DVD and seemed settled. He did not smell of smoke or petrol. Cross-examined she admits that she had been drinking spirits when out with her boy friend. This would not have impaired her memory, but it may have made it more difficult to detect the smell of petrol had there been any to smell.

Mr Wynford: My Lady, that concludes my case.

Sheriff: Thank you. Now Mr Reporter, would you like to sum up your position.

Final speech by the reporter

Reporter: I'm obliged.

The first Statement avers that William carried out what I will call the 'paint' offence of malicious mischief during the evening of 2nd November 2005. Your Ladyship will scarcely require to be addressed on what constitutes malicious mischief and my friend and I are not at issue over the matter, but for the sake of completeness I refer to the words of Lord Justice-Clerk Aitchison in *Ward v Robertson*, 1938 JC 32 wherein his Lordship, at the top of page 36, states: 'It is not essential to the offence of malicious mischief that there should be a deliberate wicked intent to injure another in his property. It is enough if the damage is done by a person who shows a deliberate disregard of, or even indifference to, the property or possessory rights of others'.

As I have said, there is no dispute between my friend and myself that the evidence established that an act amounting to malicious mischief took place, the only live issue is who performed it. In my submission the time of the action was established by the combined evidence of the science teacher Mr McNeill and the janitor Mr Donaldson as being between 5.30 and 7 pm. on the evening concerned. In my submission Stephen Green's evidence that he saw William go into the school between these times – when he had no business to go to the school – and, moreover, with an object which could well have been a can for applying spray paint concealed in his jacket provides one source of evidence for your Ladyship.

For corroboration I rely on the words of the referred child which your Ladyship have ruled admissible, 'The grassing little bastard had it coming to him'. I concede that these words are capable of having the meaning that William ascribed to them – that Stephen had invented a story about him to get him into trouble. But I submit that they are also capable of having the meaning that I would urge upon your Ladyship, namely that William was in effect saying that Stephen had acted as a 'grass' in the sense of having gone to the authorities with information as to the true identity of an offender. One reads of trials involving 'super-grasses' who apparently enable convictions to be obtained, for example in terrorist cases, by telling on the activities of their former colleagues. I have not found the word in the Oxford Dictionary but your Ladyship may be interested to hear that *Brewer's Dictionary of 20th Century Phrase and Fable* has the following definition: 'In criminal slang, to inform, which may derive from rhyming slang 'grasshopper' for copper. A supergrass is one who informs on a number of his associates.'

Sheriff: I'm impressed by your erudition, but you may take it that the meaning of a 'grass' in this context is within judicial knowledge.

Reporter: I am grateful to your Ladyship for that indication. In that event I think it will also be known to your Ladyship that it is a recognised danger that witnesses who are 'grasses' may be giving perjured evidence, but I would submit that evidence of this kind must be weighed on its merits like any other evidence. As your Ladyship is aware, that is all that is needed for corroboration since the concept was explained by Lord Justice General Rodger in *Fox v HM Advocate* 1998 JC 94 at 98, where his Lordship said in effect that it was sufficient for the corroborating witness to speak to facts and circumstances which are *capable* of supporting the direct evidence. In my submission Stephen should be believed and that, if he is believed, then the words which he reported William as having said are capable of providing the 'support' desiderated by Lord Justice General Rodger in *Fox*.

As to the fire-raising offence, your Ladyship has already ruled that there is sufficient evidence, having regard to the *Moorov* principle, to allow me to succeed in respect of this Statement of Fact. Of course all that follows from there being a 'case to answer' is that the inference of guilt is capable of being drawn provided the inference is strong enough and the witnesses are credible and reliable.

As to the strength of the inference, I would submit that the finding in a place where the boy William was known to frequent of such a remarkable combination of items produces a compelling inference that he who placed one also placed the other and that therefore the possessor of the red paint container also possessed the petrol container. The only other red paint container we know of – and they do not lie about like coke-cans or autumn leaves in Vallombrosa – is the can which William was carrying when Stephen saw him on the Wednesday night.

As to credibility and reliability, and obviously I apply this to both alleged offences, I would submit that there could be no question but that the staff witnesses from the school were unimpeachable. I would submit that Stephen Green gave his evidence in a straightforward manner and that his evidence should be preferred to that of William Brown who had to admit having told a lie to the head teacher. Also William Brown's evidence lacked inherent credibility. On both the Wednesday and the Saturday evenings he was conveniently alone at the key times. Also he was compelled to vary his evidence about Douglas not wanting to go to the swimming pool 'alone' when he realised, too late, the implications of that evidence. Interestingly, we did not hear from either Douglas or Henry who might have been able to clarify some matters.

Before leaving the 'fire-raising' charge I should mention to your Ladyship, and perhaps should have raised this earlier in my speech, that I have framed Statement 2 in the alternative, namely 'wilful' or, alternatively, 'culpable and reckless' fire-raising. In a comparatively recent case, *Byrne v HM Advocate*, (No 2) 2000 JC 155, 2000 SLT 593, 2000 SCCR 77, the distinction between the two has been examined by a bench of five judges. In this case the court re-affirmed the distinction between the two. After indicating that for wilful fireraising the 'Crown must establish beyond reasonable doubt that he intended to set fire to that item of property' Lord Coulsfield, delivering the opinion of the court, stated at page 163H of the report in the Justiciary Cases:

> '*The crime of culpable and reckless fireraising can also be committed in respect of any form of property. In that respect it is similar to wilful fireraising. The difference from wilful fireraising lies in the mens rea. Mere negligence is not enough: the property must have been set on fire due to an act of the accused displaying a reckless disregard as to what the result of his act would be*'.

> '*Contrary to what has sometimes been suggested, the distinction between the crimes remains important since the degree of blameworthiness will be relevant to penalty*.'

While of course we are not concerned with 'penalty' in a referrals case, we are concerned with disposal and in my submission the hearing are entitled to have your Ladyship's view as to which of the alternatives is appropriate. In my submission there can be no doubt on the point. A person who obtains a can of petrol and sets alight to a wooden structure is, I would maintain, acting wilfully as opposed to the person who, say, starts a bonfire beside a flammable structure which consequently catches fire. Of course no-one, apart from the fire-raiser, saw the incident, but the fire officer's report indicates that a flammable substance such as petrol was the cause and I submit that, in the absence of any competing explanation, the only conclusion is that this acting was 'wilful' and that this should be reflected in your Ladyship's determination. On the whole matter I move your Ladyship to find that both offences have been established and to remit the case to the Principal Reporter to make arrangements for a hearing to consider disposal[109].

Unless I can assist your Ladyship any further, that is my submission.

Sheriff: No, thank you, I think you have covered all the points. Mr Wynford?

Final speech for the Referred Child

Mr Wynford: I'm obliged. At the outset I can set my friend's mind at rest on the subject of 'wilful'. In the event of your Ladyship finding against my client on the second alleged offence I can concede that your Ladyship will be bound to make a finding of 'wilful fireraising'. That is the inevitable inference from the evidence and there has been no competing explanation put forward by my client for the simple reason that my client knows nothing at all about the incident or indeed about the paint incident. His defence to both charges is one of outright denial.

William's solicitor goes on to deal with the reporter's arguments, urging the sheriff as a matter of law that the Moorov argument, although in law capable of being sustained, should not, in all the circumstances, be sustained. On the facts of the paint charge he urges the sheriff to prefer William's evidence to that of Stephen. In relation to the fireraising charge he submits that the evidence of the two containers being found together amounts to almost nothing. He concludes:–

Your Ladyship has of course indicated that there was a case to answer in relation to the charge of fireraising. However, after such a finding the court has still to assess the weight of that case. As pointed out by the Lord Justice General in the case of *Byrne*, wilful fireraising is a serious, even a dire, matter and I would submit that to make a finding of guilt based upon nothing more than the contiguity of two tins would be dangerous in the extreme. William may not be an angel. He has denied the paint charge and I move your Ladyship to believe him and not to sustain the Statement in relation to that charge. In relation to the fireraising I would submit that, even if your Ladyship were against me on the schoolboy prank represented by the paint business, she should not make a finding against this child on the very grave fire charge.

Sheriff: Thank you both. I will rise for a few minutes and give an oral decision[110] presently.

---

109. Children (Scotland) Act 1995, s 68(10)(a).
110. Act of Sederunt (Child Care and Maintenance Rules) 1997 r 3.51(1).

Bar Officer: All stand.

Ten minutes later the sheriff returns.

Oral decision of the sheriff

Sheriff: I have carefully considered the evidence and the helpful speeches of Mr Somerville and Mr Wynford. In relation to the charge of malicious mischief I have to say that I found the child Stephen to be straightforward and convincing. I thought his evidence was enough to provide a firm source of evidence which, if corroborated, would leave it open to me to make a finding of guilt. The much quoted words of William about Stephen being a 'grass' were accepted by William but he said he meant that Stephen had fabricated a story against him, not that he had acted, as it were, as a police informer. I had no hesitation in concluding that the interpretation of the phrase advanced by the reporter was not only a possible one but the natural and normal one. I did not believe William's explanation and in general am sorry to say that I did not find William to be a credible witness generally. He is an intelligent young man and gave the impression of being able to work out what was in his interests to say, although, like others who seek to mislead courts, he could not quite keep it up, as in the slip about Douglas. I accordingly am in favour of sustaining the first Statement of Fact.

As to the fire-raising charge, I have already held that there was a case to answer. The only answer came from the referred child in the form of an outright denial which, if believed, would of course have resulted in my not sustaining that charge. However, for the reasons stated, I did not regard William as a credible witness. Mr Wynford pointed out that this charge was a much more serious one than the paint incident and that is correct, but that consideration is relevant to disposal rather than to assessment of evidence. I consider that there has been no adequate 'answer' to the case made out by the reporter in relation to the charge of wilful fireraising contained in the second Statement of Fact and accordingly I hold that this has been established and I accordingly sustain it under deletion, of consent, of the words 'or, alternatively, the offence of culpable and reckless fire-raising'.

[*Formally, to the sheriff clerk*] I find that the whole grounds of referral have been established by the evidence, subject to the deletion mentioned, and I accordingly remit this case to the reporter so that he may arrange a hearing. I do not intend to issue a written Note of Reasons[111] as such but will ask the sheriff clerk to send parties a copy of the transcript of this extempore opinion once it has been typed. [*In informal tone, to the child and his mother.*] I have held that the reporter was right to bring this matter to a hearing on the basis of the two offences set out in the grounds for referral. What happens to you, William, will be decided not by me but by a children's hearing. The reporter will notify you of the time and date of that hearing. That concludes today's proceedings.

---

111. Act of Sederunt (Child Care and Maintenance Rules) 1997 r 3.51(3).

Reporter: My Lady, before your Ladyship rises I have a motion in terms of section 68(10)(b) of the Children (Scotland) Act 1995.

Sheriff: Yes?

Reporter: As your Ladyship is aware this provision enables the court, on remitting a child's case to a hearing for disposal, to keep the child in a place of safety for a period not exceeding three days or not after the disposal hearing.

Sheriff: I have never been asked to grant such an order before. (*Consulting the Act.*) I see that the pre-conditions for the granting of such an order are a reasonable belief that the child may run away or that such an order is necessary in the child's best interests?

Reporter: That is correct. I would rely on the latter matter. In my submission there has been a clear and quite sudden deterioration in the conduct of the child. It is increasingly being recognised that as early as possible intervention in children's lives is in their interests.

Sheriff: But it doesn't follow that a residential disposal will be necessary to achieve this. I seem to remember that the Social Workers here are able to offer home-based intervention, yet your motion would seem to pre-suppose that a residential disposal will be made in the end of the day. Mr Wynford, what is your stance on this point on behalf of William?

Mr Wynford: Your Ladyship has to some extent anticipated me. I was aware, and a little surprised, that my friend was going to make this motion. In my submission this is not the type of case at which the section relied upon by my friend is concerned. Like your Ladyship I have not personally encountered such a motion being made, much less granted, but am aware anecdotally of one case, not in this jurisdiction, where a section 68(10)(b) order was granted, but that was in respect of a boy who had a history of appearances before hearings and in respect of whom the grounds of referral included over twenty car thefts in about two weeks. I also think your Ladyship is right about social work facilities in Kirklenton. To my fairly certain knowledge, and I have consulted both my friend and the procurator fiscal about this, William Brown has no charge pending. The situation at home is reasonably stable. In my submission the motion is totally inappropriate and should be refused.

Sheriff: I seem to recall that I had to reverse a decision of a hearing to grant a warrant at an early stage in this case?

Reporter: Yes, my Lady, but now we have the grounds established.

Sheriff: Yes, and we also have nearly three months apparently clear of further offending. Have you anything further to add, Mr Reporter?

Reporter: No, my Lady, except I suspect your Ladyship is not entirely with me.

Sheriff: You suspect correctly. The motion is refused. Now, if there is no further motion that concludes today's proceedings.

Bar officer: All stand.

The sheriff departs. That is the end of the proof.

AN APPEAL IS DISCUSSED

Monday, 30 January 2006

4.30 pm. A meeting is held in Mr Wynford's office. William Brown and his mother are there as well as Mr Wynford. The latter explains the possibilities, namely an appeal on point of law or in relation to any irregularity in the conduct of the case to the Court of Session or to the Sheriff Principal[112]. He says that in a case like this an appeal to the Sheriff Principal would be the norm and would be quicker than an appeal to the Court of Session. In any event the Scottish Legal Aid Board would be unlikely to sanction an appeal to the Court of Session.

He explains in general terms the 'Stated Case' procedures and advises that there can be no appeal against the sheriff's assessment of such matters as the relative credibility of William Brown and Stephen Green. His clients are disappointed about this. He explains that in an appeal he could argue again the point about the admissibility of the words spoken by William Brown to the police. If successful this would mean complete success because the proof of the second alleged offence depended on the first offence. However Mr Wynford now thinks that it is likely that the words were rightly held to be admissible and that, while the point is still worth arguing on appeal, he thinks his chances of success will be less than even. He says he is more hopeful of persuading the Sheriff Principal that Sheriff Grey was 'plainly wrong'[113] in inferring that the evidence of Mr Black's finding the paint container and the empty petrol can together was sufficient to identify William as the fire-raiser.

He explains that it would be well worthwhile to displace the sheriff's finding about the fire-raising incident since that would leave only the paint incident which, as little more than a school-boy prank, could not be regarded by the panel as of anywhere near the gravity of the fire-raising incident. If the more serious offence were out of the way the hearing might even discharge the referral.

Mr Wynford advises that he anticipates that there will be no problem in obtaining Legal Aid for an appeal to the Sheriff Principal and William and his mother instruct that an appeal should go ahead. They ask about the position pending appeal and Mr Wynford advises that the hearing

---

112. Children (Scotland) Act 1995, s 51(11).
113. Cf *Galbraith v L* 1981 SLT 194.

procedures will continue meantime. He will be happy to go with William to the hearing which will soon be held and says he thinks he should set in motion the procedures under the The Children's Hearings (Legal Representation) (Scotland) Rules 2002[114], whereby a legal representative may be appointed and that representative entitled to receive payment under the government's scheme. He re-assures William Brown and his mother that he does not think it very likely that a hearing will make a residential requirement, still less a secure accommodation recommendation.

---

114. Rule 3 of which provides that a business meeting (r 3(1)) or a full hearing (r 3(2)) may appoint a legal representative where (a) legal representation is required to allow the child 'to effectively participate' at the Hearing; or (b) it may be necessary to make a supervision requirement (or a review of such requirement) which includes a requirement for the child to reside in a named residential establishment and the child is likely to meet the criteria specified in Section 70(10) of the Act and the Secure Accommodation (Scotland) Regulations 1996.

APPENDIX ONE

Children (Scotland) Act 1995, as amended

52 Children requiring compulsory measures of supervision

(1) The question of whether compulsory measures of supervision are necessary in respect of a child arises if at least one of the conditions mentioned in subsection (2) below is satisfied with respect to him.

(2) The conditions referred to in subsection (1) above are that the child –

(a) is beyond the control of any relevant person;

(b) is falling into bad associations or is exposed to moral danger:

(c) is likely –

    (i) to suffer unnecessary; or

    (ii) be impaired seriously in his health or development, due to a lack of parental care;

(d) is a child in respect of whom any of the offences mentioned in Schedule 1 to the Criminal Procedure (Scotland) Act 1995 (offences against children to which special provisions apply) has been committed;

(e) is, or is likely to become, a member of the same household as a child in respect of whom any of the offences referred to in paragraph (d) above has been committed;

(f) is, or is likely to become, a member of the same household as a person who has committed any of the offences referred to in paragraph (d) above;

(g) is, or is likely to become, a member of the same household as a person in respect of whom an offence under sections 1 and 3 of the Criminal Law (Consolidation) (Scotland) Act 1995 (incest and intercourse with a child by step-parent or person in position of trust) has been committed by a member of that household;

(h) has failed to attend school regularly without reasonable excuse;

(i) has committed an offence;

(j) has misused alcohol or any drug, whether or not a controlled drug within the Misuse of Drugs Act 1971;

(k) has misused a volatile substance by deliberately inhaling its vapour, other than for medicinal purposes;

(l) is being provided with accommodation by a local authority under section 25, or is the subject of a parental responsibilities order obtained under section 86, of this Act and, in supervision in his interest or the interest of others.

(m) is a child to whom subsection (2A) below applies.

(2A) This subsection applies to a child where –

a requirement is made of the Principal Reporter under section 12(1) of the Antisocial Behaviour etc. ((Scotland) Act 2004 (asp 8) (power of sheriff to require the Principal Reporter to refer case to children's hearing) in respect of the child's case; and the child is not subject to a supervision requirement.

(3) In this Part of this Act, 'supervision' in relation to compulsory measures of supervision may include measures for the protection, guidance, treatment or control of the child.

APPENDIX TWO

Convention for the Protection of Human Rights and Fundamental Freedoms

Article 6

Right to a fair trial

1. In the determination of his civil rights and obligations or of any criminal charge against him, everyone is entitled to a fair and public hearing within a reasonable time by an independent and impartial tribunal established by law. Judgement shall be pronounced publicly by the press and public may be excluded from all or part of the trial in the interest of morals, public order or national security in a democratic society, where the interests of juveniles or the protection of the private life of the parties so require, or the extent strictly necessary in the opinion of the court in special circumstances where publicity would prejudice the interests of justice.

2. Everyone charged with a criminal offence shall be presumed innocent until proved guilty according to law.

3. Everyone charged with a criminal offence has the following minimum rights:

(a)   to be informed promptly, in a language which he understands and in detail, of the nature and cause of the accusation against him;

(b)   to have adequate time and the facilities for the preparation of his defence;

(c)   to defend himself in person or through legal assistance or, if he has not sufficient means to pay for legal assistance, to be given it free when the interests of justice so require;

(d)   to examine or have examined witnesses against him and to obtain the attendance and examination of witnesses on his behalf under the same conditions as witnesses against him;

(e)   to have the free assistance of an interpreter if he cannot understand or speak the language used in court.

Article 7

No punishment without law

1. No one shall be held guilty of any criminal offence on account of any act or omission which did not constitute a criminal offence under national or international law at the time when it was committed. Nor shall a heavier penalty be imposed than the one that was applicable at the time the criminal offence was committed.

2. This article shall not prejudice the trial and punishment of any person for any act or omission which, at the time when it was committed, was criminal according the general principles of law recognized by civilised nations.

Article 8

Right to respect for private and family law

1. Everyone has the right to respect for his private and family life, his home and his correspondence.

2. There shall be no interference by a public authority with the exercise of this right except such as is in accordance with the law and is necessary in a democratic society in the interests of national security, public safety or the economic well-being of the country, for the prevention of disorder or crime, for the protection of health or morals, or for the protection of the rights and freedoms of others.

APPENDIX THREE

Children's Hearings (Scotland) Rules 1996 (SI 1996/3261)

Service of notification and other documents

30. – (1) Any notice in writing or other document and any oral notification authorised or required under these Rules to be given or issued by the Principal Reporter may be given or issued by the Principal Reporter or by a person duly authorised by him or by any constable.

(2) Any notice in writing or other document authorised or required by these Rules to be given or issued to a child or to a relevant person may be –

(a)   delivered to him in person; or

(b)   left for him at his dwellinghouse or place of business or where he has no known dwellinghouse or place of business, at any other place in which he may at the time be resident; or

(c)   where he is the master of, or a seaman or other person employed in, a vessel, left with a person on board thereof and connected therewith; or

(d)   sent by post in a registered or first class service recorded delivery letter to this dwelling house or place of business.

(3) Where the Principal Reporter or a person duly authorised by him gives to any relevant person a notification in writing under paragraph (1) of rule 7 above, or an oral notification under that paragraph as read with paragraph (4) of that rule, he shall execute a certificate of notification in the form of Form 25.

(4) Where a notice under rule 6 or 7 or a copy of such a statement as is mentioned in rule 18 is sent by post in accordance with paragraph 2 (d) of this rule, the notification or copy shall be deemed, for the purpose of rule 6, 7 or 18, as the case may be, to have been given the day following the date of posting.

Index